Secretaries of God

Women Prophets in Late Medieval and
Early Modern England

Secretaries of God

Women Prophets in Late Medieval and Early Modern England

Diane Watt

D. S. BREWER

BR
750
. W38
1997

First published 1997
D. S. Brewer, Cambridge

ISBN 0 85991 524 7

D. S. Brewer is an imprint of Boydell & Brewer Ltd
PO Box 9, Woodbridge, Suffolk IP12 3DF, UK
and of Boydell & Brewer Inc.
PO Box 41026, Rochester, NY 14604–4126, USA

A catalogue record for this book is available
from the British Library

Library of Congress Cataloging-in-Publication Data
Watt, Diane, 1965–
  Secretaries of God : women prophets in late medieval and early
modern England / Diane Watt.
      p.   cm.
  Includes bibliographical references and index.
  ISBN 0–85991–524–7 (hardback : alk. paper)
  1. Women in Christianity – England – History. 2. Prophets –
England – History. 3. England – Church history – 1066–1485.
4. England – Church history – 16th century. 5. England – Church
history – 17th century. I. Title.
BR750.W38   1997
274.2'05'082 – dc21   97–19124

This publication is printed on acid-free paper

Printed in Great Britain by
St Edmundsbury Press Ltd, Bury St Edmunds, Suffolk

Contents

Illustrations

Abbreviations

BL	British Library
CS	Camden Society
o.s.	original (first) series
CSPD	*Calendar of the State Papers, Domestic Series* (London, 1856–1924)
CSP Spain	*Calendar of Letters, Despatches, and State Papers, Relating to the Negotiations between England and Spain,* ed. G.A. Begenroth et al. (London, 1862–1947)
Catholic Encyclopedia	*The Catholic Encyclopedia: an International Work of Reference on the Constitution, Doctrine, Discipline and History of the Catholic Church,* ed. C.G. Herbermann et al. (New York, 1907–1922)
EETS	Early English Text Society
o.s., e.s., s.s.	original series, extra series, special series
Hindle, *Bibliography*	C.J. Hindle, *A Bibliography of the Printed Pamphlets and Broadsides of Lady Eleanor Douglas the Seventeenth-Century Prophetess* (Edinburgh, 1936)
L&P	*Letters and Papers, Foreign and Domestic, of the Reign of Henry VIII,* ed. J.S. Brewer, J. Gairdner and R.H. Brodie (Vaduz, 1965)
MED	*Middle English Dictionary,* ed. H. Kurath and S.M. Kuhn (Ann Arbor, 1956–)
OED	*The Oxford English Dictionary,* prepared J.A. Simpson and E.S.C. Weiner (Oxford, 1989)
PRO	Public Records Office
SCH	Studies in Church History
SP	State Papers
STC	*A Short Title Catalogue of Books Printed in England, Scotland, and Ireland and of English Books Printed Abroad 1475–1640,* compiled A.W. Pollard and G.R. Redgrave, rev. W.A. Jackson and F.S. Ferguson, completed K. Panzer (London, 1986)
TLS	*The Times Literary Supplement*
Wing, *STC*	*Short-Title Catalogue of Books Printed in England, Scotland, Ireland, Wales, and British America and of English Books Printed in Other Countries 1641–1700,* compiled D. Wing (New York, 1972–88)

For Patricia Watt

Thus you can see clearly, dear friend, how Our Lord has often revealed his secrets to the world through women.
                    Christine de Pisan, *The City of Ladies*

Acknowledgements

I should like to thank Jane Aaron, Andrew Hadfield, Richard Phillips, Sarah Prescott and John Watts for their invaluable comments on drafts of various chapters of this book. Glenn Campbell answered my questions about legal history, and I am grateful to him for his assistance. I was intellectually stimulated by the ideas, responses and suggestions contributed by my students in the 'Women, Writing and Religion' modules 1993–1996; I can only hope that they learned as much from my teaching as I gained from them.

This book is derived from my doctoral thesis and I am indebted to the careful supervision of Julia Briggs and Douglas Gray, and to the advice of Nigel Smith. Kathryn Purkis contributed a great deal to my research, especially in its early stages. Jacqueline Tasioulas encouraged me a great deal throughout.

I would also like to express my appreciation of the staff at the Interlibrary Loan Desk at the University Library in Aberystwyth who were both cheerful and efficient in the fulfillment of their duties; of Jean Matthews who helped produce the manuscript; of Ruth C.A. Higgins who read it in its entirety with great patience; and of Caroline Palmer, from Boydell & Brewer Ltd., who gave me so much guidance and encouragement. Without the support of the English Department at the University of Wales, Aberystwyth, which granted me study leave in the first half of 1996, and without a generous bursary from the College Research Fund, this project would have taken much longer to complete.

Parts of this book first appeared in earlier publications, although they have since been revised. Parts of Chapters 2 and 3 were published as 'The Prophet at Home: Elizabeth Barton and the Influence of Bridget of Sweden and Catherine of Siena' in *Prophets Abroad: The Reception of Continental Holy Women in Medieval England*, ed. Rosalynn Voaden (Cambridge: D.S. Brewer, 1996), and as 'Reconstructing the Word: The Prophecies of Elizabeth Barton' in *Renaissance Quarterly* 1 (Spring 1997). Part of the Epilogue was published as 'The Posthumous Reputation of the Holy Maid of Kent' in *Recusant History* xxiii (October 1996). All of this material is used here with the permission of the publishers.

The author and the publishers would like to thank the following for their kind permission to use the following illustrations: Geoffrey Van Ltd: Fig. 1; The Bodleian Library, University of Oxford: Figs 3, 4, 5, 6; The Provost and Fellows of Worcester College Oxford: Fig. 7. Despite every effort to trace and contact copyright owners prior to publication this has not been possible in every case. We apologize for any apparent infringement of copyright and if notified, we will be pleased to rectify any errors or ommissions at the earliest opportunity.

1

Crossing the Great Divide:
Continuity and Change in Women's Prophetic Experience

In *The Book of Margery Kempe,* Kempe is likened (by herself or her scribe) to 'owyr Lordys owyn secretarijs whech he hath indued wyth lofe' who are disparaged and hindered by sinful men and women caught up in the cares of the world.[1] When the *Book* was written in the first half of the fifteenth century, *secretari(e)* had the meaning of 'one entrusted with private or confidential matters, a confidant; a trusted servant or counselor; one entrusted with the secrets of God'.[2] In the context in which the word appears in *The Book of Margery Kempe* the last sense is dominant. However, by this time, *secretari(e)* could also be used in the modern sense of 'one employed to write for another, a scribe, secretary'. Margery Kempe, a laywoman and a member of the middle classes, lived in a culture which was still predominantly oral rather than literate.[3] For her, to be God's secretary was to be one who communed intimately with God, and whose duty it was to communicate to others her revelations and the story of her pious and sometimes miraculous life, largely, although not entirely, through the spoken word. Three centuries later the aristocratic Lady Eleanor Davies was prophesying in very different circumstances. In a tract addressed to her daughter Lucy, Countess of Huntingdon, printed in 1644, she spoke of her first mystical experience in 1625 in which she had felt herself called to follow the Old Testament prophet Daniel, 'at what time your Mother became a Writer or Secretary'.[4] During the English Civil War, Davies published more texts than

---

1   *The Book of Margery Kempe,* ed. S.B. Meech and H.E. Allen, EETS o.s. 212 (Oxford, 1940), 71.
2   *MED,* s.v. 'secretari(e)'. The early thirteenth-century *Ancrene Wisse* describes Love as the Lord's chamberlain, counsellor and, significantly, as his wife, 'þet he ne mei nawt heole wið ah þet he þencheð': *Medieval English Prose for Women: from the Katherine Group and Ancrene Wisse,* ed. B. Millett and J. Wogan-Browne (Oxford, 1990), 128.
3   There is an extensive literature concerning late medieval literacy; see n. 27 below. On the orality of late medieval culture generally, see M.T. Clanchy, *From Memory to Written Record: England 1066–1307* (2nd ed. Oxford, 1993).
4   Eleanor Davies, *From the Lady Eleanor, her blessing* (1644), A4r. See also the discussion of the role of the seventeenth-century secretary by A. Stewart, 'The Early Modern Closet Discovered', *Representations* i (1995), 76–100, especially 83–7.

any English woman before her. For Davies, the written word *subsumed* the spoken – through her pamphlets she hoped to disseminate her prophecies quickly and effectively. For Davies, who claimed that prophecy was 'an office not a trade',[5] the role of secretary no doubt also had connotations of a governmental position, a meaning appropriate to one concerned with the political unrest of her time and whose tracts attacked what she saw as the papistry of Charles I and Archbishop Laud and expressed her support of the Protectorate of Oliver Cromwell.

Throughout the medieval and early modern periods, women and men of all social ranks and levels of education declared themselves to be prophets and visionaries inspired by God to proclaim His, or sometimes Her, message to the people. The substance of such divine revelations might be doctrinal, soteriological, apocalyptic, millenarian or chiliastic, orthodox or heretical, entirely religious or also political. It might commit God to a certain course of events by predicting the future, proclaiming God's word or interpreting Scripture, and it might also require those to whom it was addressed and sometimes the prophet her/himself to take action. While not all prophecy was oppositional or revolutionary, those persecuted or oppressed, whatever their sex, rank or education, could voice their dissatisfaction through this type of discourse. Prophecy has however been dismissed by scholars as a marginal form, largely because religious conviction and religious discourse have been seen as subservient to separately identifiable political purposes. One of the central arguments of this book is that by the later Middle Ages, there existed in Western Christendom established traditions of popular and specifically female prophecy which, although open to appropriation by the various and often conflicting power structures, have their own partial autonomy and which are, to some extent at least, independent cultural, and thus potentially political, forces.

This book takes the form of a series of studies of women in England who lived between the early twelfth and the second half of the seventeenth centuries, and who claimed to speak and act for the deity or interpret divine will. It includes Margery Kempe (*c*.1373 to sometime after 1439) and the medieval visionaries; Elizabeth Barton, the 'Holy Maid of Kent' (1506–1534); the Reformation Protestant Anne Askew (1521–1546) and other godly women described in John Foxe's *Acts and Monuments*; and Lady Eleanor Davies (*c*.1588–1652) as an example of a woman prophet of the Civil War. It looks at some of the ways in which prophecy, often perceived as feminine regardless of the sex of the speaker, gave these women's words authority. Mystical, visionary and devotional texts are frequently viewed by scholars as indifferent to and unaffected by their historical settings, but I argue that through prophecy women were often able to intervene in the religious and political discourses of their times: the role

---

[5] Eleanor Davies, *A warning to the dragon and all his angels* (1625), A3v.

of God's secretary, His confidant and trusted servant, gave women a rare opportunity to act and speak autonomously and publicly.

It would of course be wrong to assume that the role of prophet remained the same during the long period in question. At different times the word *prophecy* has meant different things and these will be explored further in the course of this book. However it will be helpful to provide some definitions at the outset.[6] *Prophet* will be used both in its earlier senses of 'one who speaks on behalf of God' and 'one who speaks for God', and in its more popular sense of 'one who predicts the future'; the prophet's revelations are primarily public utterances. *Mystic* means 'one who attains direct communion with God' and whose revelations are concerned with the way of perfection. Evelyn Underhill explained the distinction thus, 'As the prophet looks at the landscape of Eternity, the mystic finds and feels it and both know that there is laid on them the obligation of exhibiting it if they can.'[7] *Visionary* includes both *prophet* and *mystic*; it refers to one who has revelations of a transcendent reality, not necessarily of a visual nature. The extent and nature of the transformations of the prophetic role can perhaps be most succinctly illustrated by the example of semantic change given above. Unlike many of their continental counterparts Margery Kempe and almost all other late medieval women prophets and visionaries in England only intervened in matters relating to the communities in which they lived. Possible reasons for this are the conservatism of the English tradition (as I suggest in the second chapter), and also the poverty and lack of independence of the English convents before the foundation of Syon Abbey, relative to their continental counterparts and to the monasteries. However Max Weber's assertion in *The Sociology of Religion* that women are receptive to religious but not political prophecy does not bear scrutiny.[8] During and after the Reformation such secretaries of God were much more inclined to frame their denunciations of the vices of the world in political and/or apocalyptic terms.

This study does not then argue for a *single* tradition of female prophecy, or suggest that it is a consistent, transhistorical phenomenon, but, as the following chapters reveal, similarities in the lives and writings of these women do emerge. In the case of Margery Kempe, we need to see her in relation to prophecy in late medieval Europe, which was derived from the pre-Christian past, and was both widespread and diverse in its manifestations in the West. Biblical figures and Christian saints provided important

6 See K. Rahner, *Visions and Prophecies*, Quæstiones Disputatæ 10 (London, 1963), 17; K. Kerby-Fulton, *Reformist Apocalypticism and 'Piers Plowman'*, Cambridge Studies in Medieval Literature 7 (Cambridge, 1990), 3.
7 E. Underhill, 'The Mystic as Creative Artist' in *The Essentials of Mysticism and Other Essays* (London, 1920), 65.
8 Max Weber, *Economy and Society: an Outline of Interpretative Sociology*, ed. G. Roth and C. Wittich (New York, 1968), ii, 489.

role models for prophets of both sexes, and Kempe is compared to women like Hildegard of Bingen, Bridget of Sweden and Catherine of Siena, who all wielded particular spiritual and political power. Bridget's influence in England is well documented and Kempe, of course, acknowledges her devotion to the Swedish saint, but parallels can equally be drawn between Kempe's prophetic activities, which were largely confined to her immediate social and religious communities, and did not take an overtly political turn, and those of another English woman who lived three centuries earlier – Christina of Markyate.

Kempe's unconventional behaviour and extreme religious devotion, her refusal to be constrained by either her sex or by norms of spirituality, evidently provoked a great deal of hostility. All the women discussed in this book are linked by their persecution and suffering; Kempe's accounts of her examinations for heresy portray her as a 'prophet in her own country', dishonoured and persecuted like Christ, but inspired by God and thus able to confound all her enemies. In the Reformation, as in the Middle Ages, the woman who assumed a public role could find herself in conflict with the established Church. Anne Askew's self-presentation as a persecuted Christian prophet, her defiance of authority, her characterization of herself as 'harmless as a dove, wise as a serpent', undermines the conventional portrayal of the pious Protestant woman as chaste, silent and obedient. Askew's *imitatio Christi*, which in some respects resembles Margery Kempe's, is drawn from Scripture and from reformist traditions, which teach that anyone can be transformed by the Spirit, and that women and men are equal before God. Askew's autobiographical text was published by John Bale, one of the earliest English Protestant apocalyptic writers, who, in adopting it as a Protestant saint's life, tried to transform her into a model of passive feminine suffering.

A second approach to the material is empirical, combining contextualization with close readings of the texts. The hostile and often misogynous evidence concerning the life and prophecies of Elizabeth Barton, which typically represents her as either an ignorant woman who fell under the sway of conservative churchmen reacting against the reforms of Henry VIII, or as an immoral woman possessed by the devil, needs to be seen in the light of contemporary English and European Catholic piety, which highlights the impact of popular oral culture on her prophecies and visions, and draws our attention to the continuity in certain aspects of female revelatory experience from the Middle Ages into the Renaissance. From this perspective, Barton was exceptional as the first English woman political prophet, a woman represented by her supporters as being once again Christ-like, 'of the seed of Abraham', but whose divine authority was not recognized by those who were determined to silence her.

Eleanor Davies, who began to prophesy a century later, was also an exceptional figure, as is illustrated by the control she exercised over the production and publication of her contentious tracts which was much greater than that of many of her contemporaries or of any other of the women covered by this study. Her independence from religious sects and congregations and her resistance to the controlling powers of the state illustrate that women's prophecy was indeed a force of its own. Davies, a Protestant, represents her extremely sexual experience of mystical union as the Annunciation, describes her prophecies as the body and blood of Christ, and develops elaborate metaphors of giving birth and motherhood. Similarities between her discourse and that of earlier women prophets may be explained in part by the influence of contemporary Catholicism and residual elements of medieval prophecy and vision, and in part by her debt to popular political prophecy. Nonetheless the singularity of Eleanor Davies' conception of her own role as prophet is remarkable in that she identifies with the Virgin Mary as the new Redeemer, and portrays God, the creator and judge, as a Woman above all men in whom Davies herself is subsumed.

Starting in the later Middle Ages, specifically the twelfth century, does not imply that this is in any real sense a point of origin. Nor is it suggested that women's prophecy stopped with the Restoration, although its sudden but relatively short-lived flourishing during the Civil War and Interregnum makes it an appropriate rather than entirely arbitrary time at which to end. To a large extent the medieval and early Renaissance prophets in this study are self-selected because so little evidence has survived from before the seventeenth century. Nonetheless women's prophecy provides a comparatively rich field of study, given the dearth of early historical and literary texts written by and about women. Many of these women not only spoke but also wrote in an age when historical as opposed to fictional women's voices are seldom heard. The certainty that they were empowered by God encouraged them (or their supporters) to textualize their experiences. But if the decision to focus on women's (rather than women's and men's) prophecy can be justified, certain caveats have to be kept in mind. One should be wary of insisting either that women's use of language is distinctly different from that of men or that sex prevails over other factors of difference such as race, social and economic status, or cultural and historical context, and of naively asserting that a continuum exists in visionary experiences or religious practices between the twelfth and the seventeenth centuries.[9] Some of these prophets may never have heard of or read the

---

9   On *écriture féminine* and the interrelation of gender, language and religious experience, see Luce Irigaray, 'La Mystérique' in *Speculum of the Other Woman*, trans. G.C. Gill (Ithaca N.Y., 1985), 191–202; Hélène Cixous, 'The Laugh of the Medusa', trans. K. Cohen and P. Cohen, *Signs* i (1976), 875–99; Julia Kristeva, *Powers of Horror: an Essay on Abjection*, trans. L.S. Roudiez (New York, 1982). For an overview, see T. Moi, *Sexual/Textual Politics: Feminist Literary Theory* (London, 1988), 102–73. Michel de Certeau implies a continuity in religious practices from the Middle Ages into the early modern period in his chapter 'Mystic Speech' in *Heterologies: Discourse on*

works of another woman. Margery Kempe, for example, despite being aware of continental female role models, found herself struggling to develop a narrative persona and literary form. Similarly, their long-term influence was limited. The epilogue to this book, which discusses the posthumous reputations of these women and the survival of their texts, shows that connections may exist between, say, Margery Kempe and Elizabeth Barton, or more directly between Barton and Anne Askew, but these are far from strong and it would be a mistake to place too much weight on them. To argue for a tradition in this sense would result in a distortion of the significant gaps in the written records and an overemphasis on some aspects of women's writing at the expense of others. It is crucial that these women's utterances, spoken and written, not be *assumed* to have similar interests and concerns, and equally crucial that they are not artificially isolated from male discourse.

Before looking further at individual cases, we need to address some of the theoretical issues entailed in such a project. This study challenges a series of academic assumptions. Firstly, it focuses on what is usually and mistakenly taken to be a marginal and 'sub-literary' type of discourse. Secondly, it is located in that grey area between history and literature, drawing on the methodology and theoretical vocabulary of both disciplines (disciplines which are often completely separate in educational institutions). As Paul Strohm has argued, 'one reason past generations of academics maintained distinctions between "the literary," with its reliance on invention, and "the historical," with its adherence to fact, is the reassuring implication of such clearly bounded categories that fictional elements can be segregated and controlled'.[10] Yet it cannot be denied that historical texts of all sorts do contain fictional elements, or that fictional texts contain history. What is more, the distinction between the literary and the historical is itself ahistorical when applied to much of the Middle Ages. This book also extends beyond the confines of established schemes of periodization. As a result, it not only studies texts which have seldom been considered before (i.e. non-canonical texts) alongside semi-canonical ones (e.g. *The Book of Margery Kempe*), arguing that their importance to their contemporaries has often been ignored, but also and more significantly, it compares texts which would normally be isolated from one another in academic research because they come from different sides of the medieval/Renaissance barrier.

Increasingly in the past few years scholars have begun to question the

---

the *Other*, trans. B. Massumi, Theory and History of Literature 17 (London, 1986), 80–100; cf. also M. de Certeau, *The Mystic Fable, Volume One: the Sixteenth and Seventeenth Centuries*, trans. M.B. Smith (Chicago, 1992).

[10] P. Strohm, *Hochon's Arrow: the Social Imagination of Fourteenth-Century Texts* (Princeton, 1992), 5.

labels 'medieval' and 'Renaissance'.[11] The title of this chapter comes from
Judith Bennett's essay 'Medieval Women, Modern Women: Across the
Great Divide' in which she gives the following summary of the 'master
narrative' of European history,

> In our dominant vision of the past, a great chasm separates the medieval world
> from the world of early-modern Europe. This chasm partly reflects the
> genuine historical transitions of the fourteenth through seventeenth centuries:
> the development of humanism and reformed Christianity, the advance of
> capitalism and urbanisation, the rise of nationalism and national monarchies,
> the 'discovery' and exploration of 'New World' territories. Yet this breach in
> historical continuity has been deepened far beyond its natural contours by
> scholarly depictions of the great divide.[12]

One of the principal arguments against the great divide in the sense of a
transition in religious, political and social terms is that the Renaissance was
not the homogenous intellectual movement it is often seen to have been.
Even if we think of the Renaissance as, say, a 'flowering of learning' there
were in fact many renaissances all over Europe at various times in history
(for example, the twelfth-century renaissance). Indeed, it seems that the
Renaissance was pretty much 'self-fashioned' and it would be naive to
accept without questioning what the Renaissance tells us about itself. The
Renaissance invented the 'Middle Ages' in order to break with the past and
emphasize its own achievements; the term is a historical construct like any
other. Modern scholars have likewise challenged the influential view of the
nineteenth-century historian Jacob Burckhardt that people had no sense of
themselves as individuals in the Middle Ages.[13] The very terminology,
including the label 'early modern', is problematic because it implies

---

11 See D. Aers, *Community, Gender, and Individual Identity: English Writing 1360–1430*
    (London, 1988); and his essay 'A Whisper in the Ear of Early Modernists; or, Reflec-
    tions on Literary Critics Writing the "History of the Subject" ' in *Culture and History
    1350–1600: Essays on English Communities, Identities and Writing*, ed. D. Aers (Lon-
    don, 1992), 177–202. See also L. Patterson, *Negotiating the Past: the Historical Under-
    standing of Medieval Literature* (Madison WI, 1987); and L. Patterson, 'On the Margin:
    Postmodernism, Ironic History, and Medieval Studies', *Speculum* lxv (1990), 87–108.

12 J.M. Bennett, 'Medieval Women, Modern Women: Across the Great Divide' in *Culture
    and History*, ed. Aers, 147.

13 Jacob Burckhardt, *The Civilization of the Renaissance*, trans. S.G.C. Middlemore (Lon-
    don, 1944), 81. Cf. C. Morris, *The Discovery of the Individual, 1050–1200* (London,
    1972); C.W. Bynum, 'Did the Twelfth Century Discover the Individual?' *Journal of
    Ecclesiastical History* xxxi (1980), 1–17; J.F. Benton, 'Consciousness of Self and
    Perceptions of Individuality' in *Renaissance and Renewal in the Twelfth Century*, ed.
    R.L. Benson and G. Constable (Oxford, 1982), 263–96; Umberto Eco, 'Living in the
    New Middle Ages' in *Travels in Hyperreality: Essays*, trans. W. Weaver (London,
    1987), 73–85; Patterson, *Negotiating the Past*; Aers, *Community*; Patterson, 'On the
    Margin'; Aers, 'Whisper in the Ear'.

progress as well as a 'great divide' between the pre-modern and modern periods.

The strongest feminist attacks on the grand narrative of Western European cultural epochs have however come from rather different directions to those just outlined. On the one hand, critics like Margaret Ezell have shown that traditional literary histories often exclude or marginalize texts by women, especially those which were written before 1700, a period which is often characterized by illiteracy and silence, and which is described in *The Norton Anthology of Literature by Women* as the 'Dark Ages' of women's imagination.[14] On the other, in 1977 in her famous essay, Joan Kelly posed the question 'Did women have a Renaissance?', thus challenging the assumption that traditional schemes of historical periodization are equally applicable to men and women.[15] It is not surprising that subsequent feminist scholars should have renewed the attack by asking 'Did women have a Reformation?'[16] In a recent essay, Lisa Jardine suggests that most feminist historians have recognized that ' "history as a unified story was a fiction" – that all history *is* constructed narrative, textually interpreting and recreating – weaving, unweaving and reweaving – the slender residue of "evidence" which time has carried down to us', and she proposes that we adopt the motto 'One woman's fact is another man's fiction.'[17] To put this simply – the ages of history and literature do not comfortably accommodate women's writing and history, and they sometimes may seem to conspire to

---

14 *The Norton Anthology of Literature by Women: the Tradition in English*, ed. S.M. Gilbert and S. Gubar (New York, 1985), 15; cf. *Silences of the Middle Ages*, ed. C. Klapisch-Zuber, A History of Women in the West 2, gen. eds. G. Duby and M. Perrot (Cambridge MA, 1992). For a full critique of women's literary histories with special reference to the seventeenth century, see M.J.M. Ezell, *Writing Women's Literary History* (Baltimore, 1993). Women's writing in the Middle Ages is discussed in S. Delaney, ' "Mothers to Think Back Through": Who are They? The Ambiguous Example of Christine de Pizan' in *Medieval Texts and Contemporary Readers*, ed. L.A. Finke and M.S. Shichtman (Ithaca N.Y., 1987), 177–97; the introduction to *Seeking the Woman in Late Medieval and Renaissance Writings: Essays in Feminist Contextual Criticism*, ed. S. Fisher and J.E. Halley (Knoxville, 1989), 1–17; the introduction to *Women's Writing in Middle English*, ed. A. Barratt (London, 1992), 1–23; J. Boffey, 'Women Authors and Women's Literacy in Fourteenth-and Fifteenth-Century England' in *Women and Literature in Britain, 1150–1500*, ed. C.M. Meale, Cambridge Studies in Medieval Literature 17 (Cambridge, 1993), 159–82.

15 J. Kelly, 'Did Women Have a Renaissance?' reprinted in her *Women, History and Theory* (Chicago, 1984), 19–51.

16 J. Mueller, 'Autobiography of a New "Creatur": Female Spirituality, Selfhood and Authorship in *The Book of Margery Kempe*', *New York Literary Forum* vols. xii–xiii (1984), 15.

17 L. Jardine, *Reading Shakespeare Historically* (London, 1996), 146–7. For a useful summary of the theoretical debates about women's history, see J. Scott, 'Women's History' in *New Perspectives on Historical Writing*, ed. P. Burke (Cambridge, 1991), 42–66; especially 57–61.

exclude them. Adrienne Rich states that 'Re-vision – the act of looking back, of seeing with fresh eyes, of entering an old text from a new critical direction – is for women more than a chapter in cultural history: it is an act of survival.'[18]

Arguing that traditional schemes of periodization reflect a masculine view of history does not imply that women were unaffected by the religiopolitical crises of their times. Indeed it would appear that the political prophecies of both men and women were precipitated by discontent or rebellion, whether the Wars of the Roses or the overthrow of Charles I. Nonetheless, the picture which is provided by a history which focuses on what have been traditionally thought of as the major events and turning points does not tell us the *whole* story, or even, necessarily, the most important parts of it. This raises yet another theoretical question: should we simply replace the 'master narrative' with an alternative scheme of women's history? Bennett points out that this seems to be exactly what has happened. As she says,

> Both medievalists and early modernists tend to agree – without trespassing much into each other's periods – not only that women's lives changed over these centuries but also about the nature of the change: things were better for women in the Middle Ages, and they worsened during the early modern centuries.[19]

According to this paradigm, medieval women enjoyed 'rough and ready equality' with men (to use Eileen Power's phrase), but during the Renaissance, and (according to Alice Clark) especially in the course of the seventeenth century, women's status diminished. Women became increasingly confined to domestic activities relating to the needs of the family and their work was devalued. One great divide has merely been replaced by another.

To some extent this paradigm of a negative transition appears to work, as the following examples will illustrate. In terms of maintaining their independence either outwith or within the bonds of matrimony, the medieval women in this study seem to have fared rather better than their successors. Christina of Markyate ultimately succeeded in preserving her virginity, and early fifteenth-century society accommodated (although admittedly only with difficulty) Margery Kempe's celibate lifestyle, allowing her to replace

---

[18] Adrienne Rich, 'When We Dead Awaken: Writing as Re-Vision' in *On Lies, Secrets, and Silence: Selected Prose 1966–1978* (London, 1980), 35.

[19] Bennett, 'Medieval Women', 149. See, for example, Eileen Power, *Medieval Women*, ed. M.M. Postan (Cambridge, 1975); and Alice Clark, *Working Life of Women in the Seventeenth Century* (rpt. London, 1982). For an overview of recent studies by historians see R.M. Warnicke, *Women of the English Renaissance and Reformation*, Contributions to Women's Studies 38 (Westport C.T., 1983), 4–5; and also Bennett, 'Medieval Women', 149–52.

subjection to her husband with direct allegiance to God and the Church. However, Anne Askew's comparable desire for freedom of belief and movement, which she hoped to obtain by divorce, a course of action acceptable to some radical Protestants, was clearly perceived as dangerous by the reactionary authorities. On the other hand, by the seventeenth century, separation was an option available to the socially-privileged Eleanor Davies. Yet despite this she represents herself as overcoming the restraining control of both her husbands through predicting (and thus it seems supernaturally effecting) the death of the first, and the insanity of the second.[20]

The women prophets studied here lived and wrote under very different conditions. Their social and educational backgrounds, religious beliefs and specific circumstances varied greatly, and it is important that the implications of these crucial matters of difference are not underestimated. At one end of the scale is Elizabeth Barton (a former servant, either illiterate or semi-literate, who became a nun and held extremely orthodox beliefs), while at the other is Lady Eleanor Davies (an aristocrat, educated in the Classics, who had a literary husband – the politician and poet Sir John Davies – and who, despite her Protestantism, identified with the Virgin Mary and saw herself as the Redeemer). Nonetheless, given these differences, the contrasts between their experiences and discourses are not as great as might have been expected. Many of these prophets were publicly censured: Christina of Markyate was physically and psychologically abused by her family and forced to flee her home; Margery Kempe was examined for heresy; both Barton and Askew were executed; and Eleanor Davies was incarcerated a number of times in prison and also in Bedlam. The need to validate their own experiences, to vindicate themselves against accusations that they were abnormal because they rejected the sexual and social roles into which they were born, is a theme of many of their writings. As Bennett concludes, 'The paradigm of a great divide, quite simply, does not hold.'[21]

Instead of simply re-writing history in terms of an equally fixed paradigm, Bennett urges us to 'pursue our historical study of women with greater attention to the *varied* and *changing* patriarchal contexts of women's lives' [my italics].[22] And just as Judith Butler has warned against the assumption that women have a transcultural transhistorical identity,[23] so Bennett argues that we ought to think carefully about the nature of patriarchy, or more correctly, patriarchies:

---

[20] Eleanor Davies, *The Lady Eleanor her appeal* (1646), B4r-B4v and C3r-C3v.

[21] Bennett, 'Medieval Women', 164.

[22] Bennett, 'Medieval Women', 164.

[23] J. Butler, *Gender Trouble: Feminism and the Subversion of Identity* (New York, 1990).

Patriarchies have changed historically, but the institution of patriarchy has endured because of its complex and multi-faceted nature; patriarchy draws its strength from ideology, custom and affective relations as well as from politics, law, economy and society. This multi-faceted structure calls upon the attention of literary scholars as much as the attention of historians.[24]

The way forward seems to be to avoid those universalizing tendencies which falsify our understanding of the past. As Patricia Crawford puts it, 'Whiggish questions about "better" or "worse" for women obscure the fact that women are not a monolithic group; women were born into different social levels, and thus class as well as age affected their experiences.'[25] By carefully situating our studies within the appropriate cultural and historical contexts we can try to steer clear of sweeping generalizations. To sum up, in crossing the great divide between the medieval and Renaissance or early modern periods, I do not accept without questioning those grand narratives which posit a series of historical or literary periods, and imply a linear development or progression, but nor do I reject a chronological approach to history and literature. The idea behind this research is essentially straight-forward – it looks for evidence of both continuity and change in women's prophetic experience and discourse. This is still a narrative, albeit an often discontinuous one.

In the following chapters I will argue that the Reformation did signal an important turning point in English women's prophecies in some respects, but not in others. For example, in the Middle Ages, prophets and visionaries not only saw themselves as divinely-inspired teachers, but were often also consulted as seers and spiritual guides, and demonstrated physical manifestations of their gifts. In much Protestant theology, however, prophecy was understood *primarily* as the interpretation of Scripture. Furthermore, as has been suggested already, English women's prophecy became more politi-cized with the Reformation. Also relevant here is the legislation against popular prophecy: perhaps partly as a direct consequence of Elizabeth Barton's execution for treason in 1534, and partly as a consequence of the iconoclastic fervour of the Reformation, women's prophecy in England did not have an overtly political dimension throughout the rest of the sixteenth century, and even in recusant circles women were less likely to have revelatory and visionary experiences than had been the case in the previous centuries.

Yet the circumstances which limited women's freedom and those which allowed women to take public actions, and indeed to write, did not change completely in the period in question. Possibly the momentous events of the

---

[24] Bennett, 'Medieval Women', 165.
[25] P. Crawford, review of Alice Clark's *Working Life of Women in the Seventeenth Century* (1992) in *Gender and History* v (1993), 304.

Reformation – or even that other great transition with which it is often associated, the invention of the printing press, did not have such far-reaching consequences for women prophets as might be expected. While the development of the printing press made the publication and circulation of texts easier and cheaper for women as well as men, and the supporters of prophets like Barton and Askew hoped to reach larger audiences by printing their works, censorship may well have considerably limited its impact. Although scholars are divided over the question of how effective censorship really was in the first two centuries after the introduction of printing, attempts to control the press were not without their successes as the destruction of Barton's works reveals. Except for a brief period in the sixteenth century during Seymour's Protectorate (when Askew's texts were in fairly free circulation in England), it was only during the 1640s that censorship broke down more or less completely, offering subversive and heterodox writers like Davies and some of the other Civil War prophets unprecedented opportunities to make their ideas known.[26]

At least of equal importance to the transition from a manuscript to a print culture is the related question of patronage (often by men), whether in the form of religious or financial support, which provided most of these women from both the Middle Ages and early modern period with the means to produce and circulate their texts, and also an audience which would read them. But even more significant than the invention of the printing press is the issue of orality. Recent social historians have suggested that illiteracy is a dynamic force, and that it is often associated with religious heterodoxy and political nonconformity.[27] Books (especially printed books which could be produced and disseminated quickly and cheaply) were of course a potentially subversive medium (the writings of Askew, Barton and Davies were seen as such), but through increased literacy the authorities could also hope to educate and in this way pacify the unruly elements in society; thus

26 See W.W. Greg, *Some Aspects and Problems of London Publishing between 1550 and 1650* (Oxford, 1956); D. Thomas, *A Long Time Burning: the History of Literary Censorship in England* (London, 1969), 8–13; D.M. Loades, 'The Theory and Practices of Censorship in Sixteenth Century England', *Transactions of the Royal Historical Society*, 5th series, xxiv (1974), 141–57; J. Feather, *A History of British Publishing* (London, 1988). On Barton see E.J. Devereux, 'Elizabeth Barton and Tudor Censorship', *Bulletin of the John Rylands Library* xlix (1966–1967), 91–106. On the freedom of the press under Seymour, see J.N. King, *English Reformation Literature: the Tudor Origins of the Protestant Tradition* (Princeton, 1982), 76–121.

27 K.V. Thomas, 'The Meaning of Literacy in Early Modern England' in *The Written Word: Literacy in Transition*, ed. G. Baumann (Oxford, 1986), 104–105. On literacy generally, see H.J. Chaytor, *From Script to Print: an Introduction to Medieval Vernacular Literature* (London, 1966), 5–21; and D. Cressy, *Literacy and the Social Order: Reading and Writing in Tudor and Stuart England* (Cambridge, 1980), 1–18; and B. Stock, *The Implications of Literacy: Written Language and Models of Interpretation in the Eleventh and Twelfth Centuries* (Princeton, 1983).

the perceived power of printed propaganda (used to great effect against Barton). However political prophecy was often associated with oral culture, and the vision was a form of discourse which did not necessarily require the written word in its formulation or articulation.[28] The influence of oral and popular culture can be clearly seen in the examples of Kempe and Barton, but more unexpectedly even the educated Eleanor Davies drew extensively on elements of popular political prophecy, such as predictions based on anagrams, puns, monograms, heraldic devices, numbers, riddles and astrology, which have been (inaccurately) associated with those sectors of society which are often disregarded because they are thought of as uneducated and socially insignificant.

Women writing and speaking publicly between the eleventh and seventeenth centuries were confronted with the obstacle that according to their cultures their sex was inferior. They were excluded from the masculine concept of authority not only in its social sense ('power') but also in its literary sense in so far as the word *auctour* or *author* also implied 'father' and 'creator'.[29] Relegated to a position of subjection in society and of object in discourse, women had to justify their decision to speak publicly or write. Such a subjective limitation was perhaps more of an impediment than any practical difficulties like lack of education or free time, financial independence or patronage. Throughout the periods in question, prophecy was seen as a feminine activity, regardless of the sex of the speaker, but while it authorized the female voice, it was derived from and at the same time reinforced women's perceived inferiority. In *The Renaissance Notion of Woman*, Ian Maclean explains that if 'prophecy contravenes the prohibition of speech, teaching and preaching by women' it also reflects a 'prerogative of woman over man, which is only conducive to her honour in a rather doubtful way'.[30] Indeed it was their very inferiority, their perceived powerlessness and irrationality which made women prophets and visionaries, no matter their social status, humble recipients of and suitable conduits for the Holy Spirit. Sometimes early women writers felt the need to apologise for textualizing their achievements. Often they explained their decision to speak or write as an act of obedience, representing themselves as passive and compliant, and validating their experiences by emphasizing their

---

28 On the popular and oral nature of prophecy, see K.V. Thomas, *Religion and the Decline of Magic: Studies in Popular Beliefs in Sixteenth and Seventeenth Century England* (London, 1971), 389–432; A. Fox, 'Prophecies and Politics in the Reign of Henry VIII' in *Reassessing the Henrician Age: Humanism, Politics and Reform 1500–1550* (Oxford, 1986), 77–94; and S.L. Jansen, *Political Protest and Prophecy under Henry VIII* (Woodbridge, 1991).

29 *MED*, s.v 'auctour' and 'auctorite'; *OED*, s.v 'author' and 'authority'; see also the discussion of authority in *Women's Writing*, ed. Barratt, 6–7.

30 I. Maclean, *The Renaissance Notion of Woman: a Study in the Fortunes of Scholasticism and Medical Science in European Intellectual Life* (Cambridge, 1980), 21.

endurance in the face of persecution and physical or inner torment. Women prophets could claim the transcendental authority of God's command, denying that they themselves spoke or wrote and depicting themselves as transmitters of divine inspiration, and thus they succeeded in crossing an even greater divide than that between the Middle Ages and the Renaissance – they crossed from silence into discourse.

2

A Prophet In her Own Country:
Margery Kempe and the Medieval Tradition

---

*A prophet is not without honour, save in his own country, and in his
own house.*   (Matthew 13.57)

The Authority of Prophetic Experience

During the episcopate of William Alnwick at Norwich, between 1426 and
1436, a time when persecution of Lollards had been at its height, the town
of Lynn in Norfolk was divided over an issue of local politics: the granting
of baptisms and purifications to the Chapels of St Nicholas and St James.
An almost contemporaneous account of the dispute appears in *The Book of
Margery Kempe* (the first version of which seems to have been begun
around about 1430 and abandoned in 1431 with the death of the first scribe;
the revisions by another scribe, an anonymous priest, were made between
1436 and 1438):

> It happyd in a worshepful town wher was o parysch cherch & tweyn chapelys
> annexid, þe chapellys hauyng & mynystryng alle sacramentys, except only
> cristenyng & purificacyons, thorw sufferawns of þe person . . . Thorw summe
> of þe parischenys desyryng to make þe chapelys lych to þe parysch cherch,
> pursuyng a bulle fro þe Cowrt of Rome, fel gret ple & gret heuynes be-twen
> þe Priowr whech was her person & curat & þe forseyd paryschenys þat
> desyred to haue fvntys & purificacyons in þe chapelys lych as weryn in þe
> parysch cherche. & specyaly in þe on chapel whech was þe grettar & þe
> fayrare þei wold haue a funte. Þer was pursuyd a bulle, in þe whech was
> grawntyd a funte to þe chapel so it wer no derogacyon to þe parysch cherch.
> Þe bulle was put in ple, & diuers days wer kept be forme of lawe to preuyn
> wheþyr þe funte, ȝyf it wer had, xuld ben derogacyon to þe parysch chyrch
> or nowt. Þe paryschenys whech pursuyd weryn rygth strong & haddyn gret
> help of lordshyp, & also, þe most of alle, þei wer ryche men, worshepful
> marchawntys, & haddyn gold a-now, whech may spede in euery nede, & þat
> is rewth þat mede xuld spede er þan trewth. Neuyr-þe-lesse þe Priowr whech
> was her person, þei he wer powyr, manfully he wythstod hem thorw þe help
> of summe of hys paryschenys whech wer hys frendys & louedyn þe worshep
> of her parysch chyrch. So long þis mater was in ple þat it be-gan yrkyn hem

on boþe sydes, & it was neuyr þe nerar an ende. Þan was þe mater put in my Lord of Norwych Alnewyk to say if he mygth be trety bryng it to an ende.[1]

Clearly this is a partisan account of events. The narrator – in this passage Kempe's clerical scribe (rather than Kempe herself) – takes the side of the Prior of St Margaret's Church in Lynn, John Derham.[2] The dispute is constructed as a conflict between *mede,* with its connotations of a 'gift', 'reward', 'fee' and 'bribe', and *trewthe,* which can denote 'faithfulness' and 'loyalty' as well as 'veracity' and 'righteousness'.[3] The narrator draws upon the *communis sententia* of proverbial wisdom ('Gold may speed in every need' and 'Meed may speed rather than truth'[4]) to oppose the power which comes with material wealth, status and patronage against the authority of a poor servant of God who relies on the support of his devout parishioners.[5] If the merchants are 'worschepful' their honour and dignity is worldly rather than spiritual – Derham's 'manful' opposition to the bullying of these esteemed citizens echoes the descriptions of the tribulations of numerous saints.[6]

The legal system is seen to be incapable of resolving the matter which drags on to the dissatisfaction of all concerned, and even the intervention of Bishop Alnwick does not appear to hasten the proceedings. At this point the narrator (who characteristically describes himself as 'þe preste whech aftyrward wrot þis boke') gives up on the official process and turns to Kempe, as, he tells us, 'he had done be-forn in þe tyme of ple' and asks her to look into her soul and predict the outcome. Kempe's answer is instantaneous and unambiguous, 'Drede ȝe not, for I vndyrstond in my sowle, þow þei woldyn ȝeve a buschel of nobelys, þei xuld not haue it.' It is not perhaps surprising that Kempe should take Derham's part in this matter as the *Red Register of King's Lynn* records that an attempt to secure privileges for the Chapel of St Nicholas in 1378 had been opposed by her father John Brunham, the then Mayor of Lynn.[7] Despite Kempe's confidence in her own revelation, the narrator is not entirely reassured; he is aware that Alnwick

---

1 *The Book of Margery Kempe,* ed. S.B. Meech and H.E. Allen, EETS 212 (Oxford, 1940), 58–9. All references are to this edition.

2 *Book of Margery Kempe,* n. 59/2–3 and Appendix III, v, 3, 4, 5, 6.

3 *MED,* s.v. 'mede'; *OED,* s.v. 'truth'.

4 B.J. Whiting, ed., *Proverbs, Sentences, and Proverbial Phrases from English Writing mainly before 1500* (Cambridge MA, 1968), G302 and M493.

5 Compare the language of this passage to a letter dated 13 January 1431/2 from the Mayor, Alderman, Burgesses, and Commons of Lynn to the Prior of Norwich requesting privileges for the Chapel of St Nicholas, reproduced in *Book of Margery Kempe,* Appendix III, vii, 374.

6 Masculine traits are often ascribed to female saints in their militant defence of their chastity. See, for example, *The Life of Christina of Markyate: a Twelfth Century Recluse,* ed. and trans. C.H. Talbot (Oxford, 1987), 93.

7 *Book of Margery Kempe,* Appendix III, vii, 373.

has started negotiations with the merchant party. It is then, all the more remarkable that her predictions are nevertheless fulfilled: the proposed compromise is rejected and the court finds in favour of the Prior.

This narrative episode has an exemplary function within the larger narrative of Kempe's *Book*, as its conclusion makes clear:

> And so, blyssed mot God ben, þe parysch cherch stod stylle in her worshep & hyr degre as sche had don ij hundryd ʒer befor & mor, and þe inspiracyon of owyr Lord was be experiens preuyd for very sothfast & sekyr in þe forseyd creatur.[8]

Not only are the righteous rewarded, but, more significantly, experience proves the authenticity of the prophetic voice; the authority of God-given inspiration. This is only one of three extended passages in *The Book of Margery Kempe* in which it is not only possible to distinguish the voice of Kempe's principal scribe, but where he also appears as a character in his own narrative (the proem, the twenty-fourth and twenty-fifth chapters and the sixty-second chapter). On each occasion the scribe describes the resolution of doubts which he has felt concerning Kempe's piety and her devotions and thus confirms the validity of her sanctity and religious practices. Whenever possible, Kempe sought the assistance of men of religion to read to her from the Bible and devotional works and to write down the matters of God which were revealed to her, and this scribe testifies in the proem that 'sche knew & vndyrstod many secret & preuy thyngys whech schuld beffallen aftyrward be inspiracyon of þe Holy Gost'.[9] In Chapter 25, however, the scribe admits that he had not always been so convinced. As a priest, he felt a pastoral responsibility towards those who would read the treatise which he was copying and editing – he had to be sure in his own mind that he was not doing the work of the devil and in order to test Margery Kempe's spirit of prophecy he encouraged her to predict the outcome of future happenings 'vn-sekyr & vncerteyn as þat tyme to any creatur what xuld be þe ende'.[10] He even threatened that he would not help to write the book if she refused. Referring to incidents which had taken place many years earlier, he reveals that by ignoring Margery Kempe's warnings he had once been tricked into parting with money by a disarming young man.[11] Less cynical a second time, he asked for Margery Kempe's advice and thus avoided being similarly deceived by another man.[12]

It was suggested earlier that prophets appropriated authority for their

---

8 *Book of Margery Kempe*, 60.
9 *Book of Margery Kempe*, 2.
10 *Book of Margery Kempe*, 55.
11 *Book of Margery Kempe*, 55–7.
12 *Book of Margery Kempe*, 57–8.

words and deeds by representing themselves as conduits of divine inspiration. Kempe asserts that during one of her contemplations, Christ revealed to her that He spoke through her: 'I am in þe, and þow in me. And þei þat heryn þe þei heryn þe voys of God.'[13] Like the writers of saints' lives, in the episodes just described Margery Kempe's scribe is anxious to attribute supernatural powers to his subject. His 'masculine' objectifying voice confirms the veracity of her revelations and the orthodoxy of her piety and authorizes the text itself. As Janet Wilson argues, 'his confessions of wavering faith not only provide eye-witness verification; they also contribute to a rhetorical design which ultimately endorses Kempe's mysticism and guarantees an image of saintliness'.[14] What interests me here, however, is not only Kempe's 'quest for authority' (which has already been the focus of a great deal of critical attention),[15] but also the importance the scribe places on her prophetic voice, a voice which is however never direct, but always mediated by the scribe himself.

In the next sections I will discuss the meaning of prophecy in the Middle Ages, going on to focus on the European tradition of women's prophecy in particular (a tradition which included political comment and activism), and then comparing Margery Kempe to other English visionary women before considering the extent to which she was influenced by St Bridget and the controversy which surrounded her revelations. In my analysis of the ways in which prophecy functions to authorize both Kempe and her *Book*, I will

[13] *Book of Margery Kempe*, 23.

[14] J. Wilson, 'Communities of Dissent: the Secular and Ecclesiastical Communities of Margery Kempe's *Book*' in *Medieval Women in their Communities*, ed. D. Watt (Cardiff, 1997), 161–2.

[15] See, for example, K. Lochrie, '*The Book of Margery Kempe*: the Marginal Woman's Quest for Literary Authority', *Journal of Medieval and Renaissance Studies* xvi (1986), 33–55, and *Margery Kempe and Translations of the Flesh* (Philadelphia, 1991), 97–134. Lochrie argues that the voice of God and Kempe's 'dalyawns' are central to her quest for authority and to some extent replace conventional *auctoritas*. See also J.A. Erskine, 'Margery Kempe and her Models: the Role of the Authorial Voice', *Mystics Quarterly* xv (1989), 75–85; S. Beckwith, 'Problems of Authority in Late Medieval Mysticism: Language, Agency and Authority in *The Book of Margery Kempe*', *Exemplaria* iv (1992), 171–99; and D.R. Uhlman, 'The Comfort of Voice, the Solace of Script: Orality and Literacy in *The Book of Margery Kempe*', *Studies in Philology* xci (1994), 50–69. Critics are divided over the question of authorship of the *Book*: for an overview, see W. Harding, 'Body into Text: *The Book of Margery Kempe*' in *Feminist Approaches to the Body in Medieval Literature*, ed. L. Lomperis and S. Stanbury (Philadelphia, 1993), 168–9. One recent critic has contended that Kempe's scribe (whether real or a fictional creation) is a metaphor which relates 'to the author's perception of the act of producing literature': L. Staley, *Margery Kempe's Dissenting Fictions* (Pennsylvania, 1994), 37; cf. her earlier article, L.S. Johnson, 'The Trope of the Scribe and the Question of Literary Authority in the Works of Julian of Norwich and Margery Kempe', *Speculum* lxvi (1991), 820–38, and also M.J. Wright, 'What they Said to Margery Kempe: Narrative Reliability in her *Book*', *Neophilologus* lxxix (1995), 497–508.

argue that while her prophetic role may be less political than is the case with her continental predecessors, the *Book* itself can nonetheless be understood as a response to the tensions of the time. Kempe used the more widely accepted sorts of prophecy, in particular her divine revelations about the state of individuals within the church, to justify another type, the interpretation of Scripture, in an age which was anxious to deny the latter to the lay piety in general and women in particular.

Prophecy in the Middle Ages

The English word *prophet* derives from the Greek *prophetes*.[16] As Howard Dobin argues in *Merlin's Disciples,* its principal meanings are 'one who speaks forth' and 'one who speaks beforehand'; two senses of the word which were conflated in both the classical and Hebrew traditions:

> The Greeks blurred this distinction between these two meanings; the prophet was the spokesman (or spokeswoman) of the gods who interpreted the oracles and thus delivered a prediction of the future. To speak 'for' the gods always already means to speak 'in advance of' future things. The prophets of the Old Testament primarily spoke 'for' God, declaring his divine will and displeasure; however, their inspired prophecies inevitably entailed predictions, typically in the form of warnings, of the tests and punishments God would impose on his chosen people. In the political arena, the distinction between prophecy and prognostication virtually disappears. The Old Testament prophet did not simply express a divine protest to an evil king; he also predicted his imminent downfall. Prophecy is essentially a form of political discourse; the prophet invokes God as the authority superior to and more powerful than the earthly powers of church and state. Prophecy as political protest – as opposition to the reigning secular and sacred authorities – inevitably constituted a call for change and a challenge to the dominant order.[17]

Richard K. Emmerson, in his article 'The Prophetic, the Apocalyptic, and the Study of Medieval Literature', draws a distinction between the 'prophetic' and the 'apocalyptic'.[18] Emmerson's categorization is founded in biblical scholarship: the Old Testament prophets from Amos to Malachi spoke and wrote between the eighth and fifth centuries BC; the apocalyptic

16 *OED,* s.v. 'prophet'; see also *Catholic Encyclopedia,* s.v. 'prophecy' and 'prophet'.
17 H. Dobin, *Merlin's Disciples: Prophecy, Poetry and Power in Renaissance England* (Stanford CA, 1990), 27–8; cf. M. Lieb, *The Visionary Mode: Biblical Prophecy, Hermeneutics, and Cultural Change* (Ithaca N.Y., 1991), 25 n. 25.
18 R.K. Emmerson, 'The Prophetic, the Apocalyptic, and the Study of Medieval Literature' in *Poetic Prophecy in Western Literature,* ed. J. Wojcik and R.J. Frontain (London, 1984), 40–54; cf. M. Murrin, *The Veil of Allegory: Some Notes Towards a Theory of Allegorical Rhetoric in the English Renaissance* (Chicago, 1969), 21–53.

visionaries, from Daniel to John of Patmos, wrote between the second century BC and the first century AD. The two modes of discourse do sometimes overlap: the apocalyptic visionaries saw themselves as the heirs of the prophets. Nonetheless, Emmerson is able to make some useful generalizations about their distinguishing features. In summary, he argues that the prophets spoke in response to specific historical circumstances, in times of political chaos when Israel and Judah were under threat from foreign powers, and they called for moral reformation. In contrast the apocalyptic authors wrote during a long period of oppression, and their message was encouraging, offering hope for the future. While each claims to reveal God's will, the prophet, according to Emmerson, is primarily a spokesperson and participant or actor who demands change, while the visionary plays a more passive role requiring a less active response. Both use very figurative and often ambiguous language, but whereas the apoca-lyptic writer offers no hope for change in the present but speaks to the future, revealing God's secret message in esoteric terms only to the righteous, the prophet's utterance is usually more immediate, more concerned with the here and now. The apocalyptic visionary writes about the divine purpose of universal history, but the prophet's purpose is 'to proclaim God's message to the nation', and so 'the message must be specific, direct, powerful'.[19]

In the Middle Ages, the division between prophecy and apocalyptic vision was, however, far from clear.[20] As Bernard McGinn states, 'most apocalypticists were in some way prophets' but prophecy 'did not neces-sarily entail concern with the structure and imminent End of history'.[21] This collapsing of the two traditions has its roots in the Gospels, the Epistles of St Paul, and the Apocalypse of St John – the last book, for example, describes itself as a prophecy. Medieval exegesis, with its insistence that the New Testament fulfilled the Old, removed the Old Testament texts from their specific historical contexts, weakening the distinction still further. If, according to the medieval exegetes, Daniel was a prophet, so too were Virgil and the Sibyl because they were believed to have foretold Christ's mission. In the medieval period, then, prophecy was *primarily* understood to be predictive, yet it was more than simply foresight, it was also a divinely inspired utterance which might also take the form of a command or a description of how things are. In I Corinthians 14, St Paul did not confine the meaning of *prophecy* to foreknowledge of future events but used the word interchangeably with *interpret*. St Augustine of Hippo argued that dreams and visions were only prophetic if they were understood intellectu-ally, 'the man who interpreted what another had seen was more a prophet

---

[19] Emmerson, 'Prophetic', 45.
[20] Emmerson, 'Prophetic', 40–2.
[21] B. McGinn, *Visions of the End: Apocalyptic Traditions in the Middle Ages* (New York, 1979), 4.

than the man who had seen'.[22] St Thomas Aquinas insisted that Scriptural interpretation was a form of prophecy:

> The interpretation of speeches can be reduced to the gift of prophecy – in so far as the mind is enlightened so as to understand and expound whatever is obscure in speeches, whether because of the difficulty of the matters referred to, or because of the very words uttered, or because of the examples given: thus *Daniel, I have heard that you can interpret and solve problems.*[23]

Aquinas also emphasized that a prophet was also a teacher and preacher, one called by God to speak His word to the people.[24] The last prophetic or visionary work recognized by the Church is the final book of the canonical Scriptures, the Apocalypse of St John, and Aquinas argued that prophecy could serve 'not for the purpose of setting out new doctrine to be believed, but for the government of human activities'.[25] In summary, prophecy could denote divine inspiration in a much more general sense.

In the Middle Ages then, prophecy was both widespread and diverse. Commentators and writers from Origen and St Augustine to Isidore of Seville, Richard of St Victor, Bernard of Clairvaux and Thomas Aquinas were concerned with the subject. As J. Wojcik and R.J. Frontain point out, 'Old Testament prophets also served postbiblical writers as models for mystical or visionary experience, in which the spirit is purified and the mind attuned to only spiritual realities. For the desert contemplatives as for the great medieval spiritual writers and the mystics of the twelfth through sixteenth centuries, the prophet's nearness to God, his actual experience of *visio dei*, made him the example to follow in the search for divine illumination.'[26] From the twelfth century, apocalyptic visionaries drew on Scripture (in particular the Book of Daniel and the Apocalypse of St John) as well as the fourth-century sibylline tradition in their attempts to make sense of the worlds in which they lived.[27] Amongst the most famous of these

---

22 S.F. Kruger, *Dreaming in the Middle Ages*, Cambridge Studies in Medieval Literature 14 (Cambridge, 1992), 41.

23 Aquinas, *Summa theologiæ*, ed. and trans. T. Gilby (London, 1964–1976), xlv, 2a2æ. q. 176, art. 2 (127).

24 Aquinas, *De veritate*, q. 12, art. 2c, cited by Emmerson, 'The Prophetic', 48. As William Kerrigan puts it, 'glossing the prophetic visions, exegetes wrote with an authority similar to the prophets themselves', *The Prophetic Milton* (Charlottesville, 1974), 41.

25 Aquinas, *Summa theologiæ*, xlv, 2a2æ, q. 174, art. 6 (93).

26 *Poetic Prophecy*, ed. Wojcik and Frontain, 20.

27 See G. Leff, *Heresy in the Later Middle Ages: the Relation of Heterodoxy to Dissent c.1250–c.1450* (Manchester, 1967), i; M. Reeves, *The Influence of Prophecy in the Later Middle Ages: a Study of Joachimism* (Oxford, 1969); N. Cohn, *The Pursuit of the Millennium: Revolutionary Millenarians and Mystical Anarchists of the Middle Ages* (London, 1970), 29–36; R.E. Lerner, 'Medieval Prophecy and Religious Dissent', *Past and Present* lxxii (1976), 3–24; B. McGinn, trans., *Apocalyptic Spirituality: Treatises*

thinkers is Joachim of Fiore (*c.*1135–1202), who inspired radical groups of followers in the thirteenth century and thereafter.[28] Popular forms of divination were in circulation, while astrology was seen as a scientific means of interpreting history, and a type of natural theology.[29] In England, Scotland and Wales, as well as in other parts of Europe, Judeo-Christian prophecies and apocalyptic visions also combined with insular tradition, especially those prophecies attributed to Merlin, Bede, and Thomas Becket, John of Bridlington and Thomas of Erceldoune.[30] The author of the early fourteenth-century *Five Dreams of Edward II*, who identifies himself as one Adam Davy, marshal, of Stratford-at-Bow, claimed that he had been instructed by an angel to reveal his prophecy to the King.[31] Of course, seers and soothsayers who threatened the political stability of the country ran the risk of imprisonment or even execution, and Acts of Parliament were passed against the seditious prophecies.[32] Nonetheless, despite J.A.F. Thomson's claim in *The Later Lollards* that 'millenarianism was not common in late medieval England',[33] numerous examples can be found of individuals claiming that the end was approaching.[34]

Ian Maclean, in *The Renaissance Notion of Woman*, suggests that

and Letters of Lactanius, Adso of Montier-en-Der, Joachim of Fiore, the Spiritual Franciscans, Savonarola (New York, 1979); B. McGinn, *Apocalypticism in the Western Tradition* (Aldershot, 1994).

[28] See especially M. Reeves, 'History and Prophecy in Medieval Thought', *Medievalia et Humanistica* n.s. 5 (1974), 51–75. On Joachim's influence in medieval England, see K. Kerby-Fulton, *Reformist Apocalypticism and 'Piers Plowman'*, Cambridge Studies in Medieval Literature 7 (Cambridge, 1990), 162–200.

[29] See, for example, L.A. Smoller, *History, Prophecy and the Stars: the Christian Astrology of Pierre d'Ailly 1350–1420* (Princeton, 1994).

[30] For an overview, see S. Jansen, *Political Protest and Prophecy in the Reign of Henry VIII* (Woodbridge, 1991), 9–19; R.H. Robbins, 'Political Prophecies' in *A Manual of the Writings in Middle English 1050–1500*, v, ed. A.E. Hartung (New Haven C.T., 1975), 1516–36.

[31] J.E. Wells, *A Manual of Writings in Middle English, 1050–1400* (Oxford, 1916), 221–2. For an example of a fifteenth-century English woman's prophecy with political import, see M.P. Harley, 'The Vision of Margaret Edward and Others at Canterbury, 29 July 1451', *Manuscripta* xxxii (1988), 146–51.

[32] For some medieval examples, see G.L. Kittredge, *Witchcraft in Old and New England* (Cambridge MA, 1929), 226–31; and S.L. Jansen, *Political Protest and Prophecy in the Reign of Henry VIII* (Woodbridge, 1991), 18.

[33] J.A.F. Thomson, *The Later Lollards, 1414–1520* (Oxford, 1965), 240.

[34] See, for example, Thomson, *The Later Lollards*, 241; R. Bauckham, *Tudor Apocalypse; Sixteenth Century Apocalypticism, Millennarianism and the English Reformation: from John Bale to John Foxe and Thomas Brightman*, The Courtenay Library of Reformation Classics 8 (Oxford, 1978), 17–21; Kerby-Fulton, *Reformist Apocalypticism*, 133–61; P. Szittya, 'Domesday Bokes: the Apocalypse in Medieval English Literary Culture' in *The Apocalypse in the Middle Ages*, ed. R.K. Emmerson and B. McGinn (Ithaca N.Y., 1992), 383–5.

prophecy was one domain in which women were seen as superior to men.[35] Famous female prophets from the classical period include the Pythia at Delphi, the Greek oracle which flourished between 700 and 480 BC; the Sibyl, who directed Æneas into the underworld in Virgil's *Æneid*, and to whom were attributed some spurious cryptic verses; and Cassandra, granted the gift of prophecy by Apollo, who then decreed that no one should ever believe her. Women were associated with prophecy in Celtic, Germanic and Scandinavian legend. Writing in AD 98, Tacitus claimed that the Germanic tribes 'believe that there resides in women an element of holiness and a gift of prophecy, and so they do not scorn to ask their advice or lightly disregard their replies'.[36] In the Scriptures, a number of women are described as prophetesses: Mary, the sister of Moses; Hannah, the mother of Samuel; Deborah, the only woman judge of Israel; Huldah, the wife of Shallum; and, in the New Testament, Elizabeth, the mother of John the Baptist, who recognized Mary as the Mother of God; and Anna, who blessed the baby Jesus when he was presented in the temple. Nicholas of Lyra refers to such inspired women as 'illuminatae mentis'.[37] The legendary Katherine of Alexandria, a typical example of an early Christian female martyr, fits into this tradition of women inspired by God; she was famous for disputing with philosophers and triumphing over the Emperor Maxentius. Her popularity lasted right up until the Reformation: a late fifteenth- or early sixteenth-century English alabaster represents her, unusually attired as a nun, holding a sword (a symbol of her martyrdom) with which she pierces the body of her persecutor, which lies prone beneath her feet [fig. 1].[38] Private revelations by women as well as men continued to be acknowledged if not authorized throughout the Middle Ages. Indeed, in the turbulent religious and political climate of late medieval Europe, it seems that prophecy could offer women a rare opportunity for direct involvement in the political sphere.

In 'The Prophet, the Apocalyptic, and the Study of Medieval Literature', Emmerson argues that the apocalytic visionary is working within a more consciously *literary* tradition than the prophet: 'Whereas the prophet "speaks" the word of God, the apocalyptic visionary is instructed to "write" what he has seen.'[39] He cites Hildegard of Bingen (1098–1179),

---

35 I. Maclean, *The Renaissance Notion of Woman: a Study in the Fortunes of Scholasticism and Medical Science in European Intellectual Life* (Cambridge, 1980), 20–1.

36 Tacitus, *On Britain and Germany: a New Translation of the 'Agricola' and the 'Germanica'*, trans. H. Mattingley (Harmondsworth, 1948), 107; see also M. Green, *Celtic Goddesses: Warriors, Virgins and Mothers* (London, 1995).

37 Maclean, *Renaissance Notion*, 21.

38 R.S. Ferguson, 'Notes Taken at Naworth', *Transactions of the Cumberland and Westmorland Antiquarian and Archaeological Society* iv (1878–9), 510–15; E. Maclagan, 'Medieval Alabasters from Norworth Castle', *Antiquaries Journal* xii (1932), 407–10.

39 Emmerson, 'The Prophetic, the Apocalyptic, and the Study of Medieval Literature', 44.

the so-called 'German Sibyl',[40] as an example of an apocalyptic visionary who claimed secret knowledge concerning the cosmos, heaven and hell, the history of the world and the coming of the Antichrist, and whose revelations were 'highly bookish and literary'.[41] Like St John, who was instructed by God, 'Write down thy vision of what now is, and what must befall hereafter' (Apocalypse 1.19), Hildegard records in her first visionary work, the *Scivias* (1151), that she heard a voice which told her to 'tell these marvels and write them'.[42] Yet Hildegard clearly also modelled herself on the Old Testament prophets. As Gillian Ahlgren points out, a letter to Pope Anastasius which begins 'Listen, o man' echoes the prophetic exhortation 'Hear the word of Yahweh.'[43] Even more significantly, Hildegard evoked figures of authority which are traditionally female, identifying herself with the Old Testament Sapientia: 'Is not Wisdom calling, Knowledge raising her voice? On the high ground by the roadside, in the streets she takes her stand, by the gateways opening to the city, at the entries, she is crying out.' (Proverbs 8.1–3). Hildegard's deep concern about contemporary society is revealed in her many prophecies directed at the Church or about the future of certain kingdoms, including England and France. She expressed her fears about the failings of the clergy in letters to figures like the cardinals Bernard of St Clement and Gregory of St Angelus, whom she reproached for neglecting their duties. She wrote to three popes, Eugenius III, Anastasius IV and Hadrian IV, and also to various monarchs including the Emperor Frederick Barbarossa, whom she held responsible for the twelfth-century schism because he attempted to bring the Church under his own control by setting up his own anti-pope. Hildegard even reproached the Emperor for acting 'childishly, like one whose mode of life is insane'[44] and gave him severe warnings about his fate: 'Woe, woe upon the evil doing of the unjust who scorn me! Hear this, king, if you would live – else my sword will pierce through you!'[45] Barbara Newman suggests that Hildegard saw her mission

---

[40] Lerner, 'Medieval Prophecy and Religious Dissent', 9 and n. 19. On Hildegard see P. Dronke, *Women Writers of the Middle Ages: a Critical Study of Texts from Perpetua (†203) to Marguerite Porete (†1310)* (Cambridge, 1984), 144–201; B. Newman, *Sister of Wisdom: St Hildegard's Theology of the Feminine* (Berkeley, 1987); S. Flanagan, *Hildegard of Bingen, 1098–1179: a Visionary Life* (London, 1989); Kerby-Fulton, *Reformist Apocalypticism*, 26–75.

[41] Emmerson, 'The Prophetic, the Apocalyptic, and the Study of Medieval Literature', 49.

[42] Emmerson, 'The Prophetic, the Apocalyptic, and the Study of Medieval Literature', 49.

[43] G.T.W. Ahlgren, 'Visions and Rhetorical Strategy in the Letters of Hildegard of Bingen' in *Dear Sister: Medieval Women and the Epistolary Genre*, ed. K. Cherewatuk and U. Wiethaus (Philadelphia, 1993), 53.

[44] Dronke, *Women Writers of the Middle Ages*, 149.

[45] F. Beer, *Women and Mystical Experience in the Middle Ages* (Woodbridge, 1992), 21.

Fig. 1. Katherine of Alexandria, attired as a nun, stabbing Emperor Maxentius
with her sword. A late fifteenth- or early sixteenth-century English alabaster.
Copyright Geoffrey Van Ltd.

as being to 'unlock the mysteries of Scripture, to proclaim the way of salvation, to admonish priests and prelates, to instruct the people of God'.[46]

In the second half of the fourteenth century, two women in particular, St Bridget of Sweden (1303–1373) and St Catherine of Siena (1347–1380), emerged as important and influential. For both the written word was as important as the spoken: Catherine of Siena dictated her *Dialogue* to her secretaries while in ecstasy, and Bridget of Sweden did the same with the rule of the Brigittine Order. Like Hildegard, both also looked to the Old Testament for precedents, to prophets and visionaries like Jeremiah, Nathan, Daniel and Ezekiel. St Bridget, who saw herself as the 'bride' of Christ, received revelations concerning the spiritual rebirth of her own country and the reformation of the Roman Church. As Emmerson notes, 'Her warning of a terrible visitation, which many in her time took as a "prophecy" of the Black Death, has all the poetic power of the Old Testament prophetic oracles: "I shall plow the field with my wrath and pull up bushes and trees by their roots. Where a thousand people lived, barely a hundred will be left." '[47] She admonished King Magnus of Sweden about his failings, attacked the corruption of his court, and attempted to direct his policies. Concerned by international instability, she warned Pope Clement VI to make peace between England and France. St Catherine attempted to negotiate an end to a conflict which broke out between Florence and the Papacy. St Bridget and St Catherine urged the return of the Papacy from Avignon; during the Great Schism, St Catherine supported the Roman claimant, Urban VI, and worked for his cause. Somewhat later, at the end of the second decade of the fifteenth century, Joan of Arc (1412–1431), driven by her visions of St Michael, St Margaret of Antioch and St Katherine of Alexandria, took a leading part in the Anglo-French conflicts, persuading the Dauphin Charles that she had a divine mission to drive the English out of France.

These medieval women prophets came from a range of social and religious backgrounds. St Hildegard of Bingen and St Bridget of Sweden were of aristocratic birth; the former was a powerful abbess, the latter had married and had children but lived as a penitent after the death of her husband. St Catherine of Siena was the daughter of a lower-class tradesman; she remained unmarried and became a Dominican tertiary. Joan of Arc was a laywoman from a peasant family. The prophetic roles of all four were eventually endorsed by the Church. Urban VI is reported to have said to his cardinals of Catherine of Siena:

> This little woman shames us. I call her a little woman not out of contempt for her, but as an expression of her female sex which is by nature fragile, and for

---

[46] Newman, *Sister of Wisdom*, 4.

[47] Emmerson, 'The Prophetic, the Apocalyptic, and the Study of Medieval Literature', 48.

our own instruction. This woman by nature ought to fear, while we ought to be secure: and yet while now we tremble, she is without fear and comforts us with her persuasive words. A great shame must arise in us now.[48]

Hildegard of Bingen's visions were approved in part by Eugenius III, Bridget of Sweden's by Boniface IX, and Catherine of Siena's by Gregory XI. Although the controversy surrounding Bridget's revelations continued well into the fifteenth century, both Bridget and Catherine were canonized relatively soon after their deaths; progress towards Hildegard's canonization had begun by the third decade of the thirteenth century; and twenty-five years after her execution, a rehabilitation commission declared Joan of Arc's condemnation invalid.

Kempe and the Medieval Women Prophets

The *TLS* review of the EETS edition of *The Book of Margery Kempe* gave the work the accolade of the first autobiography in English, yet it has proved to be a controversial text and its mystical and contemplative content has often been derided.[49] Nonetheless, autobiography, biography and prophecy are closely linked: paradoxically it is only through surrendering the self to God that the prophetic voice can speak. Margery Kempe's consistent representation of herself as 'þis creatur' formulates her identity in terms of her dependency on God, and her *Book* reveals the workings of God on and through the individual. A great deal of work has already been done on *The Book of Margery Kempe* and on Kempe's devotions and piety and the influence of continental women visionaries and English mystics, but she has seldom been discussed as a prophet or considered in such a broad context of medieval and early modern women religious writers.[50] This

---

48 Quoted by K. Scott, ' "*Io Catarina*": Ecclesiastical Politics and Oral Culture in the Letters of Catherine of Siena' in *Dear Sister*, ed. Cherewatuk and Wiethaus, 95.

49 'Margery Kempe of Lynn, First English Autobiographer: a Mystic at Home and Abroad' in the *TLS*, 8 March 1941, 111 and 120. David Knowles claimed that Margery Kempe 'can only improperly and accidentally be classed among the English mystics', *The English Mystical Tradition* (London, 1961), 149. For a brief overview of the controversy, see R.B. Bosse, 'Margery Kempe's Tarnished Reputation: a Reassessment', *Fourteenth Century English Mystics Newsletter* v (1979), 9–19; N.F. Partner, 'Reading *The Book of Margery Kempe*', *Exemplaria* iii (1991), 31–2 and 62–3.

50 But see, for example, M.G. Mason, 'The Other Voice: Autobiographies of Women Writers' in *Autobiography: Essays Theoretical and Critical*, ed. J. Olney (Princeton, 1980), 207–35. Kempe is compared to Mary Astell in V.E. Neuburger's *Margery Kempe: a Study in Early English Feminism* (Berne, 1994), and to a range of authors which includes Virginia Woolf, Antonia White and Sylvia Plath by G. Claridge, R. Pryor and G. Watkins in *Sounds from the Bell Jar: Ten Psychotic Authors* (London, 1990).

section will examine the relationship between the prophetic revelations of Kempe and the traditions of visionary women in England.

Within the communities in which she lived, Margery Kempe was evidently consulted as a spiritual guide and seer; indeed fortune-telling of this sort does not seem to have been uncommon in late medieval England.[51] Kempe records that the Abbess of Denny, a community of Poor Clares with strict rules of enclosure, often sent for her to speak with her and her sisters.[52] According to her own account, Margery Kempe was able to foretell future events (including natural occurrences such as plagues and earthquakes)[53] and make predictions about, for example, the sick (revealing if they would be healed or if their illnesses would prove fatal).[54] *The Book of Margery Kempe* orders this sort of episode in such a way as to reveal the accuracy of her predictions.[55] Kempe also received revelations concerning the fate of the dead (if they were damned or saved),[56] and she could advise friends and relatives of the deceased on how the sufferings of those in purgatory could be reduced by pious acts, such as almsgiving.[57] Closely related to this was her ability to see the secrets of people's hearts, discern true piety from hypocrisy, and suggest how sinners might reform their lives.[58] In Rome, for example, Kempe perceived a priest whom she saw celebrating mass to be 'a good man & deuowte'.[59] These kinds of prophecy were often associated with supernatural abilities and phenomena: sensory experiences such as sweet smells confirmed some of Margery Kempe's prognostications.[60] Her gift of prophecy gained her many followers and the dying called for her to be with them in their final hours, to help them prepare for their judgement.[61]

---

[51] In the later Middle Ages, hermits and anchorites were sometimes consulted as seers: R.M. Clay, *Hermits and Anchorites of England* (London, 1914), 146. For the influence of anchorites and anchoresses, who claimed to have prophetic powers, on the Lancaster family, see A.K. Warren, *Anchorites and their Patrons in Medieval England* (Berkeley, 1985), 203–6. For an example of an English woman recluse who said that she had seen a vision, see *Nova legenda anglicæ: as Collected by John of Tynemouth, John Capgrave and Others*, ed. C. Horstman (Oxford, 1901), ii, 71.

[52] *Book of Margery Kempe*, 202.

[53] *Book of Margery Kempe*, 47 and 185–6.

[54] *Book of Margery Kempe*, 53.

[55] See, for example, Kempe's prediction concerning the repayment of a debt and its fulfilment: *Book of Margery Kempe*, 92 and 106; for an analysis of prophecies relating to Kempe's pilgrimage to Jerusalem and white clothes, see Wilson, 'Communities', 169–70.

[56] *Book of Margery Kempe*, 144. When challenged, Kempe did not assert that she knew with certainty whether the living would be saved or damned: *Book of Margery Kempe*, 136.

[57] *Book of Margery Kempe*, 46–7.

[58] *Book of Margery Kempe*, 55–8.

[59] *Book of Margery Kempe*, 82.

[60] See, for example, *Book of Margery Kempe*, 170–2.

[61] *Book of Margery Kempe*, 172–3.

Parallels might be drawn between Kempe's prophetic vocation and that of another English woman, one who lived some three hundred years earlier and of whom Kempe is unlikely to have heard, the recluse and then nun and prioress, Christina of Markyate (1096/8–c.1160).[62] Just as Kempe portrayed herself as enjoying frequent 'dalyawns' with the Lord, so, in Christina of Markyate's anonymous *vita*, we are told that Christ spoke intimately to Christina as if he were present in the flesh.[63] Christina, like Kempe, could predict whether or not the sick would recover from their illnesses;[64] received assurances of not only her own salvation, but also of those close to her;[65] warned people of their wrongdoing and knew about the sins they kept hidden in their hearts;[66] and was granted physical confirmation of her revelations and prayers in the form of the sensation of a caress, a bird fluttering in her breast, or bright shining lights.[67] Elizabeth Alvida Petroff acknowledges that because Christina's visions were often predictive they 'conferred personal power onto her', but she also argues that they were 'intended to provide guidance to her individually without commenting on a larger community',[68] or, as Christopher Talbot puts it, they 'lack public import'.[69] Yet others around her shared Christina's gift of prophecy, including Roger, the hermit, with whom she lived for four years, and Sueno, Canon of Huntingdon;[70] and some members of her 'familiar circle' were granted visions, such as one Simon of Bermondsey, and also her close associate for many years, Geoffrey, Abbot of Saint Albans.[71]

Christina's own predictions relate mainly to one man, Geoffrey of St Albans.[72] Within the *vita*, Geoffrey plays a role similar to that of the priest-scribe in *The Book of Margery Kempe*. Like many of Kempe's supporters, Geoffrey initially refused to believe Christina's visions and warnings about his own corrupt activities, but learnt through hard

---

62 In addition to the texts cited below, see P. Dinzelbacher, 'The Beginnings of Mysticism Experienced in Twelfth-Century England' in *The Medieval Mystical Tradition in England*, ed. M. Glasscoe, Exeter Symposium 4 (Cambridge, 1987), 119–21; S. Elkins, *Holy Women of Twelfth Century England* (Chapel Hill N.C., 1988), 27–42; S. Thompson, *Women Religious: the Founding of English Nunneries after the Norman Conquest* (Oxford, 1991), 16–37.
63 *Life of Christina of Markyate*, 37.
64 *Life of Christina of Markyate*, 141–2 and 147.
65 *Life of Christina of Markyate*, 79, 157, 159 and 183.
66 *Life of Christina of Markyate*, 135, 141, and 191.
67 *Life of Christina of Markyate*, 171, and cf. 91.
68 E.A. Petroff, *Body and Soul: Essays on Medieval Women and Mysticism* (Oxford, 1994), 10.
69 *Life of Christina of Markyate*, 32.
70 *Life of Christina of Markyate*, 83, 97, 101 and 107.
71 *Life of Christina of Markyate*, 153–5 and 175–6.
72 For Christina's prophecies about other people in her community, see, for example, *Life of Christina of Markyate*, 191–3.

experience that he should not ignore them.[73] Although he found her fore-knowledge disconcerting,[74] and on occasion tried to test her,[75] the writer of the *vita* records that 'ever after the man often visited the servant of Christ, heard her admonitions, accepted her advice, consulted her in doubts, avoided evil, bore her reproaches'.[76] Between 1136 and 1139, Geoffrey was summonsed to journey to Rome: first, for the confirmation of Stephen's election as monarch; then as a delegate in a Council called by Innocent III; and finally to defend the rights of the Church after the bishops of Salisbury and Lincoln had been imprisoned.[77] On each occasion Geoffrey consulted Christina, whose prayers were answered, and Geoffrey remained in England. Likewise, in *c.*1140 Geoffrey was summoned to the royal court, but Christina was able to assure him that all would go well.[78] The episodes are comparable to those in *The Book of Margery Kempe* in which Kempe's scribe appears, and which function to authorize her devotions and her text. Petroff suggests that the relationship between Christina and Geoffrey was one of interdependency: 'Geoffrey's role as abbot made Christina's life simpler and safer, and Christina's role as prophet and confidante strengthened Geoffrey.'[79] Geoffrey was head of one of the wealthiest abbeys in England, and he apparently helped found the priory at Markyate of which Christina was to be superior.[80] Christopher Holdsworth contends that prophets like Christina achieved their status by existing 'on the margin, or the frontier, of society' or, in Victor Turner's words, in 'a permanent condition of sacred "outsiderhood" ' not only literally by living as hermits, but also by cutting themselves off from their families, and by preserving their chastity.[81] Kempe too, in her imitation of Christ, constructs herself as a holy fool, and she often lived and travelled without her husband, deliberately associating herself with those on the margins of the community, such as the mad, the poor, and lepers.[82] However, Christina's marginal status, like that

---

[73] *Life of Christina of Markyate*, 135–9.

[74] *Life of Christina of Markyate*, 151–3.

[75] *Life of Christina of Markyate*, 145.

[76] *Life of Christina of Markyate*, 139.

[77] *Life of Christina of Markyate*, 161–9.

[78] *Life of Christina of Markyate*, 169–71.

[79] Petroff, *Body and Soul*, 144.

[80] *Life of Christina of Markyate*, 29.

[81] C.J. Holdsworth, 'Christina of Markyate' in *Medieval Women: dedicated and presented to Professor Rosalind M.T. Hill on the Occasion of her Seventieth Birthday*, ed. D. Baker, Studies in Church History subsidia 1 (Oxford, 1978), 203–4.

[82] See R. Maisonneuve, 'Margery Kempe and the Eastern Tradition of the "Perfect Fool" ' in *The Medieval Mystical Tradition in England: Papers read at Dartington Hall, July 1982*, ed. M. Glasscoe (Exeter, 1982), 1–17; D. Gray, 'Popular Religion and Late Medieval English Literature' in *Religion and Drama of the Late Middle Ages in England*, ed. P. Boitani and A. Torti (Cambridge, 1990), 18–22; Lochrie, *Translations of the Flesh*, 156–60.

of Margery Kempe, should not be over-emphasized. Kempe came from a successful and relatively affluent family living in an important English port.[83] Christina is represented in her text as a powerful and influential woman who corrected church leaders, and who was invited to join the communities at Fontevrault and Marcigny and turned down an offer by Archbishop Thurstan to become Superior of the convent of St Clement's in York.[84]

Kempe is often considered alongside Julian of Norwich, whom Kempe records that she consulted about her meditations and revelations, 'for þe ankres was expert in swech thyngys & good cownsel cowd ȝeuyn'.[85] But although Julian is evidently cited by Kempe as a figure of authority, she is not represented, either in this account or in her own writings, as a prophet.[86] This is a crucial point: in many respects Julian of Norwich and Margery Kempe were contributing to quite distinct, if overlapping, modes of discourse. A significant strand of prophetic revelation is the vision of the otherworld, common in continental and medieval texts written by or about both men and women.[87] Descriptions of the sufferings of intransigent bishops and kings are found in the revelations of Hildegard of Bingen, Bridget of Sweden and Catherine of Siena, and other examples which can be cited include the vision of purgatory seen by the mother of Guilbert of Nogent, Rannveig's revelation of her own torment, and the salvation of certain Icelandic bishops, as well as Christina Mirabilis's experience of purgatory and hell.[88] The relevance of such visions to nuns, for whom saying prayers for the dead was an important duty, is manifest. In England in the twelfth century, Ælred of Rievaulx reported that the sisters of Watton in Yorkshire were 'often taken in ineffable raptures' and would offer prayers

---

[83] Kempe's family and social background are considered by A. Goodman, 'The Piety of John Brunham's Daughter of Lynn' in *Medieval Women*, ed. Baker, especially 351–3; and by D. Aers, 'The Making of Margery Kempe: Individual and Community' in *Community, Gender, and Individual Identity: English Writing 1360–1430* (London, 1988), 73–116.

[84] *Life of Christina of Markyate*, 127.

[85] *Book of Margery Kempe*, 42.

[86] Staley, *Dissenting Fictions*, 27.

[87] H.A. Patch, *The Other World according to Descriptions in Medieval Literature* (Cambridge MA, 1950); C.J. Holdsworth, 'Visions and Visionaries in the Middle Ages', *History* xlviii (1963), 141–53; F.A. Foster, 'Legends of the Afterlife' in *A Manual of the Writings in Middle English, 1050–1500*, ed. J. Burke Severs (Hamden C.T., 1970), ii, 452–7, 645–9; J. Le Goff, *The Birth of Purgatory* (Chicago, 1984); J. Hughes, *Pastors and Visionaries: Religion and Secular Life in Late Medieval Yorkshire* (Woodbridge, 1988); E. Gardiner, *Visions of Heaven and Hell before Dante* (New York, 1989); A. Morgan, *Dante and the Medieval Other World*, Cambridge Studies in Medieval Literature 8 (Cambridge, 1990), 201–33; E. Gardiner, *Medieval Visions of Heaven and Hell: a Sourcebook* (New York, 1993).

[88] See C. Larrington, *Women and Writing in Medieval Europe: a Sourcebook* (London, 1995), 92–4, 123, 138–41.

for their dead sisters until they were granted a vision to assure them of their salvation.[89] While Margery Kempe claimed that her revelations of the damnation of souls sometimes drove her to the verge of despair,[90] Julian of Norwich conceded that those who were of the devil's condition would be damned, but did not see a vision of hell itself:

> And for ought þat I culde desyer, I ne culde se of thys ryght nouȝt but . . . that I saw þe devylle is reprovyd of god and endlessly dampned. In whych syȝt I vnderstond þat all the creature þat be of the devylles condiscion in thys lyfe and ther in endyyng, ther is no more mencyon made of them before god and alle his holyn then of the devylle, notwythstondyng that they be of mankynde, wheder they haue be cristened or nought; for though the reuelation was shewde of goodnes, in whych was made lytylle mencion of evylle, ȝett I was nott drawen ther by from ony poynt of the feyth þat holy chyrch techyth me to beleue.[91]

Julian's assertion of doctrinal orthodoxy is undercut by a spiritual optimism which almost comprehends the notion of universal salvation and which may derive from her feminization of God.[92] The absence of the revelation of a general hell seems implicitly to admit the theologically-radical possibility that, in Julian's understanding, it does not exist. Very different to this is the anonymous but apparently authentic English letter, known as *A Revelation of Purgatory*, which was written in the first half of the fifteenth century either by a pious laywoman or a vowess, and which gives a graphic account of the pains endured by the dreamer's friend, a nun called Margaret, and detailed instructions about what prayers, pilgrimages and masses will speed her into heaven.[93] Nicholas Watson has recently argued in his

---

[89]   G. Constable, 'Ælred of Rievaulx and the Nun of Watton: an Episode in the Early History of the Gilbertine Order' in *Medieval Women*, ed. Baker, 206; cf. Elkins, *Holy Women*, 106–11.

[90]   *Book of Margery Kempe*, 54–5 and 144–6.

[91]   *A Book of Showings to the Anchoress Julian of Norwich*, ed. E. Colledge and J. Walsh (Toronto, 1978), ii, 427–8.

[92]   See R. Harries, 'On the Brink of Universalism' in *Julian: Woman of Our Day*, ed. R. Llewelyn (London, 1985), 41–60; S. McNamer, 'The Exploratory Image: God as Mother in Julian of Norwich's *Revelations of Divine Love*', *Mystics Quarterly* xv (1989), 21–8; F. Riddy, 'Women Talking about the Things of God: a Late Medieval Subculture' in *Women and Literature in Britain, 1150–1500*, ed. C.M. Meale, Cambridge Studies in Medieval Literature 17 (Cambridge, 1993), 116.

[93]   *Yorkshire Writers: Richard Rolle of Hampole and his Followers*, ed. C. Horstmann (London, 1895–96), i, 383–92; *A Revelation of Purgatory by an Unknown Fifteenth Century Woman Visionary: Introduction, Critical Text and Translation*, ed. M.P. Harley, Studies in Women and Religion 18 (Lewiston N.Y., 1985); M.P. Harley, 'The Origin of a Revelation of Purgatory', *Reading Medieval Studies* xii (1986), 87–91; G.R. Keiser, 'St Jerome and the Brigittines: Visions of the Afterlife in Fifteenth-Century England' in *England in the Fifteenth Century: Proceedings of the 1986 Harlaxton Symposium*, ed. D. Williams (Woodbridge, 1987), 143–52. For similar

revisionary article on the dating of Julian's Short and Long Texts that the wider context does have an impact on our understanding of Julian's work and its composition.[94] Nonetheless, Julian's text is less historically specific in its points of reference than either *The Book of Margery Kempe* or *A Revelation of Purgatory* – as Watson says, its significance is universal rather than local.[95]

If Kempe was writing within a broad tradition of women's prophetic writing which included texts like the *vita* of Christina of Markyate or *A Revelation of Purgatory* but excluded Julian's *Showings*, in defining her role as visionary, she modelled herself to some extent on the Virgin Mary and biblical and medieval women saints,[96] and had, as many critics have recognized, a particular devotion to Bridget of Sweden, who had lived a generation before her.[97] Shortly after her death, St Bridget gained some popularity in England, and Norfolk may well have been affected by this cult.[98] Adam Easton, who served on St Bridget's canonization commission and wrote a series of works in defence of her revelations and her rule, had been a monk at Norwich, and in his cardinalate maintained an interest in his former monastery and its cell at Lynn.[99] One cleric who is reported to have encouraged Kempe, and even to have offered to write down her experiences, was the Carmelite Alan of Lynn,[100] a pious and scholarly man who is known to have compiled indices to Bridget's *Revelations* and the *Prophecies*.[101] In *The Book of Margery Kempe*, Bridget's 'boke' (that is, her

---

texts, see M.P. Harley, 'A Fifteenth-Century Revelation of a Cistercian Nun', *Vox Benedicta* vi (1989), 120–7; and Harley, 'Vision of Margaret Edward'.

[94] N. Watson, 'The Composition of Julian of Norwich's *Revelation of Love*', *Speculum* lxviii (1993), 637–83.

[95] Watson, 'Composition', 643 n. 16.

[96] See G.M. Gibson, *The Theatre of Devotion: East Anglian Drama and Society in the Late Middle Ages* (Chicago, 1989), 49–65.

[97] See, for example, C.W. Atkinson, *Mystic and Pilgrim: the Book and the World of Margery Kempe* (Ithaca N.Y., 1983), 34–6 and 168–79; S. Dickman, 'Margery Kempe and the Continental Tradition of the Pious Woman' in *The Medieval Mystical Tradition in England: Papers Read at Dartington Hall, July 1984*, ed. M. Glasscoe (Cambridge, 1984), 150–68; G. Cleve, 'Margery Kempe: a Scandinavian Influence on Medieval England' in *The Medieval Mystical Tradition in England*, ed. M. Glasscoe, Exeter Symposium 5 (Cambridge, 1992), 163–78.

[98] F.R. Johnson, 'The English Cult of St Bridget of Sweden', *Analecta Bollandiana* ciii (1985), 75–92. For an account of one English noblewoman's devotion to St Bridget, see C.A.J. Armstrong, 'The Piety of Cicely, Duchess of York: a Study in Late Medieval Culture' in *For Hilaire Belloc: Essays in Honour of his Seventy-Second Birthday*, ed. D. Woodruff (London, 1942), 88–9.

[99] On Adam Easton, see *Book of Margery Kempe*, n. 47/26; W.A. Pantin, *The English Church in the Fourteenth Century* (Cambridge, 1955), 175–81; and J.A. Schmidtke, ' "Saving" by Faint Praise: St Birgitta of Sweden, Adam Easton and Medieval Antifeminism', *American Benedictine Review* xxxiii (1982), 149–61.

[100] *Book of Margery Kempe*, 6; n. 6/9.

[101] *Book of Margery Kempe*, n. 22/11–12; n. 6/9sq.

Revelations) is mentioned as one of those works Kempe heard read to her.[102] Furthermore during Kempe's pilgrimage to Rome and the Holy Lands, her residence in Rome in 1414 and 1415 coincided with the confirmation of Bridget's canonization, and on Bridget's feast-day, Kempe made a devotional visit to the saint's former lodgings and attended a sermon preached about her visions and life.[103] Certain aspects of Kempe's life have parallels in Bridget's experiences, for example the conflict between her social roles of wife and mother and her religious vocation, or her decision to travel on pilgrimage in her old age.[104] Similarly, Kempe's self-representation as the bride of Christ, her visions of Christ's nativity and passion, and her predictions concerning her personal redemption and the salvation of others reflect the revelations given to her predecessor.

It comes somewhat as a surprise then to find little evidence in Kempe's *Book* of the influence of Bridget's political prophecies. In one passage in *The Book of Margery Kempe* (located in a chapter which mentions the saint by name three times), the Lord speaks of the pains which will befall those who do not reform their evil ways:

> I send hem prechyng & techyng, pestylens & bataylys, hungyr & famynyng, losse of her goodys wyth gret sekeness, & many oþer tribulacyons, & þei wyl not leuyn my wordys ne þei wyl not knowe my vysitacyon. & þerfore I xal sey to hem þat I made my seruawntys to prey for ȝow, & ȝe despysed her werkys & her leuyng.[105]

This admonishment clearly echoes the vehement language of St Bridget's prophetic warnings, but it is an isolated example. A possible reason for this absence may be that although prophetic and eschatological material was often excerpted from her *Revelations* in Middle English compilations, many of the *vitae* in circulation in fifteenth-century England did not foreground this aspect of Bridget's vocation.[106] However, in a recent review, Robert Glück makes the point that Kempe's lack of interest in contemporary politics is in itself remarkable, given that she visited Constance immediately prior to the meeting of the Council to settle the Schism and travelled through Europe when England was engaged in war.[107] The explanation for Kempe's comparative restraint may lie in the debate over women visionaries.

While St Bridget certainly provided Kempe with a role model, even

---

102 *Book of Margery Kempe*, 143.
103 *Book of Margery Kempe*, 95.
104 Atkinson, *Mystic and Pilgrim*, 168–79.
105 *Book of Margery Kempe*, 48.
106 Johnson, 'English Cult'; R. Ellis, ' "Flores ad Fabricandam . . . Coronam": an Investigation into the Uses of the Revelations of St Bridget of Sweden in Fifteenth-Century England', *Medium Ævum* li (1982), 163–86.
107 R. Glück, 'Bursting into Modernity: Margery's Excess of Noisy Self', *TLS*, 4 August 1995, 5.

canonized saints were vulnerable to attack from within the Church, and contention over the authenticity of Bridget's revelations and visions was still rife during Kempe's lifetime.[108] Kempe herself was sensitive to this. The same day that she visited the house of St Bridget there was a terrible storm which she interpreted as an indication that God wanted the people to venerate the saint more than they had hitherto.[109] Bridget's example validated Kempe's own activities – on one occasion, Christ assured her of the authenticity of a certain vision with the words, 'My dowtyr, Bryde, say me neuyr in þis wyse', and on another he promised that a revelation would be fulfilled with the affirmation, 'Ryght as I spak to Seynt Bryde ryte so I speke to þe'[110] – but elsewhere Kempe found herself defending Bridget's revelations, relating the Lord's emphatic statement that 'trewly it is trewe euery word þat is wretyn in Brides boke, & be þe it xal be knowyn for very trewth'.[111] Kempe's personal testimony would itself resolve the doubts of the people. Later in her life, Kempe visited the newly-founded Brigittine house of Syon in order to receive plenary indulgence, and the example of her pious weeping encouraged a young man who was intending to become a monk.[112]

The theologian Jean Gerson was one of those who stood against the Swedish prophet: during the Council of Constance, when the debate over her revelations was at its most intense, he wrote his tract 'De probatione spirituum' in which he gave clear guidance on the discernment of spirits and emphasized the need to exercise sober judgement in this sensitive area. Elsewhere Gerson also attacked the prophecies of Catherine of Siena, although he did write in defence of Joan of Arc.[113] In his 'De probatione' it is clear that Jean Gerson was concerned that many ordinary people would be deluded into imitating St Bridget.[114] While not directly condemning the *Revelations*, he thought that women in particular should come under close scrutiny because, he argued, their enthusiasm was inclined to be excessive and unstable. He warned against those who constantly occupied their religious instructors in confession and with discussions about their visions, and claimed that women are often given to a curiosity and gullibility which makes them easily deceived. Catherine Brown, in her study of Gerson, has

---

108 See E. Colledge, '*Epistola solitarii ad reges*: Alphonse of Pecha as Organizer of Brigittine and Urbanist Propaganda', *Medieval Studies* xviii (1956), 19–49.

109 *Book of Margery Kempe*, 95.

110 *Book of Margery Kempe*, 47.

111 *Book of Margery Kempe*, 47.

112 *Book of Margery Kempe*, 245–6.

113 D.C. Brown, *Pastor and Laity in the Theology of Jean Gerson* (Cambridge, 1987), 209–26, especially 222–4.

114 J. Gerson, 'De probatione spirituum' in *Oeuvres Complètes*, ed. Mnr P. Glorieux (Paris, 1960–1973), ix, 180 and 184; cf. Brown, *Pastor and Laity*, 222.

shown that he seems to have regarded many of the women in his pastoral care, and a number of women visionaries, as 'deviants and cranks'.[115]

Fifteenth-century churchmen like Gerson were suspicious of the growing numbers of laywomen who were being revered as saints, fearing that they would either overtly undermine the authority of the Church by openly criticizing and challenging it (claiming to do so in the voice of God), or more indirectly destabilize it through their popularity. In response to the publication of women's revelations, in particular those of St Bridget and St Catherine, Gerson argued that women were prohibited by apostolic authority from teaching in public, not only in words, but also in writing. He contended that 'all women's teaching, particularly formal teaching by word and by writing' must be held in doubt until it had been carefully examined, 'and much more fully than men's'.[116] Gerson went much further than other church leaders in his censuring and censoring not only of women's preaching but also their writing, but his views may well have been shared by many. Nicholas Watson notes that 'the spirituality of England differed markedly in its caution (some would say parochialism) from that of Northern Continental Europe'.[117] Certainly, contemplative writers like Hilton, Rolle and the authors of the *Ancrene Wisse*, *The Cloud of Unknowing*, and *The Chastising of God's Children* warned their readers against visions and discouraged excesses in the spiritual life of women in particular.[118] As Watson puts it, 'the English women visionaries continued to be prophets without much honour in their own countries (and none elsewhere) and . . . English enthusiasm for Continental women writers did not have as liberating an effect on their insular counterparts as we might expect'.[119] Nonetheless, while they were aware of the need to justify Kempe's life and prophecies, neither Margery Kempe nor her scribe ultimately felt that such strictures applied to their book. Kempe's scribe had been both hostile and supportive, but the stance he finally took was that of the convert, of one who had been brought to the realization that Kempe was a woman blessed with divine gifts, and he intended to draw the reader with him.

An important function of prophecy was to reveal divine disapproval of the contemporary world, and woman visionaries as diverse as Christina of Markyate, Hildegard of Bingen, Bridget of Sweden and Catherine of Siena all took upon themselves, to varying extents, the role of inspired social commentator and exposer of corruption. Margery Kempe did not become involved in larger political issues, but, as will be seen, she too was outspoken

---

115 Brown, *Pastor and Laity*, 215.
116 Quoted in translation in Julian's *Showings*, ed. Colledge and Walsh, i, 151.
117 Watson, 'Composition', 646.
118 See the introduction to *The Chastising of God's Children and the Treatise of Perfection of the Sons of God*, ed. J. Bazire and E. Colledge (Oxford, 1957), 54–61.
119 Watson, 'Composition', 657.

in her reproaches of figures in positions of secular and religious power. However, prophecy was also defined as interpretation of Scripture. The next section reveals that in believing that she was privileged to know the secrets of the Holy Ghost, Kempe saw herself as an inspired teacher, facing opposition and incredulity as a prophet 'in her own country' – a country in which the piety of lay people in general and of women in particular could be tolerated only with difficulty.

Conflict, Controversy and Prophetic Identity

Kempe's spiritual vocation, her pilgrimages and her enthusiastic devotions brought her considerable public attention, and even though she eventually received a letter from Archbishop Chichele legitimizing her religious practices,[120] at least once in 1413 and four times in 1417 she was brought before the authorities and examined for heresy. Her first examination occurred at Norwich.[121] She was also interrogated at Leicester,[122] and later questioned by a doctor of divinity at York and then by the Archbishop of York himself.[123] Following her arrest by men in the service of the Duke of Bedford, she was brought to Beverley where she was once more taken before the Archbishop of York.[124] The objections to Kempe raised during these trials are indicative both of the religious tension caused by the widespread fear of heresy prompted by Oldcastle's failed uprising, and also of the prevalent attitudes to and suspicion of women, orthodox as well as heterodox, who transgressed gender boundaries. No details are given about her 1413 interrogation conducted by the officers of the Bishop of Norwich, but it is clear from her accounts of her later examinations that her questioners (the Mayor of Leicester, the Abbot of Leicester and his officers, Henry Bowet Archbishop of York, and a number of other clerics) were unsettled by her extreme religious devotion and unconventional behaviour. Although these trials occurred many years before Kempe began dictating her book, they are given prominence in the middle of her narrative. It is through her struggles and victories as well as her suffering that her literary identity is created: Kempe is depicted as prophetically inspired, strong and disputatious. In this respect, she can usefully be considered alongside Anne Askew and Foxe's godly women, who will be discussed below in Chapter Four.

Kempe's active religious life coincided with the start of the Lollard trials,

---

[120] *Book of Margery Kempe*, 136. In 1413, Kempe received a letter from Archbishop Arundel which gave her permission to choose her own confessor and be houselled every Sunday: *Book of Margery Kempe*, 36.

[121] *Book of Margery Kempe*, 40.

[122] *Book of Margery Kempe*, 111–17.

[123] *Book of Margery Kempe*, 121–8.

[124] *Book of Margery Kempe*, 129–35.

and her own locality seems to have been a centre of unorthodox belief and practice – in 1401, William Sawtrey, a parish priest from Kempe's home town, became the first heretic to be executed in England.[125] In her study of East Anglia, Gail McMurray Gibson describes the area as 'the most troublesome area of non-conformist thought in England in the fifteenth century'.[126] It is significant that Kempe was repeatedly denounced as a Lollard and actually associated with the Lollard knight, Sir John Oldcastle, at a time when he was still at large and his notoriety was at its height. During one examination, men in the service of the Duke of Bedford alleged that she was Oldcastle's daughter, entrusted with carrying letters around the country.[127] The Duke of Bedford had been present at Oldcastle's trial and was a great opponent of heresy and sedition; his retainers said that he had called for Kempe's imprisonment.[128] The intensity of popular hatred of Lollards is reflected in the *Book*, and Kempe's accounts of her examinations reveal her very real danger at these times. This is not to say that she was a heretic. Kempe was a follower of the Norwich vicar, Richard Caister, who supported her during the first formal ecclesiastical examination of her beliefs, and who may have had radical sympathies.[129] However, there is little trace of heterodoxy in the beliefs she expresses in her trial accounts, and throughout the book she emphasizes her personal obedience to the Church. When she was first examined in York, she asserted, 'I wil neiþer meynteyn errowr ne heresy, for it is my ful wil to holdyn as Holy Chirche holdith & fully to plesyn God.'[130]

Kempe's self-portrayal in the accounts of her examinations challenges many common-place medieval stereotypes about women. When she had first sought an interview with Richard Caister in Norwich, he exclaimed, 'Benedicte. What cowd a woman ocupyn an owyr or tweyn owyrs in þe lofe of owyr Lord?'[131] The assumption that women were intellectually inferior, and the awareness that they were unlikely to have received any formal education, convinced some that she was divinely inspired, while others feared that she must be possessed by a devil. After questioning Kempe and

---

125 On Lollardy generally, see M. Aston, *Lollards and Reformers: Images and Literacy in Late Medieval Religion* (London, 1984); M. Aston, *England's Iconoclasts: Laws against Images* (Oxford, 1988); and A. Hudson, *The Premature Reformation: Wycliffite Texts and Lollard History* (Oxford, 1988). On Lollardy in Norwich, see *Heresy Trials in the Diocese of Norwich, 1428–1431*, ed. N.P. Tanner, CS 4th series 20 (London, 1977); see also Gibson, *Theatre of Devotion*, 19–46.

126 Gibson, *Theatre of Devotion*, 21.

127 *Book of Margery Kempe*, 132.

128 *Book of Margery Kempe*, 129 and cf. n. 129/22–33.

129 *Book of Margery Kempe*, 38–40 and 147; cf. N.P. Tanner, *The Church in Late Medieval Norwich, 1370–1532* (Toronto, 1984), 231–3; Wilson, 'Communities', 165–6.

130 *Book of Margery Kempe*, 122.

131 *Book of Margery Kempe*, 38.

finding no fault in her answers, the Steward of Leicester said aggressively, 'Þu xalt telle me wheþer þu hast þis speche of God er of þe Devyl, er ellys þu xalt gon to preson', and he was forced to conclude that she was either 'a ryth good woman er ellys a ryth wikked woman'.[132] Kempe does her best to leave us in no doubt that her wisdom comes from God. Lawyers in Lincoln were amazed by her words, observing that 'we han gone to scole many ʒerys, & ʒet arn we no sufficient to answeryn as þu dost'.[133] In reply to their question, 'Of whom has þu þis connyng', Kempe said, 'Of þe Holy Gost', and cited Christ's words in Matthew 10.19–20, 'Stody not what ʒe schal sey, for it schal not be ʒowr spiryt þat schal spekyn in ʒow, but it schal be þe spiryt of þe Holy Gost.' Shortly after her conversion, Christ had revealed to Kempe that through fasting, daily meditation and receiving the Sacrament of the Altar weekly, she would receive the grace to experience in her life His redemptive suffering, 'Þow xalt ben etyn & knawyn of þe pepul of þe world as any raton knawyth þe stokfysch', but that, despite her lack of learning, she would have victory over all her enemies because He would bless her with the ability 'to answer euery clerke in þe loue of God'.[134] Throughout her interrogations, Kempe is depicted as self-assured and in control, while her opponents, whom she outwits with her pragmatic arguments and greater understanding of Scripture, are made to appear disorganized and uncertain.

As God's spokeswoman, Kempe was willing to stand against those in positions of secular and religious power, and at times her opprobrium appears to shade into Lollard beliefs about grace and dominion. She characterized the Mayor of Leicester as her deadly enemy,[135] and when he asked her to explain why she wore white, her response was forthright to the point of arrogance, ' "Syr',," sche seyth, "ʒe xal not wetyn of my mowth why I go in white clothys; ʒe arn not worthy to wetyn it. But, ser, I wil tellyn it to þes worthy clerkys wyth good wil be þe maner of confessyon. Avyse hem ʒif þei wyl telle it ʒow." '[136] The Mayor was not one to whom the secrets of God could be revealed. Kempe made it clear that in spiritual matters she would remain obedient to the Church but that she was not willing to submit to the secular authorities. This did not mean that she never opposed individuals within the Church. In her account of her interview with Thomas Arundel, Archbishop of Canterbury, she reports that she rebuked the church leader about his unruly household in unequivocal terms:

---

[132] *Book of Margery Kempe*, 113.
[133] *Book of Margery Kempe*, 135.
[134] *Book of Margery Kempe*, 17.
[135] *Book of Margery Kempe*, 115.
[136] *Book of Margery Kempe*, 116.

'My Lord, owyr alderes Lord al-myty God hath not ȝon ȝow ȝowyr benefys
& gret goodys of þe world to maynten wyth hys tretowrys . . . ȝe schal answer
fro hem les þan ȝe correctyn hem or ellys put hem owt of ȝowr seruyse.'[137]

Kempe claimed that 'vndyr þe abyte of holynes is curyd meche wyk-
kydnes'.[138] During her persecution by a distinguished preacher who came
to Lynn in 1420 or shortly thereafter, tentatively identified as the Franciscan
William Melton,[139] the Lord told her, 'Dowtyr, ȝyf he be a preyst þat
despisith the, knowing wel wher-for þu wepist & cyrsit, he is a-cursyd.'[140]
Another time it was revealed to her that any cleric who denounced her holy
life 'is not Goddys clerk; he is þe Deuelys clerk'.[141] Her response to the
Archbishop of York's accusation that he had heard reports that she was a
very evil woman was also one of defiance: 'Ser, so I her seyn þat ȝe arn a
wykkyd man. And, ȝyf ȝe ben as wikkyd as men seyn, ȝe xal neuyr come
in Heuyn les þan ȝe amende ȝow whil ȝe ben her.'[142]

Kempe was, nonetheless, careful not to utter reproofs which could be
perceived to undermine the sacred role of the priesthood. She did not attack
the sacramental power of priests; on the contrary, she declared that she was
innocent of a charge that she believed she could receive contrition whenever
she wanted to.[143] On being asked about her understanding of the mass, she
explained:

'Serys, I beleue in þe Sacrament of þe Awter on þis wyse, þat what man hath
takyn þe ordyr of presthode, be he neuyr so vicyows a man in hys leuyng,
ȝyf he sey dewly þo wordys ouyr þe bred þat owr Lord Ihesu Criste seyde
whan he mad hys Mawnde a-mong hys disciplys þer he sat at þe soper, I
be-leue þat it is hys very flesch & hys blood & no material bred ne neuyr may
be vnseyd be it onys seyd.'[144]

Her answer not only revealed her belief in transubstantiation (the denial of
which was held to be one of the central tenets of Lollardy), but also refuted
the heretical views that an evil priest can corrupt the Sacrament and that
transubstantiation is not a permanent phenomenon.[145] That her answer is so
precisely and unequivocally orthodox may indicate either that at the time
of her questioning she had been well-versed in the questions she might be
expected to answer, or that retrospectively either she or her scribe was

137 *Book of Margery Kempe*, 37.
138 *Book of Margery Kempe*, 158.
139 *Book of Margery Kempe*, n. 148/28–9.
140 *Book of Margery Kempe*, 155.
141 *Book of Margery Kempe*, 158.
142 *Book of Margery Kempe*, 125.
143 *Book of Margery Kempe*, 132.
144 *Book of Margery Kempe*, 115.
145 For a discussion of Lollard beliefs about the eucharist, see Hudson, *Premature Reformation*, 281–90.

concerned to clear away any doubts which might remain about her orthodoxy.

In these accounts, Kempe appears as an articulate woman, defiant in the
face of the male authorities who repeatedly misunderstood her beliefs and
practices. Many churchmen were suspicious of lay study of the Bible,
fearing that misinterpretation resulted in error. This suspicion is also expressed by the poet Hoccleve, in his opprobrium of women who 'thogh hir
wit be thynne, / Wole argumentes make in holy writ', directing them to
'kakele of sumwhat elles, for your wit / Is al to feeble to despute of it'.[146]
The Lollards, who called for reform of the Church, were known as Bible
men and emphasized the importance of close reading of the vernacular
Bible. When Kempe cited the Gospel in her own defence, her questioners
picked this up as evidence of her heresy: ' "A ser," seyd þe clerkys, "her
wot we well þat sche hath a deuyl wyth-inne her, for sche spekyth of þe
Gospel." '[147] Kempe's examiners raised all the traditional objections to lay
study of the Bible in general and women's public involvement in matters
of religion in particular. Her response was to refute these arguments within
the limits of orthodoxy while presenting herself as an exceptional Christian
woman unjustly persecuted by her enemies. In 1 Timothy 2.12–14, St Paul
said,

> Women are to keep silence, and take their place, with all submissiveness, as
> learners; a woman shall have no leave from me to teach, and issue commands
> to her husband; her part is to be silent. It was Adam that was created first,
> and Eve later, nor was it Adam that went astray; woman was led astray, and
> was involved in transgression.

Some Lollards challenged the orthodox interpretation of these verses.[148] In

---

146 Thomas Hoccleve, 'Address to Sir John Oldcastle', lines144–9: *Hoccleve's Works: the
Minor Poems*, ed. F.J. Furnivall and I. Gollancz, rev. J. Mitchell and A.I. Doyle, EETS
e.s. 61 and 73 (London, 1970), no. 2.

147 *Book of Margery Kempe*, 126. Cf. M. Aston, 'Lollardy and Literacy', *History* lxii
(1977), 347–71; R.M. Haines, ' "Wilde Wittes and Wilfulnes": John Swetstock's
Attack on those "Poyswunmongeres", the Lollards' in *Popular Belief and Practice*,
ed. G.J. Cuming and D. Baker, Studies in Church History 8 (Cambridge, 1972),
143–53; Hudson, *Premature Reformation*, 174–277; *Heresy and Literacy, 1000–1531*,
ed. A. Hudson and P. Biller (Cambridge, 1994); A. Blamires, 'The Limits of Bible
Study for Medieval Women' in *Women, the Book and the Godly*, ed. L. Smith and J.
Taylor (Cambridge, 1995), 1–12.

148 C. Cross, ' "Great Reasoners in Scripture": the Activities of Women Lollards
1380–1530' in *Medieval Women*, ed. Baker, 359–80; and M. Aston, 'Lollard Women
Priests?' *Journal of Ecclesiastical History* xxxi (1980), 441–61; but cf. S. McSheffrey,
'Literacy and the Gender Gap in the Late Middle Ages: Women and Reading in
Lollard Communities' in *Women, the Book and the Godly*, ed. Smith and Taylor,
157–70; and S. McSheffrey, *Gender and Heresy: Women and Men in Lollard Communities 1420–1530* (Philadelphia, 1996). On women's preaching generally, see G.R.

his *Doctrinale antiquitatum fidei catholicæ ecclesiæ*, the theologian Thomas Netter refuted the claim made by the Lollard scholar Purvey that lay preaching was not only to be tolerated but an obligation which even extended to women.[149] Netter conceded that women were allowed to teach privately, for example they could instruct other women or boys, but he cited St Paul and quoted many orthodox authorities to support his argument that women's public teaching went against law and nature (undermining the very structure of society by placing women above men), and that women preachers were liable to seduce people into error.

Kempe's public instruction did resemble preaching: while imprisoned in Beverley, for example, she took the opportunity to stand at the window and relate 'many good talys' to passers-by.[150] During her first examination before the Archbishop of York, Kempe was accused of speaking publicly on matters of religion. In her own defence, she claimed that neither God nor the Pope and the Church had forbidden the laity to speak of God, citing Luke 11.27–8:

> 'Þe Gospel makyth mencyon þat, whan þe woman had herd owr Lord prechyd, sche cam be-forn hym wyth a lowde voys & seyd, "Blyssed be þe wombe þat þe bar & þe tetys þat ȝaf þe sowkyn." Þan owr Lord seyd a-ȝen to hir, "Forsoþe so ar þei blissed þat heryn þe word of God and kepyn it." And þerfor, sir, me thynkyth þat þe Gospel ȝeuyth me leue to spekyn of God.'[151]

As Karma Lochrie observes, Christ's words here do not actually give women permission to speak of God, however the Lollard William Brute interpreted them similarly: 'If they are blessed who hear and keep the word of God, they are even more blessed who preach and keep it, because it is more blessed to give that to receive.'[152] One priest's response to Kempe's interpretation was to show her St Paul's proscription, but, undaunted, Kempe replied by drawing a distinction between preaching and teaching: 'I preche not, ser, I come in no pulpytt.'[153]

The suspicions expressed by the Archbishop of York and his clerics about her subversive influence, even after her orthodoxy had been established,

Owst, *Preaching in Medieval England: an Introduction to Sermon Manuscripts of the Period c.1350–1450* (New York, 1965), 4–6.

149 Thomas Netter, *Doctrinale antiquiatum fidei catholicæ ecclesiæ*, ed. F.B. Blanciotte (Venice, 1757–1759; republished Farnborough, 1967), i, 636ff and passim; on Netter generally, see Aston, *Lollards and Reformers*, 65–8 and passim; and D.J. Dubois, 'Thomas Netter of Walden, OC (c.1372–1430)' (B.Litt. thesis, University of Oxford, 1978), 1–50.

150 *Book of Margery Kempe*, 130.

151 *Book of Margery Kempe*, 126.

152 Lochrie, 'Marginal Woman's Quest', 44–5.

153 *Book of Margery Kempe*, 126.

reflect the Church's concern over aspects of her piety. Many people from Kempe's home town were turned against her by the vitriol of the visiting friar preacher. This friar objected to the disturbances during his preaching caused by Kempe's crying and roaring and he forbade her from attending his sermons, even speaking out against her from the pulpit. He refused to believe that Kempe's crying was a gift of God, blaming it instead on 'a cardiakyl er sum oþer sekenesse'.[154] At this time, 'sum enuyows personys' complained about Alan of Lynn to Thomas Netter in his capacity as Prior Provincial of the Carmelite order because the former was 'to conuersawnt with þe sayd creatur, for-as-mech as he supportyd hir in hir wepyng & in hir crying & also enformyd hir in qwestyons of Scriptur whan sche wolde any askyn hym'.[155] Netter was a cautious man. The Norwich Carmelite Thomas Scrope earned his anger in 1425 after he left his priory to proclaim his apocalyptic visions of the New Jerusalem. As Prior Provincial, Netter was responsible for discipline within the order – in response to his reprimands Scrope withdrew from public life, living as a recluse for the next twenty years.[156] Although millennianism and politics are absent from Kempe's prophecies, Netter's response to the complaints about Kempe was to forbid Alan of Lynn, for a time at least, from speaking with her, or explaining any Scriptural text to her. Netter was a patron of anchoresses in Norwich and Lynn, but evidently he did not entirely approve of Kempe, even if he did not actually suspect her of error.

Despite her apparent orthodoxy, Kempe's refusal to live as a 'good wyfe', confining her piety to devout practices while living a life of virtuous domesticity, rendered her vulnerable to particular suspicion at this time of unrest. Lynn Staley contends that 'In achieving a spiritual identity, Margery must place herself in opposition to those orthodox ideas of family and authority sanctioned by the *civitas hominis*. By describing a conflict that goes back at least as far as the account of the martyrdom of Saint Perpetua or the apocryphal early church biography of Thecla, Kempe insinuates Margery into the ranks of the "holy woman." '[157] A doctor of divinity who interviewed her in the York Chapter House asked her if she had a letter from her husband permitting her to go on pilgrimage.[158] The absence of her husband increased her examiners' hostility as they suspected her of being unchaste. In Leicester, Kempe asserted her fidelity to her husband, declaring, 'I neuyr had part of mannys body in þis worlde in actual dede be wey of synne, but of myn husbondys body, whom I am bowndyn to be þe lawe

---

154 *Book of Margery Kempe*, 151.

155 *Book of Margery Kempe*, 168; cf. n. 168/5.

156 Dubois, 'Netter', 45.

157 Staley, *Dissenting Fictions*, 89; and also her earlier article, L.S. Johnson, 'Margery Kempe: Social Critic', *Journal of Medieval and Renaissance Studies* xxii (1992), 159–84.

158 *Book of Margery Kempe*, 122.

of matrimony, & be whom I haue born xiiij chulderyn.'[159] When the Steward of Leicester spoke to her lewdly she sought protection in her claim that she was 'a mannys wife'.[160] Clearly Kempe's freedom of movement was perceived by some as subversive licentiousness. Bowet opened his first examination by asking, 'Why gost þu in white? Art þu a mayden?'[161] Assuming the colour of her dress to indicate the perfect state of virginity,[162] on discovering that she had a husband, he quickly formed the opinion that she was travelling under false pretences and immediately called for her to be fettered.

Some of Kempe's interrogators feared that she might encourage women to rebel against the institution of marriage. The Mayor of Leicester, for example, suspected that Kempe was a member of some sort of sect. He told her, 'I wil wetyn why þow gost in white clothys, for I trowe þow art comyn hedyr to han a-wey owr wyuys fro us & ledyn hem wyth þe.'[163] While some Lollard women may have been forced to leave husbands who opposed their beliefs, others found Scriptural authority to separate from them in I Corinthians 7.13–15: 'nor is there any reason for a woman to part with her husband, not a believer, if he is content to live with her ... if the unbelieving partner is for separating, let them separate'. But there is reason to think that the Church was apprehensive that Kempe had been corrupted by other heresies with which she could have come into contact, particularly on her foreign travels. She was asked by a clerk in York to explain her understanding of the command, 'Crecite et multiplicamini.'[164] Lochrie has argued that Kempe's reply that 'þes wordys ben not vndirstodyn only of begetyng of chyldren bodily, but also be purchasyng of vertu ...' is a conventional interpretation, frequently used to qualify St Paul's teaching in the redemptive function of childbirth.[165] Nonetheless the question itself may have been raised to elicit an answer which would reveal the kind of sexually immoral tenets thought to be characteristic of the Free Spirit movement,[166] and it has even been suggested that the Mayor of Leicester feared that Margery Kempe's white dress indicated that she was a member of the heretical imitators of Christ known as the Flagellants, although it is far from clear that he would have known about the sect.[167] At the end of Archbishop

---

[159] *Book of Margery Kempe*, 115.

[160] *Book of Margery Kempe*, 113.

[161] *Book of Margery Kempe*, 124.

[162] On the symbolism of Kempe's white dress, see Wilson, 'Communities', 170–1.

[163] *Book of Margery Kempe*, 116.

[164] *Book of Margery Kempe*, 121; Genesis 1.22.

[165] *Book of Margery Kempe*, 121; Lochrie, 'Marginal Woman's Quest', 49.

[166] *Book of Margery Kempe*, n. 121/2–3; cf A. Hudson, 'A Lollard Mass' in *Lollards and their Books* (London, 1985), 14. The Free Spirit movement and its infiltration of the béguinages is discussed by Leff, *Heresy*, i, 308–407; and R.E. Lerner, *The Heresy of the Free Spirit in the Later Middle Ages* (Berkeley, 1972).

[167] Cf. *Book of Margery Kempe*, n. 124/13; and J.C. Hirsch, *The Revelations of Margery*

Bowet's first examination, his clerics complained that although Kempe knew the Articles of the Faith, they would not allow her to live amongst them 'for þe pepil hath gret feyth in hir dalyawnce, and perauentur sche myth peruertyn summe of hem'.[168] Bowet gave Kempe safe escort from his diocese 'for qwietyng of þe pepil',[169] but the earlier fears concerning her soon resurfaced and in a second examination presided over by the Archbishop, his suffragan reported new rumours that she had advised a woman of high rank, Elizabeth Lady Greystoke, to leave her husband.[170]

When he had finished questioning Kempe, and before dismissing her, Bowet told her that in his opinion 'þer was neuyr woman in Inglond so ferd wyth-al as sche is & hath ben'.[171] Kempe's devotions and contemplations, her vow of chastity and her white clothes were her equivalent of a nun's more formal renunciation of the world, but a number of critics have argued that early fifteenth-century English society could not easily accommodate men and women like her, who insisted on following Christ while living in its midst, constantly threatening its values. Anthony Goodman calls her 'an anti-social virus in the body politic', while Lochrie describes her as 'a woman on the margin of church and society'.[172] It is important not to over-emphasize Kempe's isolation, but at times she did find herself without the protection of her husband and friends. In her constant refusal to conform to the narrower precepts of Church and society her status was insufficient to protect her from prejudice and hostility. While Thomas Peverel, Bishop of Worcester, welcomed her into his presence with the assurance, 'I haue not somownd þe, for I knowe wel j-now þu art Iohn of Burnamys dowtyr of Lynne',[173] the Mayor of Leicester was less impressed when she told him of her father and husband. He dismissed her words with the threat, 'Seint Kateryn telde what kynred sche cam of & ʒet ar ʒe not lyche, for þu art a fals strumpet, a fals loller, & a fals deceyuer of þe pepyl, & þerfor I xal haue þe in preson.'[174]

During Kempe's trials, a number of clerics who had formerly supported her changed sides for their own safety; one who had promised to stand by her in her first examination in York 'drow on bakke tyl he knew how þe cawse xulde gon, whedyr wyth hir or a-ʒen hir'.[175] As Kempe tried to escape from the sort of persecution she had experienced in York, men advised her

---

Kempe: Paramystical Practices in Late Medieval England, Medieval and Renaissance Authors 10 (Leiden, 1988), 7.

168 *Book of Margery Kempe*, 125.

169 *Book of Margery Kempe*, 131.

170 *Book of Margery Kempe*, 133.

171 *Book of Margery Kempe*, 134.

172 Goodman, 'Piety', 356; Lochrie, 'Marginal Woman's Quest', 34.

173 *Book of Margery Kempe*, 109.

174 *Book of Margery Kempe*, 111–12.

175 *Book of Margery Kempe*, 121.

to 'forsake þis lyfe þat þu hast, & go spynne & carde as oþer women don, & suffyr not so meche schame & so meche wo',[176] a recommendation which echoes the poet Hoccleve's instructions to women who dispute about Scripture to 'sitteth doun and spynne'.[177] In the early years of her religious life, during a visit to Canterbury, a monk came upon Kempe after her husband had left her alone for a short time. He grew angry when he heard her speak of God and said to her that he would have her 'closyd in an hows of ston þat þer schuld no man speke wyth þe'.[178] It is not clear whether he was suggesting that she should be walled up in an anchoress's cell or imprisoned.

From the evidence of the *Book*, it would seem that Kempe was repeatedly censured for her decision to reject the relative prosperity, security and status of her married life in order to serve God. People accused her of failing as a wife and mother: in his old age, her husband fell down stairs and was badly injured, and Margery Kempe was held responsible, 'þe pepil seyd, ȝyf he deyd, hys wyfe was worthy to ben hangyn for hys deth, for-as-meche as sche myth a kept hym & dede not'.[179] Similarly, when her dissolute son contracted a dreadful disease, she was blamed for using her prophetic powers as a curse: 'sche had don ryth euyl, for thorw hir prayer God had takyn veniawns on hir owyn childe'.[180] People doubted her celibacy and even when she had lived with and gone on pilgrimage with her husband, they had slandered her, claiming that the couple breached their vow of continence.[181] Some of her supporters were turned against her by such rumours. Thomas Brakleye, a Norwich anchorite, had heard that she had conceived and given birth to a child during her travels to Jerusalem and Rome, and he was one of many who disapproved of her adoption of white clothes and tried to persuade her to abandon them.[182]

Certain passages in the *Book* reveal that Kempe internalized these suspicions and reproofs, at times doubting even her own salvation. She admits that in the years following her conversion, she was vulnerable to sexual temptation, although in later life it was the threat of violation which troubled her most.[183] She was particularly distressed by the teaching that virgins are loved more by Christ than spouses.[184] Before she had taken her vow of chastity, Kempe feared that she would be deprived of Christ's love

---

[176] *Book of Margery Kempe*, 129.
[177] Hoccleve, 'Address to Sir John Oldcastle', line 147.
[178] *Book of Margery Kempe*, 27.
[179] *Book of Margery Kempe*, 179.
[180] *Book of Margery Kempe*, 222.
[181] *Book of Margery Kempe*, 179–80.
[182] *Book of Margery Kempe*, 103; cf. n. 103/1sq.
[183] Cf. *Book of Margery Kempe*, 13–16, 144–6, 112, 241.
[184] For Jerome's teaching on virginity, see 'Against Jovinianus' and 'To Eustochium, on the Preservation of Virginity' in *The Principal Works of Saint Jerome*, trans. W.H.

and that she was unworthy 'to heryn þe spekyn & þus to comown wyth myn husbond'.[185] Christ reassured her with a promise that no one is deprived of his love, and that she would dance with virgins in heaven:

'3a, dowtyr, trow þow rygth wel þat I lofe wyfes also, and specyal þo wyfys whech woldyn levyn chast, 3yf þei mygtyn haue her wyl . . . for, þow þe state of maydenhode be more parfyte & mor holy þan þe state of wedewhode, & þe state of wedewhode more parfyte þan þe state of wedlake, 3et dowtyr I lofe þe as wel as any mayden in þe world.'[186]

Christ's words to Kempe closely echo a revelation given to St Bridget: 'Þerefor þi doghtir, wheþir scho schall be wyfe or maiden still, sho pleses me yf hir will and desir be to me.'[187]

Writing allowed Kempe to defend herself against misconceptions that she was a heretic and a rebellious wife. The narrative constantly emphasizes her role as God's messenger. At the time of the examinations, her life was certainly at risk – when she was first called before the Archbishop of York she is described as shaking and trembling so much that she had to hide her hands under her clothes so that no one would notice, and when the interrogation began she 'meltyd al in-to terys'.[188] Nonetheless, she remained steadfast in her faith. Her aptitude for speaking and teaching is repeatedly demonstrated; she was self-possessed under questioning and able to refute the arguments of her opponents and reveal their failings. She was also aware that her examinations offered her an opportunity to instruct others through both her words and her demeanour. Before she was questioned by the officials of Leicester she knelt down and prayed to God that He give her enough grace, wit and wisdom to answer in ways which would not only honour Him most, and profit her own soul, but also be the best example to the people.[189] Her prayers were answered – she found support amongst the people of Leicester,[190] and a cleric who had spoken against her in her first examination before the Archbishop of York now begged for her forgiveness.[191] One of the retainers of the Duke of Bedford regretted his part in her arrest, pleading 'Damsel, yf euyr þu be seynt in Heuyn, prey for me.'[192]

Freemantle, G. Lewis, and W.G. Hartley, A Select Library of Nicene and Post-Nicene Fathers of the Christian Church, 2nd series, 4 (Oxford, 1893), 346–416 and 22–41.
[185] *Book of Margery Kempe*, 48.
[186] *Book of Margery Kempe*, 49.
[187] *The Liber Celestis of St Bridget of Sweden*, ed. R. Ellis, EETS o.s. 291 (Oxford, 1987), 316.
[188] *Book of Margery Kempe*, 124.
[189] *Book of Margery Kempe*, 114–15.
[190] *Book of Margery Kempe*, 123.
[191] *Book of Margery Kempe*, 118.
[192] *Book of Margery Kempe*, 130.

Although the accounts of her interrogations are only episodes in a much larger work, suspicion of her piety as a layperson and woman frames the entire narrative of Kempe's life. Goodman argues that the *Book* bears 'the stamp of clerical analysis and controversy',[193] while Wilson suggests that from a socio-historical perspective, the evidence of her disruptive influence 'points to a deeply disturbed social and religious milieu'.[194] The differing responses of her confessors to her religious fervour reflect the spiritual climate of her age.[195] Master Robert Spryngolde, parish priest of St Margaret's Church, was particularly firm with her. At times he paid little heed to her visions, frowned upon her desire for physical experiences, directed her towards moderation and encouraged her to perform humble and menial tasks. His early response to her experiences had been one of scepticism; he had dismissed them as 'but tryfelys & japys',[196] and counselled Kempe to suppress her loud prayers and to concentrate instead on quiet contemplation on the sacrifice and love of God.[197] Even after he became more confident of the authenticity of her spirituality, Spryngolde remained a restraining influence. Following the slander of the visiting friar preaching in Lynn, Kempe was almost driven away from her town and even Spryngolde despaired of what to do, claiming, 'Þer is no more a-ȝen ȝow but þe mone & vij sterrys. An-ethe is þer any man þat heldith wyth ȝow but I a-lone.'[198] Nonetheless, like Kempe's scribe, in a crisis Spryngolde put his faith in her prophetic abilities.[199] Following her advice, when the Guildhall of the Trinity was consumed by flames and St Margaret's Church was itself in danger, he carried the Blessed Sacrament to the fire, trusting in its supernatural power as a relic of Christ to save the Church. Seemingly in response to Kempe's prayer, the fire was suddenly extinguished by a snowfall.

In contrast to Spryngolde, Kempe's first confessor, an anchorite attached to the Dominican Friary in Lynn, encouraged her enthusiasm. In the early years after her conversion this anchorite was appointed by God to listen to the 'preuyteys' and 'cownselys' revealed to her.[200] He too was gifted with

---

[193] Goodman, 'Piety', 349.

[194] Wilson, 'Communities', 156.

[195] For a full discussion of Kempe's relationships with her confessors, see J. Dillon, 'Holy Women and their Confessors or Confessors and their Holy Women? Margery Kempe and Continental Tradition' in *Prophets Abroad: the Reception of Continental Holy Women in Late-Medieval England*, ed. R. Voaden (Cambridge, 1996), 115–40.

[196] *Book of Margery Kempe*, 44; cf. 216–17 and n. 217/33sq.

[197] *Book of Margery Kempe*, 217–18; cf. 89–90 for Kempe's internalization of this injunction.

[198] *Book of Margery Kempe*, 155.

[199] *Book of Margery Kempe*, 162–4.

[200] *Book of Margery Kempe*, 17.

the spirit of prophecy and had confidence in his own ability to discern the authenticity and integrity of her gifts.[201] He declared her pilgrimage to Rome and Jerusalem to be a miracle, and did not doubt her piety in the face of malicious rumours which circulated about her.[202] One of her opponents at her second examination before Archbishop Bowet reported that only the intervention of this confessor's order had saved Kempe from being burnt to death in Lynn.[203] Both Kempe's confessors were encouraged by her prophecies and supported her in the face of the opposition of some of her contemporaries, which was directed against her as a layperson and as a woman. As Goodman puts it, *The Book of Margery Kempe* is a 'manifesto in favour of one sort of clerical reaction to current manifestations of feminine piety which were provoking alarm and controversy'.[204]

Unlike the *Showings* of Julian of Norwich or Bridget of Sweden's *Liber Celestis*, *The Book of Margery Kempe* is not only or even primarily an account of her prophecies and visions, and, as the next chapter will show, Kempe's imitation of St Bridget is markedly different from that of Elizabeth Barton, the so-called 'Holy Maid of Kent', in the following century. Despite the fact that Kempe often spoke out, denouncing the spiritual laxities of her age, I am inclined to agree that, at least to some extent, the *Book* 'implicitly disavows her role as a social critic' and 'is less a critique than a sacred biography'.[205] In its anxiety to refute charges of heresy and irreligiousness, the *Book* is reminiscent of times of defensive hagiographies like the *Life of Mary of Oignies*, the *vita* of a béguine written by her confessor Jacques de Vitry at least in part to prove her orthodoxy (a work which Kempe's scribe cites to justify her uncontrollable weeping),[206] but in its lengthy accounts of her trials and sufferings, it patterns her life according to the *imitatio Christi*. *The Book of Margery Kempe* describes its subject as a woman

---

[201] *Book of Margery Kempe*, 44–5, 60, 76–7.
[202] *Book of Margery Kempe*, 37–8, 46.
[203] *Book of Margery Kempe*, 132.
[204] Goodman, 'Piety', 349.
[205] Staley, *Dissenting Fictions*, 79.
[206] For an edition of a Middle English translation see 'Prosalegenden. Die legenden des ms Douce 114', ed. C. Horstmann, *Anglia* viii (1885), 134–84. Cf. P.D. Kurtz, 'Mary of Oignies, Christine the Marvelous, and Medieval Heresy', *Mystics Quarterly* xiv (1988), 186–96; B.M. Bolton, '*Vitae Matrum*: a Further Aspect of *Frauenfrage*' in *Medieval Women*, ed. Baker, 253–73; and *The Book of Margery Kempe*, 152–3. On the influence of this and other texts on *The Book of Margery Kempe*, see Erskine, 'Margery Kempe and her Models'; R. Ellis, 'Margery Kempe's Scribe and the Miraculous Books' in *Langland, the Mystics and the Medieval English Religious Tradition: Essays in honour of S.S. Hussey*, ed. H. Phillips (Cambridge, 1990), 161–75; A. Barratt, 'Margery Kempe and the King's Daughter of Hungary' in *Margery Kempe: a Book of Essays*, ed. S.J. McEntire (New York, 1992), 189–201. It should be noted, however, that Watson contends that Julian's *Showings* emerge from a similar milieu of controversy: Watson, 'Composition'.

whose conversion motivated her to reject familial ties and the social values which she had formerly held dear, such as economic ambitions and pride in her birth and 'pompows aray'.[207] As a prophet in her own country, Kempe demonstrated her ability to withstand temptation patiently, to bear reproof, and to live amidst affliction and persecution consoled by the grace of God and the blessings He gave her during her contemplations, and by the knowledge that such tribulations were a gift which proved the righteousness of her vocation. Kempe is depicted as voluntarily accepting all that befell her – when asked by God if she would that He take away her suffering, she replied, 'Nay, good Lord, late me be at þi wille & make me mythy & strong for to suffyr al þat euyr þi wilt þat I suffyr, and grawnt me mekenes & pacyens þerwyth.'[208] She is represented as a participator in the gifts of the Lord and a teacher of spiritual truths, and her role within the orthodox church is repeatedly validated. Ultimately, Kempe's decision to have her autobiography written was a decision not only to describe the mercy of the Lord who 'meued & stered a synful caytyf vn-to hys love',[209] but also to *convince* the reader that she was a true secretary of God.

---

[207] *Book of Margery Kempe*, 9–11.
[208] *Book of Margery Kempe*, 119–20.
[209] *Book of Margery Kempe*, 1.

3

Of the Seed of Abraham:
Elizabeth Barton, the 'Holy Maid of Kent'

Art thou greater than our father Abraham, which is dead? and the
prophets are dead: whom makest thou thyself?   (John 8.53)

Reassessing Barton's Infamy

On 20 April 1534, a 28-year-old Benedictine nun from the convent of St
Sepulchre's in Canterbury was hanged at Tyburn alongside her confessor
and a number of their associates. The nun was Elizabeth Barton, a former
servant from the parish of Aldington in Kent. Barton and her companions
were attainted of treason by a Parliamentary Act which asserts that they
maliciously opposed Henry VIII's divorce from Katherine of Aragon and
'traterously attempted many notable actes intendyng therbye the distur-
baunce of the pease and tranquyllytie of this Realme'.[1] The Act goes on to
specify that those attainted claimed that Elizabeth Barton had received a
revelation from God,

> that in case hys Highnes proceded to thaccomplishment of the seid devorce
> and maried another, that then hys Majestie shulde not be kynge of this Realme
> by the space of one moneth after, And in the reputacion of God shuld not be
> kynge one day nor one houre.[2]

Deliberately couching her prophecy in ambiguous terms, Barton did not
state exactly how Henry VIII would lose his kingdom, but this did not make
her words any the less compromising. The King's reign was understood to
be divinely ordained; to rebel was a sin against God, and to envisage the
King's death could be a crime of treason. Whether or not Barton was at the
centre of a conspiracy against Henry, as the Act of Attainder argued, her
claim that God had revealed to her that He no longer recognized Henry's
monarchy could have both sanctioned and inspired an insurrection in a

---

[1] 25 Henry VIII, c. 12, *Statutes of the Realm*, ed. A. Luders et al. (1810–1828), iii, 446.
[2] 25 Henry VIII, c. 12, 446. Many sources record this prophecy, although there are some
variations in the content.

country already stirring with opposition to his reforms – to overthrow the King might even be perceived as a duty by zealous reactionaries.[3]

Elizabeth Barton is represented in the Act of Attainder as a false prophet who was encouraged by her adherents to feign saintliness in order to persuade others to stand against the monarchy. Hitherto historians have accepted, almost without questioning, this evaluation of Barton as a hypocrite and a fraud. While some Reformation studies ignore Elizabeth Barton completely, others have defined her mainly in terms of her connections with others implicated in the affair, especially Bishop John Fisher and Sir Thomas More.[4] Previous discussions of her life and death have also tended to focus on her moral character and even relatively sympathetic accounts have been marred by their obsession with the question of her authenticity.[5] Retha M. Warnicke, for example, does not directly challenge Barton's reputation for 'virile sanctity' but she remains sceptical about her trances, asserting that 'sometimes their messages, especially the ones opposing the royal divorce, were invented', and she follows David Knowles in suggesting that 'as Bocking and her other associates were all hostile to the King's marital schemes, it is likely that their opinions had an effect, "if only a subconscious one" upon her revelations'.[6] Warnicke's depiction of Barton is typical in the way in which it characterizes her as a victim of clerical exploitation rather than as an active political agent.

There is an abundance of sixteenth-century material which could be cited in justification of such an interpretation of Elizabeth Barton's career. One anonymous anti-clerical satire, written the year before her death, accuses Thomas More of hypocrisy, and connects him with Barton, who is 'from the devill sent', but whose deceit has not yet been publicly exposed:

> A virgyne ffayre and gent,
> That hath our yees blent:
> Alas, we be myswent!
> for yf the false intent
> were knowen of this witche,
> It passeth dogg and bitche:
> I pray god, do so mutche

---

3   For a sixteenth-century discussion of the probable effect of Barton's prophecies on the realm see Public Record Office, State Papers 1/81, f. 85r (*Letters and Papers, Foreign and Domestic, of the Reign of Henry VIII*, ed. J.S. Brewer, J. Gairdner and R.H. Brodie (Vaduz, 1965), vii no. 72 (1)).

4   See, for example, J. Guy, *Tudor England* (Oxford, 1988), 138.

5   See, for example, D. Knowles, *The Religious Orders in England* (Cambridge, 1948–1959), iii, 182.

6   R.M. Warnicke, *Women of the English Renaissance and Reformation*, Contributions to Women's Studies 38 (Westport C.T., 1983), 69. For a more positive interpretation of Barton's career, see P. Crawford, *Women and Religion in England, 1500–1720* (London, 1993), 29.

To fret her on the itche,
And open her in tyme![7]

Yet, although historians have tended to minimize the significance of Barton's contribution to the conservative resistance to the Reformation and very few give detailed accounts of her life and prophecies,[8] at the time Barton's execution was something of a *cause célèbre*. Thomas More succeeded in defending his relations with Barton to Cromwell (who was leading the investigation); Bishop Fisher did not, and his name was included in the indictment against her. In a letter written a year after the event, John Mason linked Barton's death to Fisher's martyrdom and commented, 'What end this Tragedy wyll com to God wot. Iff that may be callid a Tragedye *quae inceperit a nuptiis.*'[9] Elizabeth Barton clearly articulated an anger at the political developments of the time which was widely felt, and she had direct links with Syon Abbey, a centre of late medieval feminine devotion and also of opposition to the Act of Supremacy in the early Reformation. According to notes taken during Barton's investigation, her prophecies were told to Abbess Agnes Jordan, the confessor of Syon John Fewterer, the scholar and future martyr Richard Reynolds, and a number of women there including the wife of the Lieutenant of the Tower, Lady Kingston.[10] Barton herself confessed that Agnes Jordan had encouraged her to meet with the Marchioness of Exeter, whose antipathy to the King was well-known,[11] and subsequent government investigations uncovered evidence which suggests that such meetings were indeed treasonous in intent.[12] Thomas More reported that certain of the monks at Syon were somewhat suspicious of Barton and of the things that she said,[13] but this did not prevent her from receiving an enthusiastic reception at the neighbouring Charterhouse at Sheen.[14] In a letter written less than a year before Barton's execution, the Procurator, Henry Man, declared that the knowledge of her pious works was

---

7   'The Image of Ypocresye', part 3, lines1687–95: *Ballads from the Manuscripts*, ed. F.J. Furnivall (London, 1868), i, part 1, 233–4.

8   The best short narrative accounts of Elizabeth Barton's life and prophecies are those by Knowles, *Religious Orders*, iii, 182–91; and A.D. Cheney, 'The Holy Maid of Kent', *Transactions of the Royal Historical Society* n.s. xviii (1904), 107–29. The only book-length study is A. Neame, *The Holy Maid of Kent: the Life of Elizabeth Barton, 1506–1534* (London, 1971).

9   H. Ellis, ed., *Original Letters Illustrative of English History* (London, 1827) 2nd series, i, 58.

10   *L&P*, vi, no. 1468 (1).

11   PRO, SP 1/80, ff. 142r–143v (*L&P*, vi, no. 1468 (7)).

12   See PRO, SP 1/138, f. 210r (*L&P*, xiii, part 2, no. 802); SP 1/139, f. 16r (*L&P*, xiii, part 2, no. 827 (2)); SP 1/139, ff. 77r–77v (*L&P*, xiii, part 2, no. 831 (liv and lv)); SP 1/140, ff. 5r–8v (*L&P*, xiii, part 2, no. 961 (2)).

13   *The Correspondence of Sir Thomas More*, ed. E.F. Rogers (Princeton, 1947), 484.

14   *Correspondence*, ed. Rogers, 485–6.

more edifying to his soul than anything that he had read in Holy Scripture.[15] He also wrote of her charismatic ability to turn people away from their sins, and described her as a woman 'ex semine Abrahæ'.[16] Even Thomas More, in a letter of advice to Barton, compared himself to Jethro counselling the 'highe prophet Moyses'.[17]

To some extent, the assumption that Barton could not have played a serious role in the resistance to the Reformation simply because she was a woman may lie behind the misinterpretation of history which has led to her marginalization. However Barton's significance has been denied not only on the basis of her gender, but also because of a more general trend in recent scholarship. As Donna B. Hamilton and Richard Strier explain,

> The great efflorescence in historicized literary studies of the early modern period in England has not been very mindful of religious issues; indeed some of these studies have tended to drive a wedge between scholars who emphasize 'religious' issues and scholars who emphasize 'political' ones.[18]

Traditionally, Barton's prophecies have been seen as part of some larger machiavellian plan. In this chapter, I argue instead that they are related to the established and partially autonomous traditions of female and popular prophecy discussed in the second chapter.

Studies of popular prophecy have revealed that they proliferated at times of discontent and rebellion.[19] Prophecies often functioned as a form of political commentary and protest, but sometimes they not only articulated, but also *inspired* social and political unease. In 1521 Edward Suffolk, the third Duke of Buckingham, was executed after the revelations of a Carthusian monk encouraged him in his aspirations to the throne. Indeed, sometime before Elizabeth Barton's arrest, Thomas More wrote a letter to her in which he tried to dissuade her from talking with anyone about affairs of the King or the state and to illustrate this warning he specifically alluded to Buckingham's downfall: 'I thinke you have harde how the late Duke of Buckingham moved with the fame of one that was reported for an holye monke and had suche talkinge with hyme as after was a grete parte of his distruction. . . .'[20] Thomas Cromwell was fully aware of the subversive power of prophetic discourse, arguing that 'if credence shuld be gyven to euery suche lewd person as wold affirme himself to haue reuelations from

---

15 PRO, SP 1/79, f. 76r (*L&P*, vi, no. 1149 (2)).
16 PRO, SP 1/77, f. 237r (*L&P*, vi, no. 835); cf. John 8.33.
17 *Correspondence*, ed. Rogers, 465.
18 *Religion, Literature, and Politics in Post-Reformation England, 1540–1688*, ed. D.B. Hamilton and R. Strier (Cambridge, 1996), 2.
19 K.V. Thomas, *Religion and the Decline of Magic: Studies in Popular Beliefs in Sixteenth and Seventeenth Century England* (London, 1971), 389–432. See also S.L. Jansen, *Political Protest and Prophecy under Henry VIII* (Woodbridge, 1991).
20 *Correspondence*, ed. Rogers, 465–6.

god what redyer wey were there to subuert al common welthes and good orders in the worlde',[21] while Eustace Chapyus observed that the English people were especially 'given to prophecies and divinations ... and thereby exceedingly prone to riots and revolutions'.[22] This problem was by no means peculiar to England. By the early sixteenth century figures like Joachim of Fiore, Amadeus of Portugal and Girolamo Savonarola were extremely influential, especially in Italy, and the spread of prophecy throughout Europe was perceived to have become such a serious concern that the Fifth Lateran Council (1512–1517) issued decrees which were intended to circumscribe its abuses: members of the clergy were forbidden to date forthcoming catastrophes; and they were banned from deriving such predictions from scriptural interpretation or claiming that they were received as divine inspiration.[23]

Elizabeth Barton's example illustrates that prophecy could offer women as well as men an opportunity for direct involvement in the public sphere on a national level. In the previous chapter it was seen that continental precedents for such female intervention did exist, particularly in the prophetic activities of Bridget of Sweden and Catherine of Siena. I suggested there that there are few indications of English holy women taking part in similar activities in the centuries leading up to the Reformation, despite the evidence of there being quite a number of women renowned for their miracles and visions. The anonymous author of the fifteenth-century *Revelation of Purgatory*, which describes a woman's vision of the pains experienced by a sinful nun, may well reflect the influence of St Bridget's *Revelations*, but it does not address issues relating to national politics, and, as I have suggested already, even the devout lay-woman Margery Kempe, who is generally recognized to have had St Bridget as a spiritual model, was very much a *local* prophet, concerned only with questions involving her immediate communities.

To give some more examples, the theologian Thomas Netter, in his *Doctrinale*, described a pious fifteenth-century Norfolk woman called Joan the Meatless who survived by eating the bread of the sacrament and was able to discern a consecrated host from an unconsecrated one.[24] A century

---

[21] *Life and Letters of Thomas Cromwell*, ed. R.B. Merriman (Oxford, 1968), i, 375.

[22] *Calendar of Letters, Despatches, and State Papers, Relating to the Negotiations between England and Spain*, ed. G.A. Begenroth et al. (London, 1862–1947), iv part 2, no. 1154.

[23] N.H. Minnich, 'Prophecy and the Fifth Lateran Council (1512–1517)' in *Prophetic Rome in the High Renaissance Period*, ed. M. Reeves (Oxford, 1992), 85–6.

[24] Thomas Netter, *Doctrinale antiquitatum fidei catholicæ ecclesiæ*, ed. F.B. Blanciotte (Venice, 1757–1759; republished Farnborough, 1967) ii, 376–7. For further examples of medieval and early modern miraculous fasts, see H.E. Rollins, 'Notes on some English Accounts of Miraculous Fasts', *Journal of American Folk-Lore* xxxiv (1921), 357–76.

later, Thomas More, in his *Dialogue Concerning Heresies*, discussed Elizabeth the so-called 'Holy Maid of Leominster' who, although she subsequently was exposed as a fraud, became famous after fasting for a long time and performing Eucharist miracles.[25] Yet even though Elizabeth of Leominster became the focus of public attention neither she nor Joan of Norfolk seem to have been associated with divinely inspired utterances of any sort. Another example, taken this time from the early sixteenth century, and more closely linked to Barton's case, is that of Anne Wentworth. Wentworth is also cited by Thomas More in his *Dialogue*, this time as a genuine holy maid.[26] As an adolescent Wentworth was afflicted by a form of prophetic madness which was cured during a pilgrimage to the shrine to the Virgin in Ipswich:

> She prophesyed and tolde many thynges done and sayd at the same tyme in other places whiche were proued trewe and many thynges sayd lyenge in her traunce of suche wysdome & lernyng that ryght connyng men hyghly meruayled to here of so yonge an vnlerned mayden whan her selfe wyst not what she sayd suche thynges vttered and spoken as well lerned menne myght haue myssed with a longe study.[27]

As will be seen in the next section, Wentworth's story bears a remarkable similarity to Barton's earliest experiences which began more than eight years before her execution, when she was nineteen years old. Both these young women impressed spectators with their psychic abilities and seemingly profound insights. However it appears that neither Wentworth's utterances nor Barton's early revelations had an *overtly* political agenda, and before Barton began to prophesy about Henry VIII's actions and policies, there is little reason to think that other English holy women showed any interest in matters of government. Barton was, then, an exceptional figure in English history, both as one of only very few Catholic women to die for opposing Henry VIII, and as a pre-Civil War female political prophet.

Elizabeth Barton's career as a prophet seems then to have fallen into two distinct phases. The first began in 1525 when Barton, at that time still a servant in a country house, acquired her supernatural gifts during an extended illness. After her parish priest Richard Master reported the matter, the Archbishop of Canterbury sent an ecclesiastical commission to examine her. It was led by Edward Bocking, a monk from the Benedictine house of Christ Church, Canterbury. When Barton was questioned, she was found orthodox on the points of faith. The commission was present when she was

---

[25] Thomas More, *A Dialogue Concerning Heresies*, ed. T.C. Lawler, G. Marc'hadour and R.C. Marius, *The Yale Edition of the Complete Works of St Thomas More*, iii (New Haven, 1981) part 1, 87–8.

[26] More, *Dialogue*, part 1, 92–4.

[27] More, *Dialogue*, part 1, 93.

miraculously healed of her disease at the Chapel of Our Lady in the village
of Court-at-Street during Lent 1526. She subsequently entered the convent
of St Sepulchre in Canterbury and was given special permission to come
under Edward Bocking's spiritual direction. During this first phase, Barton
became renowned as a miracle worker and seer, and as her reputation for
sanctity became widespread she came to be known as the 'Holy Maid of
Kent'. She was held in some esteem by the nuns at Syon Abbey, monks at
the Charterhouses of Sheen and London, and the friars at Canterbury,
Greenwich and Richmond. She had audiences with Henry VIII, Cardinal
Wolsey, Sir Thomas More, Archbishop Warham and Bishop Fisher. However, in a rapidly changing political situation, her prophecies became
increasingly contentious: this political involvement characterizes the second phase of her career. An investigation carried out by Cromwell and
Cranmer revealed links between Barton and some of the most learned and
powerful of the King's critics and resulted in her execution. The following
sections will consider each of these phases of Barton's visionary experiences and their implications for the religious and political history of the
early Reformation, before going on to examine the ways in which her
prophecies were disseminated and the processes of their suppression.

Illness and Inspiration

Largely as a result of Barton's fate, very little of the surviving information
concerning her life is reliable. A number of works relating to Barton's
prophecies were written in her lifetime, two of which are of particular
relevance to this discussion.[28] The first was a printed tract, attributed to a
layman, Edward Thwaites, and entitled *A marueilous woorke of late done
at Court of Streete in Kent*. The second was a large manuscript written by
Barton's confessor, Edward Bocking, which was known as the Nun's book,
or Bocking's 'great book'. At one time several miraculous letters also
existed; they were said to have been written in Heaven and given to Barton
by an angel.[29] The most well-known was the illuminated 'letter of Mary
Magdalene',[30] which was later discovered to have been produced by a monk
called William Hawkhurst.[31] None of these texts escaped the censorship

which followed Barton's arrest, with the exception of a single unsigned fragment, a sheet written in Latin which is thought to be a draft of the introduction to Bocking's book.[32] In other words, almost all the first-hand evidence concerning Barton's life and revelations has been destroyed. While it is my intention, in so far as it is possible, to reconstruct Barton's prophecies and the writings about her, it has to be acknowledged that there is no direct access to her words. Furthermore, the evidence provided by the Protestant propaganda which was circulated against Barton after her execution was both hostile and often conflicting, and the surviving image of Barton is the one created by those who suppressed her visions and prophecies, and were responsible for her death.

The first printed account of Barton's miracles and prophecies, *A marueilous woorke*, was published by the London printer Robert Redman in 1527 or thereabouts.[33] Writing in 1533, Archbishop Cranmer observed that the pamphlet was still very popular,[34] and there may well have been more than one edition.[35] Initially it escaped ecclesiastical censorship. Almost fifty years later William Lambarde published a refutation of *A marueilous woorke* in his *A perambulation of Kent*.[36] It is probable that his extremely condemnatory summary of its contents is quite accurate: Lambarde promises to follow the original story closely in order to preserve it.[37] Other early discussions of Barton's first spiritual experiences can be found in a range of sources which include Tyndale's *An Answer to Sir Thomas More's Dialogue* (published in 1531);[38] a sermon against Barton and her associates delivered at their public penance at St Paul's Cross and in the precincts of Canterbury Cathedral at the end of 1533;[39] a letter written by Archbishop Cranmer to Archdeacon Hawkins on 20 December 1533;[40] the Act of Attainder against Barton and her associates passed in 1534;[41] and

---

[32] PRO, SP 1/80, f. 140r (*L&P*, vi, no. 1468 (6)); edited by J.R. McKee in *Dame Elizabeth Barton, O.S.B. The Holy Maid of Kent* (London, 1925), 60–3.

[33] See William Lambarde's *A perambulation of Kent: conteining the description . . . of that shyre* (1576), T3r. Unless otherwise stated, all references will be to this edition. Edward Thwaites is named as the author of *A marueilous woorke* in the second edition of Lambarde's work: *A perambulation of Kent . . . now increased and altered* (1596), N3v.

[34] *Works*, ed. Cox, ii, 273.

[35] A large number of the books which Redman issued were reprints rather than original productions: E.J. Devereaux, 'Elizabeth Barton and Tudor Censorship', *Bulletin of the John Rylands Library* xlix (1966–1967), 99.

[36] Lambarde, *A perambulation of Kent*, T2v–T5r.

[37] Lambarde, *A perambulation of Kent*, T2v–T3r.

[38] William Tyndale, *An Answer to Sir Thomas More's Dialogue*, ed. H. Walter (Cambridge, 1850), 89–92.

[39] PRO, SP 1/82, ff. 89r–96v (*L&P*, vii, no. 72 (3)); published as 'Sermon', ed. Whatmore, 463–75. All references are to this edition.

[40] *Works*, ed. Cox, ii, 272–4.

[41] 25 Henry VIII, c. 12, 446–51.

Richard Morison's *Apomaxis calvmniarum* (a piece of propaganda written in 1535 to justify the royal divorce and other of the more scandalous events which had taken place in the recent years of Henry's reign).[42] Only Lambarde and the writer of the penitential sermon refer to *A marueilous woorke* by name, but it is probable that the other texts drew on it either directly or indirectly, and to varying degrees they confirm and supplement Lambarde's version of the story.

A marueilous woorke was a treatise intended for the edification of the pious; it may have been written to stimulate devotion to the shrine of Our Lady at Court-at-Street.[43] For several years after Barton's cure the chapel was a popular destination for pilgrimages,[44] and miracles of the Virgin continued to be reported there after Barton's entry into religion.[45] *A marueilous woorke* was also a celebration of Barton's prophetic calling, the first indication of which occurred after she had been ill for several months: during a fit, Barton predicted the imminent death of a child who was being nursed in the same room.[46] Soon afterwards Barton revealed other uncanny abilities: for example, she could see with her mind's eye events happening in other places, especially in Church – a knowledge which she revealed not only by her words but also 'by the signes proceeding from her', possibly some sort of gesticulations.[47] Lambarde reports that Barton was even able to tell the people who had gathered to witness these strange happenings what the hermit at Court-at-Street was eating for his supper.[48]

According to Lambarde's transmission, *A marueilous woorke* described in detail the symptoms of the disease which precipitated Barton's demonstration of supernatural talents. This illness affected her throat: intermittent swelling inhibited her breathing and caused her such agonizing pain that in its extremity onlookers thought that she was about to die.[49] As a result Barton could only utter her prediction 'with great pangs and groning'.[50] The surprise of those attending her was increased when in subsequent fits Barton fell into a trance-like state. Although Barton's body became completely passive she was now able to speak quite clearly, or to be spoken through.[51] Her later trances were accompanied by bodily and facial contortions which amazed and entranced growing numbers of spectators: as her body shook, she changed colour and her legs collapsed beneath her; lying prostrate on

---

42 Richard Morison, *Apomaxis calvmniarum* (1537), T1r–V2v.
43 For this suggestion, see Neame, *Holy Maid*, 19.
44 *Works*, ed. Cox, ii, 272.
45 Lambarde, *Perambulation*, T4v.
46 Lambarde, *Perambulation*, T3r.
47 Lambarde, *Perambulation*, T3v.
48 Lambarde, *Perambulation*, T4r.
49 Lambarde, *Perambulation*, T3r; cf. 'Sermon', ed. Whatmore, 464.
50 Lambarde, *Perambulation*, T3r.
51 Lambarde, *Perambulation*, T3v.

the ground, her arms and legs flailed around, her eyes protruded, her jaw appeared to dislocate, and her tongue stuck out of the side of her mouth.[52] Such fits are clearly reminiscent of those experienced by Anne Wentworth.[53] Archbishop Cranmer states that the words which were heard spoken during Barton's most dramatic and public trance were not uttered naturally, but came from a 'a voice speaking within her belly, as it had been in a tun; her lips not greatly moving; she all that while continuing by the space of three hours of more in a trance'.[54]

Lambarde summarizes the whole of *A marueilous woorke*, about twenty-four leaves in all,[55] in six quarto pages and is obviously very selective in his synopsis. According to another source, Barton's trance-like state was caused by her inability to eat or drink for long periods during her illness.[56] *A marueilous woorke* may well have described this inedia, but Lambarde makes no mention of it. Similarly, while Lambarde gives no spiritual explanation for Barton's sickness, such an interpretation seems to have been present, either explicitly or implicitly, in *A marueilous woorke*. *A marueilous woorke* probably shared with other hagiographic and devotional works a tendency to exaggerate and stereotype, but, while one cannot determine either Barton's actual experiences or her own understanding of them, it is possible to make some generalizations about late medieval attitudes towards disease. Whereas modern readings such as Warnicke's have suggested that Barton's illness and trances were the result of hysteria or epilepsy,[57] and even Lambarde tells us that she appeared to be inflicted by 'the falling Euill', in other words epilepsy,[58] in the later Middle Ages many people, including churchmen, were willing to accept that visionary trances could be brought on by natural diseases, and believed that while the senses were suspended, the soul could transcend the limits of the body and foresight would become possible.[59] To individuals of exceptional piety sickness could be a blessing. Whereas ordinary people suffered terribly in affliction, the saintly found reason to rejoice because illness brought with it not only the opportunity to share some of the torments of the crucified

---

52 See, for example, the description given in the 'Sermon', ed. Whatmore, 466.

53 Wentworth and Barton were so similar that Tyndale mentioned them together in *The Obedience of a Christian Man* in *Doctrinal Treatises and Introductions to Different Portions of Holy Scripture*, ed. H. Walter (Cambridge, 1848), 325–7, comparing them at greater length a couple of years later in *Answer*, 89–92.

54 *Works*, ed. Cox, ii, 273. However, Cranmer's account is indebted to More's narrative about Anne Wentworth in *Dialogue*, part 1, 92–4.

55 Lambarde, *Perambulation*, T3r.

56 25 Henry VIII, c. 12, 446–7.

57 Warnicke, 69. See also Cheney, 'Holy Maid', 115; and Neame, *Holy Maid*, 76–7.

58 Lambarde, *Perambulation*, T4v.

59 See the study of the history of epilepsy by O. Temkin, *The Falling Sickness: a History of Epilepsy from the Greeks to the Beginnings of Modern Neurology* (Baltimore, 1945), especially 83–192.

Christ, but also the hope that death approached and entry into heaven was imminent.[60] The link between illness and prophecy is to some extent a gendered one: accounts of prolonged physical suffering are especially common in the lives of female saints and visionaries in the Middle Ages and thereafter, and women's fasting in particular carried with it supernatural and superhuman implications in both the medieval and early modern periods.[61] A number of late medieval narratives about religious women, such as the *Showings* of Julian of Norwich and *The Book of Margery Kempe*, begin with illness, and in the seventeenth century illness re-emerged as an important aspect of the inspiration of women like Anna Trapnel and Sarah Wight. For such women, illness and physical suffering signified their liminal status between this world and the next and their physical submission to the divine, while at the same time emphasizing the disjunction between the prophetic voice and the sinful female flesh.

Elizabeth Barton's miraculous healing was a clear indication of the power and grace of the divine: in a revelation Our Lady of Court-at-Street commanded her to make it known to all Christians that she had rescued her from death, and to have the church bells rung to celebrate this miracle.[62] At the time appointed for Barton's cure the roads to the chapel were lined with people. Barton prostrated herself beneath the image of the Virgin in front of an assembled audience of two or three thousand.[63] Yet although Barton was relieved of her afflictions, the act of healing is itself anti-climactic; Lambarde even omits to mention the purpose of this public display.[64] In fact, most sources agree that not only Barton's trances but also her illness continued in the years which followed.[65] The crisis of her narrative is not the cure itself but the events which led up to it: the raptures and utterances – reappearances in sixteenth-century England of the sort of spirit of prophecy recorded in the Bible and in countless saints' lives. For all their horrific appearance, Barton's unnatural and supernatural experiences seem to have been interpreted by those who gave credence to her not as merely God-

---

[60] D. Weinsten and R.M. Bell, *Saints and Society: the Two Worlds of Western Christendom, 1000–1700* (Chicago, 1982), 156.

[61] See, for example: R. Bell, *Holy Anorexia* (Chicago, 1985); C.W. Bynum, *Holy Feast and Holy Fast: the Religious Significance of Food to Medieval Women* (Berkeley, 1987); and D. Purkiss, 'Producing the Voice, Consuming the Body: Women Prophets of the Seventeenth Century' in *Women, Writing, History 1640–1740*, ed. I. Grundy and S. Wiseman (London, 1992), 139–58.

[62] Lambarde, *Perambulation*, T3v.

[63] Lambarde claims that the audience numbered more than three thousand: Lambarde, *Perambulation*, T4v. Elsewhere the figure is reduced to above two thousand people: 'Sermon', ed. Whatmore, 465; and 25 Henry VIII, c. 12, 447.

[64] For Barton's cure see the 'Sermon', ed. Whatmore, 466; *Works*, ed. Cox, ii, 273; 25 Henry VIII, c. 12, 447–8.

[65] *Three Chapters of Letters Relating to the Suppression of Monasteries*, ed. T. Wright, CS o.s. 26 (London, 1843), 21; cf. Lambarde, *Perambulation*, T4v.

ordained but actually as works of the Holy Ghost. The voice which spoke through Barton announced that her physical affliction was a warning to the people of the punishment for sin.[66] Watching her bodily contortions, her audience saw her enact the eternal conflict of good and evil, and she alternately encouraged them in virtue and piety and warned of the horror of eternal damnation. Thomas Cranmer wrote that the ventriloquial voice which was heard while she lay in ecstasy spoke so sweetly when it described the joys of heaven 'that every man was ravished with the hearing thereof', but when it talked of hell 'it spake so horribly and terribly, that it put the hearers in a great fear'.[67] It is significant that Barton's disease attacked her throat – she was silenced so that God could speak through her. The location of the miraculous voice in Barton's belly (or womb) made it clear that her own subjectivity had been suppressed. As Diane Purkiss explains, 'prophetic utterance necessarily involves a radical dislocation of the voice from the body, since in authentic prophecy the voice comes from God, while the body through which it speaks is a passive conduit'.[68]

As a result of Barton's experiences, her status in her immediate community was improved: it was claimed in the sermon preached at her penance that Thomas Cobb, her master, was so convinced of her holiness that he invited her to eat at his table.[69] It is impossible to tell from the surviving evidence whether Cobb's reaction was a common one, but the sheer numbers of people who are said to have flocked to view her cure might suggest that it was. Certainly Barton's prophecies brought her a position in the church. The high point of her early career came when she claimed that the Virgin had revealed to her that she must join a convent,[70] and dedicate her life to her service.[71] The Virgin also dictated that Edward Bocking should become Barton's confessor – an appointment which had to be authorized by the Archbishop of Canterbury himself.[72] Lambarde ends his synopsis of *A marueilous woorke* with the wry comment that Barton was advanced from the condition of a base servant to that of a glorious nun.[73] Yet from another point of view, her entry into a convent and submission to Bocking can be seen as the re-integration into a male-controlled church of a religious enthusiasm which would otherwise be difficult to restrain.

Given the accusations made in the Act of Attainder and elsewhere that Barton feigned her prophecies and revelations, two related questions arise:

[66] Morison, *Apomaxis calvmniarum*, T1v–T2r.
[67] Works, ed. Cox, ii, 273.
[68] Purkiss, 'Producing the Voice', 141.
[69] 'Sermon', ed. Whatmore, 465.
[70] Lambarde, *Perambulation*, T4v.
[71] Morison, *Apomaxis calvmniarum*, T2r.
[72] 'Sermon', ed. Whatmore, 466; 25 Henry VIII, c. 12, 447.
[73] Lambarde, *Perambulation*, T4v. Wentworth also took the veil after her cure: More, *Dialogue*, part 1, 94.

to what extent might she actually have comprehended what she said during these early trances; and how likely is it that she framed these utterances herself or was dictated to by others? Barton's prophecies were so holy and wise that Edward Thwaites, the author of *A marueilous woorke* was one of those who believed that she could not possibly be responsible for them herself.[74] She is said to have been unable to remember the words which she had spoken when she regained consciousness from her trances.[75] Although many of her utterances, rather than appearing inspired, seemed to some to have been at best frivolous and at worst nonsensical,[76] apparent irrationality could be considered appropriate to esoteric discourse which attempted to represent that which was by its very nature beyond representation – the divine *logos*. Nonetheless, much of Barton's inspiration could have come from within her own experience. Even if she had received no formal schooling she would almost certainly have been able to recite in Latin both the Pater Noster and the Creed.[77] From the outset she knew the points of the Catholic faith, or at least her beliefs were not found to be heterodox when they were examined by the Archbishop's commission.[78] Her prophetically-inspired teaching on the seven deadly sins and the ten commandments may well have been based on elementary church instruction.[79] Even her revelation that the Son does not physically sit at the right hand of the Father, but that 'One was before Any Other, and One in Neither', seems to be a simple exposition of the doctrine of the Trinity.[80]

Barton may well have been influenced by religious ceremonies and processions, music, miracle and mystery plays as well as images such as statues, crucifixes, windows and paintings.[81] Her vision of heaven clearly reflects medieval iconographic conventions: the 'home' to which she felt herself drawn in her ecstasies was a place 'Where she sawe and hearde the ioyes of heauen, where S. Michael wayed soules, where Sainct Peter carried the keyes, and where she her selfe had the companie of our Lady at Court of Strete.'[82] Barton uttered her early prophecies in rhyme and is described (with some irony) by Tyndale as a 'goodly poetess'.[83] These rhyming

---

[74] Lambarde, *Perambulation*, T3v.

[75] 'Sermon', ed. Whatmore, 464; 25 Henry VIII, c. 12, 447.

[76] The penitential sermon and Act agree that her words were foolish: 'Sermon', ed. Whatmore, 465; and 25 Henry VIII, c. 12, 447. Morison claims that they were without sense: Morison, *Apomaxis calvmniarum*, T1v.

[77] See M.T. Clanchy, *From Memory to the Written Record: England 1066–1307* (2nd ed. Oxford, 1993), 189.

[78] Lambarde, *Perambulation*, T4r.

[79] 'Sermon', ed. Whatmore, 464.

[80] 'Sermon', ed. Whatmore, 472 and 472 n. 1.

[81] For a full study of late medieval piety, see E. Duffy, *The Stripping of the Altars: Traditional Religion in England c.1400–c.1580* (New Haven, 1992).

[82] Lambarde, *Perambulation*, T3v.

[83] Tyndale, *Answer*, 92; cf. Lambarde, *Perambulation*, T4v.

revelations integrate superstition and simple theology, and are probably more closely related to Marian devotion and medieval prayer charms (which were widely believed to help avert unexpected disasters) than to the sung outpourings of later prophets like Anna Trapnel.[84] One of her revelations warned:

> If thou the Sunday see not God in the face;
> If thou die that week suddenly without confession,
> Thou standest, man, in the way of damnation.[85]

This verse is traditional and a version of it is given a century and a half earlier in 'A Treatise of the Manner and Mede of the Mass':

> A Fair grace . God haþ þe ȝiuen
> Of þi sunnes . and þou be schriuen
> Þat day . þou has god se.
> Ȝif þou be ded . þe same day,
> Þou schalt be founden . I þe fay,
> Hoseled . as þou hed be.[86]

In fact, such promises are frequently found in the lists of the merits of the mass which became increasingly popular during the thirteenth century.[87]

Another example of Barton simply repeating a commonplace on the utility of certain religious practices is her assurance that:

> If any departe this life soudainly, or by mischance, in deadly sinne, if he be vowed to our Lady heartely, he shal be restored to life againe, to receiue shrift, and housell, and after to depart this worlde with Gods blessing.[88]

Similarly, the anonymous woman visionary responsible for *A Revelation of Purgatory* was promised that sinners suffering from doubt or despair would

---

84 D. Gray, 'Popular Religion and Late Medieval English Literature' in *Religion in the Poetry and Drama of the Late Middle Ages in England*, ed. P. Boitani and A. Torti (Cambridge, 1990), 4–5; cf. Duffy, *Stripping of the Altars*, esp. 233–65. On Marian devotion, see also *The Middle English Miracles of the Virgin*, ed. B. Boyd (San Marino CA, 1964). On Trapnel's sung prophecies, see N. Smith, *Perfection Proclaimed: Language and Literature in English Radical Religion 1640–1660* (Oxford, 1989), 50–1.

85 'Sermon', ed. Whatmore, 472.

86 'A Treatise on the Manner and Mede of the Mass', lines 113–18, in *The Lay Folks Mass Book or the Manner of Hearing Mass*, ed. T.F. Simmons, EETS o.s. 71 (London, 1879), 131.

87 M. Rubin, *Corpus Christi: the Eucharist in Late Medieval Culture* (Cambridge, 1991), 63, 108 and 341–2; Duffy, *Stripping of the Altars*, 91–130; Thomas, *Religion*, 33–6. Cf. John Lydgate's 'Virtutes missarum', lines 21–4 in *Lay Folks Mass Book*, ed. Simmons, 367–8; and John Audelay's 'De meritis misse; quodomo debemus audire missam', lines 56–9 in *The Poems of John Audelay*, ed. E.K. Whiting, EETS o.s. 184 (London, 1931) no. 9.

88 Lambarde, *Perambulation*, T4r; also cited in the 'Sermon', ed. Whatmore, 472.

be brought to a knowledge of their faults and delivered from temptation if they recited certain prayers, psalms and hymns.[89] As was noted in chapter two, dreams of heaven, hell and purgatory such as those which Barton was reported to have experienced were not uncommon amongst ordinary people in the fifteenth century.

Just as some of Barton's early utterances reflect the influence of visual images and popular prayers, others may have been derived from sermons which she had heard delivered by conservative churchmen. In 1525 the threat to the orthodox Church was a serious one – it was the year in which Tyndale began printing his English New Testament in Cologne. Two years later, after Tyndale was outlawed, he was aware that both Elizabeth Barton and Anne Wentworth were encouraging people in their superstitious beliefs and endangering his cause.[90] In her trances Barton certainly condemned the spread of heresy and she spoke in defence of the existence of purgatory and the authority of the Pope, urging Church attendance, mass, confession, prayer to the Virgin Mary and the saints, worship of images, and pilgrimage.[91] Despite the diversity of the influences on Barton's first miracles and predictions, the possibility remains that, as the Act of Attainder and other sources claim, the conservative faction of the Church quickly identified her political usefulness. However, as the next section will illustrate, Barton's prophecies continued to have a dynamic of their own.

Prophecy and Politics

In the years which followed Barton's entry into the convent, Edward Bocking compiled his 'great book' of her miracles and revelations. Many of the alleged heresies and crimes recorded in Bocking's book are enumerated both in the sermon preached at Barton's public penance and in the Act of Attainder. Documents confiscated or collected as evidence during Cromwell's investigation (for example the testimonies and correspondence of witnesses and suspects like Thomas Goldwell, Prior of Christ Church, and Thomas More) contribute to what is known of Barton's later prophecies and experiences.[92] It is important to reiterate that many sources are

---

89 *A Revelation of Purgatory* in *Yorkshire Writers: Richard Rolle of Hampole: an English Father of the Church and his Followers*, ed. C. Horstman (London, 1895–1896), i, 385.

90 Tyndale, *Obedience*, 325–7; cf. Tyndale, *Answer*, 92.

91 For Barton's prophecies concerning heresy: 25 Henry VIII, c. 12, 447; Morison, *Apomaxis calvmniarum*, T3v; and cf. *Works*, ed. Cox, ii, 273. For her prophecies in support of the orthodox faith: Lambarde, *Perambulation*, T3v; *Works*, ed. Cox, ii, 273; Morison, *Apomaxis calvmniarum*, T3v.

92 Many of these documents are found in *L&P*, vi–vii. An important letter exists written from Thomas Goldwell to Cromwell: British Library, MS Cleopatra Eiv, f. 92r–92v (*L&P*, vi, no. 1470). It is printed in *Three Chapters*, ed. Wright, 19–22. All references

unreliable or biased: one letter to Cromwell lists thirty miracles, visions and predictions; it is not signed, but L.E. Whatmore believes the writer to be Thomas Woolfe, a criminal imprisoned in the Tower, who may have hoped that his co-operation would secure his release.[93] However, from the combined evidence of the Act of Attainder and other documents, there can be no doubt that Bocking's book contained seditious material.

Within the convent of St Sepulchre, under the guidance of her confessor and other advisors and adherents, Elizabeth Barton learnt to emulate St Bridget of Sweden and St Catherine of Siena.[94] The penitential sermon asserts that Bocking read to Barton daily from the revelations of these saints, and taunted her if she failed to receive any new visions.[95] The accusation that Bocking deliberately tried to induce Barton to prophesy obviously gives fuel to the idea that she was merely the pawn of conservative churchmen. Yet there exist precedents for similar activities going on under rather less sinister circumstances: as we saw in Chapter Two, Margery Kempe also listened to a priest reading to her from the writings of St Bridget and other mystical texts and internalized the models of piety which she encountered there. It was in the interests of both Kempe's priest (who was also her amanuensis) and Barton's confessor Bocking that they should present their spiritual protégées as being in the same class as figures of religious authority. It is not then necessary for us to dismiss out of hand the evidence of the penitential sermon as simply defamatory. It is perfectly plausible that Barton was familiar with the prophecies of both St Bridget and St Catherine in some form. Well before the 1520s, the works of both saints were certainly reasonably accessible: in the first decades of the fifteenth century, the Brigittine convent of Syon had in its possession vernacular translations of the huge collection of St Bridget's revelations known as the *Liber Celestis* and St Catherine's long religious treatise, *Il Dialogo*; and Barton's Syon and Sheen connections may also have played no small part in her spiritual development.

Like Bridget of Sweden and Catherine of Siena, Barton was not afraid to champion the Church against bishops, the King and even the Pope. She

are to Wright's version. For More's letters concerning Elizabeth Barton see *Correspondence*, ed Rogers, 464–507.

[93] BL, MS Cleopatra Eiv, ff. 87r–90r (*L&P*, vi, no. 1466). It is printed in *Three Chapters*, ed. Wright, 14–18. All references are to Wright's version. For the attribution to Woolfe, see Neame, *Holy Maid*, 114. Another account of Barton's activities was provided by the government informer John Lawrence, Friar Observant at Greenwich: PRO, SP1/80, f. 138r (*L&P*, vi, no. 1468 (5)); for the attribution to Lawrence, see Neame, *Holy Maid*, 127 and n. 11.

[94] For a full analysis, see my essay, 'The Prophet at Home: Elizabeth Barton and the Influence of Bridget of Sweden and Catherine of Siena' in *Prophets Abroad: the Reception of Continental Holy Women in Late-Medieval England*, ed. R. Voaden (Cambridge, 1996), 161–76.

[95] 'Sermon', ed. Whatmore, 469.

obtained interviews with some of the most powerful people in the realm. Just as St Bridget had turned bishops and monks away from their corrupt practices, so Barton attempted to manipulate the English churchmen who were facilitating the royal divorce. Archbishop Warham, who had sent the original commission to examine Barton, subsequently interviewed her on a number of occasions. Through Warham, Barton obtained a meeting with Cardinal Wolsey,[96] and Wolsey gained Barton admission to the King himself.[97] According to one Greenwich friar, Barton enjoyed royal favour for a time: the King offered to make her an abbess, and Anne Boleyn asked Barton to remain at the Royal Court in attendance upon her.[98] Henry VIII's apparent acceptance of Barton, despite her troublesome revelations, may reflect his continuing sympathies with the old order. Wolsey's fall in 1529 resulted in the King placing a layman in charge of ecclesiastical policy, but the new Lord Chancellor, Thomas More, was nonetheless devoutly orthodox in his beliefs. Similarly, both Stokesley, appointed Bishop of London in 1530, and Lee, appointed Archbishop of York in 1531, were conservative humanists rather than radical reformers. It is plausible that the King hoped that if Barton accepted his patronage, she could be persuaded against continuing her opposition to the divorce. If this was the case, the King's plan clearly did not work.

Inspired by the two saints on whom she modelled herself, Barton wrote letters to Clement VII encouraging him to stand against the English king.[99] She communicated directly with his ambassadors;[100] they are said to have pledged the Pope's support, prostrating themselves in front of her, and kissing her feet.[101] Barton was outspoken in the presence of such worldly authorities. One account tells that during an interview with the King at Hanworth, Barton attempted to discourage him from pursuing the course he had taken, for the safety of his soul and the preservation of the realm.[102]

---

[96] The letter which Warham wrote to Wolsey requesting that he grant an interview to Barton has survived: PRO, SP 1/50, f. 163r (*L&P*, iv, part 2, no. 4806).

[97] Thomas More and Thomas Goldwell were amongst those who believed that Barton had seen the King as well as Wolsey: *Correspondence*, ed. Rogers, 481; and *Three Chapters*, ed. Wright, 20. From Eustace Chapuy's reports it appears that Barton had spoken with the King as late as 1532: *CSP Spain*, iv, part 2, no. 1153.

[98] PRO, SP 1/80, f. 138r (*L&P*, vi, no. 1468 (5)). Figure 2 shows an eighteenth-century engraving of Henry VIII and Anne Boleyn in the House of Lords, by Sutton Nicholls. Neame suggests that the two holy women may represent Barton before and after her entry into the convent: Neame, *Holy Maid*, 256.

[99] Barton's communications with the Pope are mentioned in a considerable number of sources: for example, *Works*, ed. Cox, ii, 273.

[100] 25 Henry VIII, c. 12, 449–50.

[101] Morison, *Apomaxis calvmniarum*, T4v; PRO, SP 1/143, f. 205r (*L&P*, xiv, part 1, no. 402).

[102] Richard Hall, *Vie du bienheureux martyr Jean Fisher, Cardinal, Évêque de Rochester (†1535)*, ed. Fr. van Ortroy (Brussels, 1893), 251.

Time with its Iron Teeth devours all,
And Time will come when ẙ last Trump shall call,
That erring Man shall know, & stand the Test
Of what Religions in this World were best.

Sutton Nicholls sculp:

Fig. 2. Henry VIII, Anne Boleyn and two representations of feminine piety (a laywoman and a nun). An eighteenth-century engraving by Sutton Nicholls. Originally reproduced in Alan Neame, *The Holy Maid of Kent* (London: Hodder and Stoughton, 1977), p. 256.

Barton issued Archbishop Warham and Cardinal Wolsey with threats of the divine punishment which would follow if they continued to support the King in his plan to remarry,[103] and she warned Pope Clement VII that God would plague him if he failed to rule in favour of Katherine of Aragon,[104] and that the stroke of God was already suspended over his head.[105] Barton's later visions of hell and purgatory may have been inspired directly by the descriptions in St Bridget's revelations of the sufferings of intransigent bishops and kings.[106] Barton claimed to have had foreknowledge of Wolsey's fall: it was the consequence of his disobedience of the commands which she had given him.[107] After his death in 1530 she was able to describe the fate of his soul: she declared that he had died fifteen years before his time, and that his judgement was being postponed by God.[108] Barton also received a revelation that Henry VIII would be damned and claimed that she had seen 'the particular place and spot destined to him in hell'.[109]

God's anger at Henry VIII during his attempted reconciliation with the French king in October 1532 was demonstrated to Barton in an openly seditious eucharistic vision.[110] She was miraculously transported from her convent to the Church of Our Lady in Calais where she remained invisibly present during the mass. As the King prepared to receive the bread of the sacrament an angel took it out of the hands of the priest and offered it to Barton instead. Such miracles in which the Eucharist is brought to the recipient by divine means are not unusual, especially amongst women mystics and saints.[111] Blessed Raymond of Capua describes one occasion when a particle of consecrated bread which had fallen from the chalice apparently flew straight to St Catherine of Siena at the other end of the church.[112] This miracle occurred after Catherine had been discouraged from receiving the sacrament by her companions who knew that her trances displeased some of Raymond's fellow friars. Thus clerical authority could be seen to be circumvented by divine intervention on behalf of the woman

---

103 See, for example, the 'Sermon', ed. Whatmore, 467; cf. *Works*, ed. Cox, ii, 273. For one famous prediction concerning Wolsey see: *Correspondence*, ed. Rogers, 482; and cf. *Three Chapters*, ed. Wright, 15.

104 *Three Chapters*, ed. Wright, 20.

105 *Works*, ed. Cox, ii, 273; cf. *Three Chapters*, ed. Wright, 16.

106 See the Middle English translation of *The Liber Celestis of St Bridget of Sweden*, ed. R. Ellis, EETS o.s. 291 (Oxford, 1987).

107 *Three Chapters*, ed. Wright, 15.

108 'Sermon', ed. Whatmore, 470.

109 *CSP Spain*, iv, part 2, no. 1149.

110 25 Henry VIII, c. 12, 448; cf. *Three Chapters*, ed. Wright, 15. Thomas More and Prior Goldwell knew of this vision: *Correspondence*, ed. Rogers, 483; and *Three Chapters*, ed. Wright, 20.

111 Bynum, *Holy Feast*, 77 and passim.

112 Raymond of Capua, *The Life of Saint Catherine of Siena*, trans. G. Lamb (London, 1960), 286–91.

dedicated to serving God.[113] Elizabeth Barton's eucharistic vision confirmed her prophecies against the King: for Henry VIII to be deprived of the host in this way was a sign that he was no longer a member of the community of the Church and may have been intended as a prediction of his excommunication; Barton's own reception of the host from the angel attested to her role as God's chosen messenger.

If the prophecies and visions of the second phase in Elizabeth Barton's prophetic career reveal that she followed the examples set by Bridget of Sweden and Catherine of Siena, they also drew extensively on another tradition: popular political prophecies. Again, this dimension of Barton's prophecies has previously been completely neglected. In *Political Protest and Prophecy under Henry VIII*, Sharon L. Jansen relegates her predictions to a footnote and dismisses them with the comment that they only '*may* have been influenced by the techniques of political prophecy'.[114] Yet, as Jansen herself admits, some of Barton's utterances are completely characteristic of this sort of discourse. For example, many popular predictions played on combinations of letters and numbers. One famous prophecy announced 'that A, B and C should sit all in one seat, and should work great marvels', where A, B and C stood for Anne Boleyn and Cranmer or alternatively Cromwell; another concerned 'K L M' (Katherine and Lady Mary).[115] Similarly, Barton is recorded to have spoken of the 'Letters "A F G" and of the numbers "9 9 9" ' (unfortunately the interpretations of these portents remain obscure).[116] Another type of popular prophecy took the form of warnings of devastation and division combined with predictions which used animal or plant symbolism. Cavendish records that Cardinal Wolsey knew of a saying that 'when this Cowe rideth the bull / than prest beware thy skull', and he identified the cow as the King and the bull as Anne Boleyn from their heraldic emblems.[117] Elizabeth Barton spoke figuratively of the proponents of the divorce as a root with three branches: she interpreted the root to be Wolsey, the first branch to be Henry VIII, the second to be the Duke of Norfolk and the third the Duke of Suffolk; and she declared that England should never be merry until the root were plucked up.[118] Again this prediction falls firmly into the popular political tradition: it is derived from

---

[113] For a discussion of a similar circumvention of authority in the *vita* of Ida of Lau, see Bynum, *Holy Feast*, 118.

[114] Jansen, *Political Protest*, 25–6 n. 7 [my emphasis].

[115] M.D. Dodds, 'Political Prophecies in the Reign of Henry VIII', *The Modern Languages Review* xi (1916), 278; Jansen, *Political Protest*, 14.

[116] *Three Chapters*, ed. Wright, 18.

[117] George Cavendish, *The Life and Death of Cardinal Wolsey*, ed. R.S. Sylvester, EETS o.s. 243 (London, 1959), 128.

[118] 25 Henry VIII, c. 12, 449.

one of the ancient prophecies of Merlin which are found in Geoffrey of Monmouth's *History of the Kings of Britain* and elsewhere.[119]

In identifying the influence of popular prophecy on Barton's predictions, the notion that they had no political force or momentum of their own becomes considerably weakened. Barton articulated a fear of Henry's policies which was shared by many of his subjects. The anticipated breach with Rome made the citizens of England insecure about the future stability of the realm, and prognostications concerning the state of the country abounded.[120] Barton was not alone in foretelling that wars and plagues would soon rack the country;[121] or in prophesying that the King would be overthrown,[122] that his death was imminent,[123] and that he would die as a villain.[124] Many people were discussing such prophecies, by means of which they could 'objectify their fears and hopes' in an age of change and disruption.[125] In the early 1530s rumours circulated that the King's marriage to Anne Boleyn would take place during his visit to France.[126] When they proved wrong, Barton announced that only her intervention had prevented the wedding from taking place.[127] The same year, Mrs Gold, one of Barton's adherents, insisted that the King had not married at the feast of Pentecost as some people were claiming, but only pretended to be married. She knew however that the wedding would take place.[128] At this sort of time of crisis it was hermits and mystics who were most often consulted in the belief that they could see into the future: one of those implicated with Barton, Friar Hugh Rich, decided to consult an Observant called Nesiwick who showed him marvellous matters involving pens and inkhorns and letters of prophecy and foretold the trouble that would follow Barton's arrest.[129] Mrs Gold had

---

[119] Cf. Geoffrey of Monmouth, *History of the Kings of England*, trans. S. Evans, rev. C.W. Dunn (London, 1963), 143. A detailed discussion of Galfridian prophecy is found in Taylor's work, originally published in 1911, in which he notes the continuity of English political prophecy between the twelfth and seventeenth centuries: R. Taylor, *The Political Prophecy in England* (New York, 1967), especially 83–4.

[120] Thomas, *Religion*, 398.

[121] *Works*, ed. Cox, ii, 274. PRO, SP 1/82, f. 85v (*L&P*, vii, no. 72 (1)). See also Barton's prophecies recorded in a badly mutilated document: PRO, SP 1/140, ff. 6r–8r (*L&P*, xiii, part 2, no. 961 (2)).

[122] *CSP Spain*, iv, part 2, nos. 1149 and 1153; and PRO, SP 1/138, f. 210r (*L&P*, xiii, part 2, no. 802).

[123] PRO, SP 1/80 f. 138r (*L&P*, vi, no. 1468 (5)).

[124] 25 Henry VIII, c. 12, 449.

[125] A. Fox, 'Prophecies and Politics in the Reign of Henry VIII' in *Reassessing the Henrician Age: Humanism, Politics and Reform 1500–1550*, A. Fox and J. Guy (Oxford, 1986), 78.

[126] For an example, see G. Elton, *Policy and Police: the Enforcement of the Reformation in the Age of Cromwell* (Cambridge, 1972), 54.

[127] PRO, SP 1/80, f. 138r (*L&P*, vi, no. 1468 (5)); cf. *Three Chapters*, ed. Wright, 17.

[128] PRO, SP 1/80, f. 138r (*L&P*, vi, no. 1468 (5)); cf. *Three Chapters*, ed. Wright, 17.

[129] *Three Chapters*, ed. Wright, 18.

asked Barton to tell her how things stood for Katherine of Aragon,[130] and her husband Thomas Gold, his brother Henry and the Abbess of Syon had all requested Barton to present their petitions to Our Lady of Court-at-Street.[131] Thomas More was aware that many people wished to speak with Barton about matters concerning the King, and he attempted to dissuade her from talking with lay people about such affairs.[132]

Jansen argues that by the 1530s popular prophecies were the weapons of 'ordinary men and women farthest from all sources of political decision and control'.[133] But it was not only the poor or uneducated who sought these answers and even the learned monks of Syon Abbey were said to have studied books of Merlin's prophecies.[134] Barton's main supporters were men of religion, but her prophecies were also communicated to various members of the nobility, including some courtiers.[135] While many churchmen, along with certain members of the court (such as the Countess of Salisbury), were concerned with promoting the interests of Katherine of Aragon and the Princess Mary, another major motivating factor behind their open support of Barton was the defence of Church privileges. Other courtiers, such as the Marquis of Exeter, heir apparent to the throne, also recognized that Anne Boleyn and her faction threatened their political influence over Henry VIII, and the Marchioness was reported to have had secret interviews with Barton in which the possibility of overthrowing the King may have been discussed.[136] A third group influenced by Barton was made up of London merchants, possibly disillusioned by the number of heretics in their midst.[137] The many women in Barton's circle included attendants at the Court, nuns and wives of merchants.[138] It is impossible to say whether these women, evidently from quite disparate backgrounds, formed a community in any sense, or even if they were known to one another, although it is entirely possible that many would have had connections with Syon Abbey as a centre of lay and religious feminine spirituality.

---

130 *Three Chapters*, ed. Wright, 17–18.
131 PRO, SP 1/73, ff. 27v–28r (*L&P*, v, no. 1698 (2)).
132 *Correspondence*, ed. Rogers, 466.
133 Jansen, *Political Protest*, 19.
134 Thomas, *Religion*, 400.
135 *L&P*, vi, no. 1468 (1).
136 For Barton's confession concerning her dealings with the Marchioness of Exeter, see PRO, SP 1/80, f. 142r–142v (*L&P*, vi, no. 1468 (7)). For the evidence given by the Marchioness's servants, see: PRO, SP 1/138, f. 210r (*L&P*, xiii, part 2, no. 802); PRO, SP 1/139, f. 16r (*L&P*, xiii, part 2, no. 827 (2)); PRO, SP1/139, f. 77r–77v (*L&P*, xiii, part 2, no. 831 (liv and lv)). One of these witnesses testified that Barton had said that the King would one day flee the realm. The only document which might suggest that Barton prophesied that Courtenay would take the throne is very badly mutilated: PRO, SP 1/140, ff. 5r–8v (*L&P*, xiii, part 2, no. 961 (2)).
137 *L&P*, vi, no. 1468 (1).
138 *L&P*, vi, no. 1468 (1).

In summary, during the critical years at the end of the 1520s and early 1530s, Elizabeth Barton entered the second phase in her career as a visionary: she became involved in the dangerous arena of Reformation politics, and gathered around herself a group of powerful adherents. Finding her inspiration in the examples of St Bridget and St Catherine and drawing on various strains of popular political prophecy, her revelations became increasingly concerned with the King's government. In 1525, when Barton began to prophesy, it was evident that Katherine of Aragon was unlikely to bear Henry VIII a male heir, but despite some debate over women's fitness to rule it still seemed probable that Princess Mary would become Queen regent.[139] As Eamon Duffy has shown, England was one of the most Catholic countries of late medieval Europe, and the process of the Reformation was far from inevitable.[140] In 1521 the King had gained the title 'Defensor fidei' by writing a pamphlet against Luther. By the beginning of the next decade, Henry had imprisoned Katherine, and his intention to divorce her and remarry was well-known. The split with Rome was imminent. Barton took the part of Katherine of Aragon and of orthodoxy. As well as predicting that if the King continued his divorce proceedings and married again, he would not be king a month later, Barton prophesied that the Princess Mary would not be deprived of her birthright.[141] She also spoke against the removal of the liberties of the Church,[142] and warned Henry against depriving the Pope of his rights, estates and revenues.[143] Henry's new ambivalence towards the orthodox Church became fully apparent in 1530 when he openly patronized the Protestants, but Barton continued to insist that it was Henry's duty to destroy both the heretics and their publications.[144] As the concluding section will illustrate, Barton's interference in political affairs threatened the stability of the realm to such an extent that the government was forced to take extreme measures in order to silence her.

[139] For a discussion of models for woman's rule in the sixteenth century, see C. Jordan, *Renaissance Feminism: Literary Texts and Political Models* (Ithaca N.Y., 1990), 104–33, especially 104–6 and 116–19.

[140] Duffy, *Stripping of the Altars*.

[141] 25 Henry VIII, c. 12, 450; cf. Hall, *Vie du Fisher*, 249. It appears that Barton had petitioned God to find out if war would break out over the succession issue: PRO, SP 1/82, f. 85v (*L&P*, vii, no. 72 (1)).

[142] *Works*, ed. Cox, ii, 273.

[143] *Three Chapters*, ed. Wright, 14.

[144] *Three Chapters*, ed. Wright, 14. Cf. *Works*, ed. Cox, ii, 273; and Morison, *Apomaxis calvmniarum*, T3v.

Silencing the Lamb

By the time of their arrest, Barton and some of those implicated alongside her had discussed the prophecies with many people of rank and office. Henry Gold, a priest who had formerly received the patronage of Archbishop Warham, was accused of acting as translator between Barton and the papal ambassadors.[145] He was also said to have travelled around the country telling Barton's prophecies to conservative sympathizers such as nuns and monks at Syon or the Marquis and Marchioness of Exeter, and it was reported that he had even taken messages from the nun to Katherine of Aragon,[146] although Katherine had repeatedly refused Barton's requests to speak with her.[147] In a semi-literate society, an address from the pulpit was a more effective means of mass communication than a published tract:[148] Barton's clerical supporters had made an agreement that at a time which the nun herself would appoint they would preach her prophecies to the people.[149] Barton told these monks and priests that they were elected by God for this purpose, and in preparation for their task she made them perform extreme bodily penance: some wore hair shirts, others iron chains, and some fasted until 'the sharpness of their bones had almost worn through their skin'.[150] These clerics who circulated Barton's prophecies, who helped her to gain audiences with those in political power, and who preached about her piety, formed a closely knit group, reminiscent of the *famiglia* which surrounded both St Bridget and St Catherine. Although there may be some truth in the accusation that Barton's political involvement was prompted by this circle of supporters, there is good reason to think that they genuinely believed in her experiences and prophecies. If Barton was encouraged to imitate Saints Catherine and Bridget, it should not come as a surprise that her adherents perceived her to be a leader rather than a follower.

But although the more contentious predictions were put about largely by word of mouth, Barton's adherents did not rely on purely oral means to disseminate them – knowledge of the revelations was also derived directly from Bocking's manuscript, which was circulated amongst Barton's devotees. Furthermore, the success of Thwaites's printed tract, *A marueilous woorke*, which was said to have reached a very wide audience, must have

---

145 25 Henry VIII, c. 12, 450.
146 For Gold's connections with Syon and with the Marquis of Exeter: *L&P*, vi, no. 1468 (1) and PRO, SP 1/139 f. 16r (*L&P*, xiii, part 2, no. 827). For Gold as messenger to Katherine of Aragon, see 25 Henry VIII, c. 12, 450; and PRO, SP 1/82, f. 86r (*L&P*, vii, no. 72 (1)).
147 *CSP Spain*, iv, part 2, no. 1149.
148 Elton, *Policy and Police*, 211.
149 'Sermon', ed. Whatmore, 468–9; and 25 Henry VIII, c. 12, 449.
150 'Sermon', ed. Whatmore, 469.

encouraged Barton and her followers to exploit the new technology of the press. In 1533, when they came under suspicion of making and spreading factious prophecies, Edward Bocking's room was searched and his papers confiscated.[151] The ensuing investigation revealed that a fair copy of Bocking's manuscript had been made in preparation for its printing.[152] The book was seized at the press, and the printer responsible admitted that he had produced seven hundred copies.[153] These printed texts must have been destroyed soon after as no mention was made of them at the penance at St Paul's Cross when Bocking's holograph was held up by the preacher for public derision.[154] Subsequently, the government tried to control the circulation of political prophecies: some eight years after Barton's death an act was passed against seditious prophecies printed, written, spoken or sung, without privilege of clergy.[155] It was repealed by Edward VI, only to be replaced three years later by another enacted against fond and fantastical prophecies. Although this latter statute was in turn repealed by his successor and not reimposed until the reign of Elizabeth, Mary also feared and tried to suppress prophetic protest.

The campaign to defame Barton started well before her execution. Although Barton denied her revelations and prophecies under interrogation,[156] the fidelity of many of her supporters initially continued. On Barton's behalf, Thomas Gold conveyed a message to them that she had only retracted at the command of God.[157] However when Barton was induced for a second time to recant her heresy and make a full confession of her treason, few of her former adherents dared to speak out again on her behalf. In a desperate attempt at self-preservation the religious houses which had fostered her as a visionary turned their backs on her. Prior to the passing of the Act of Attainder the Lord Chancellor made a speech, with Barton present, denouncing her before a special assembly made up of the King's councillors, judges, prelates and the nobility.[158] The public penance was imposed in order that her crimes should be made known to a wider audience. The Spanish ambassador described this as a comedy staged 'to blot out from people's minds the impression they have that the Nun is a saint and a prophet'.[159] The penitential sermon laid out in no uncertain terms the

---

[151] *L&P*, vi, no. 1194 (1).

[152] 25 Henry VIII, c. 12, 448.

[153] *L&P*, vi, no. 1194.

[154] 'Sermon', ed. Whatmore, 468.

[155] See H. Dobin, *Merlin's Disciples: Prophecy, Poetry, and Power in Renaissance England* (Stanford, 1990), 41–5. For the State's use of prophecy to support its own agenda, see 50–60.

[156] 'Sermon', ed. Whatmore, 474.

[157] 'Sermon', ed. Whatmore, 474, and 25 Henry VIII, c. 12, 450.

[158] *CSP Spain*, iv, part 2, no. 1153.

[159] *CSP Spain*, iv, part 2, no. 1154.

crimes which had been committed: it was delivered in London and in Canterbury, locations chosen because they were the centres of Barton's influence. The sermon formed the basis of the preamble of the Attainder, which was put to the press shortly after its enactment.[160] Originally it had been planned that the public penance should be re-enacted in every town in the country,[161] and although this proved impractical it was decreed that a proclamation to the effect of the Act should be made throughout the realm.[162] In England until the late seventeenth century the appropriate form of execution for women found guilty of treason was burning at the stake – the hanging of women was felt to offer an indecent spectacle.[163] Consequently, it is likely that Barton's death by public hanging was intended to be understood as a symbolic act – her body was shown to be vulnerable, broken and therefore impure. The date of her execution (20 April 1534) was significant: on the same day, the citizens of London were required to make the Oath of Succession.[164] Barton's corpse and the mutilated bodies of her supporters were visual statements of the government's determination to silence its detractors; they were explicit warnings to those who criticized Henry VIII's policies and reforms.[165]

The Act of Attainder called upon the public to surrender any books, scrolls or other writings about the revelations and miracles attributed to Barton and her adherents, on pain of imprisonment and imposition of a fine.[166] This specific requirement that every piece of literature written about Barton be confiscated by the authorities reiterated the message that all opposition to the King would be destroyed. The censorship of Barton's books was certainly successful: William Lambarde clearly had access to a copy of *A marueilous woorke* when he wrote *A perambulation of Kent* in 1570, but it seems that even then the tract was scarce because he complains that although the end of Barton's story is known to all and still remembered by many, the beginning is known by few and very likely to be completely forgotten.[167] The prohibitions also affected the pulpit: some months after

---

160 Elton, *Policy and Police*, 210–11 and n. 3. The Act was presented as a petition from the Houses of Parliament to the King – a form which would suggest public outrage at the offences described therein: S.E. Lehmberg, 'Parliamentary Attainder in the Reign of Henry VIII', *Historical Journal* xviii (1975), 682.

161 *CSP Spain*, iv, part 2, no. 1154.

162 25 Henry VIII, c. 12, 451.

163 C. Naish, *Death Comes to the Maiden: Sex and Execution 1431–1933* (London, 1991), 9.

164 See *The Lisle Letters*, ed. M. St C. Byrne (Chicago, 1981), ii, 130 (*L&P*, vii, no. 522); R. Rex, 'The Execution of the Holy Maid of Kent', *Historical Research* lxiv (1991), 216–20.

165 See M. Foucault, *Discipline and Punish: the Birth of the Prison*, trans. A. Sheridan (London, 1975), 3–69.

166 25 Henry VIII, c. 12, 451.

167 Lambarde, *Perambulation*, T2v.

Barton's execution John Rudd was imprisoned in the Tower for preaching that she had wrongly been accused of abusing the sacraments of confession and penance.[168]

The following decades saw the production of a notable amount of literature denouncing Barton, and Protestant texts like *A Confutation of Unwritten Verities*; Richard Morison's *Apomaxis calvmniarum*; or the sixteenth-century histories written by Hall, Foxe and Lambarde have all coloured more recent accounts of her life.[169] Morison, for example, depicted her ecstasies in implicitly pornographic terms, describing the audience converging on the spectacle of the woman prostrated on the floor, emphasizing her convulsing body, and focussing on her open mouth out of which (he claimed) poured heretical and abhorrent words – clearly a vicious image of female sexuality.[170] While visionaries like Margery Kempe (who describes herself writhing on the ground and roaring loudly) sometimes found themselves accused of diabolical possession, there seem to be no direct precedents for Morison's voyeuristic parody of the eroticism of mystical fervour. By depicting Barton's body as unsealed and permeable, Morison, in effect, denied her virginal innocence. In Hall's *Chronicle*, Barton's last words before her execution are quoted: in this almost certainly fictional confession, Barton did not accept full responsibility for her crimes but blamed her supporters, learned men who knew that she was not inspired by God but because the matters which she feigned were profitable to them, praised her and encouraged her to believe that the Holy Spirit was working within her.[171]

Such representations of Barton as ignorant, frail and vulnerable, self-deluded, susceptible to the sins of lust and pride, and completely reliant on her confessor and other churchmen, are not atypical of misogynistic attacks on pious women. It is all the more surprising therefore that they should continue to be accepted so uncritically in studies as recent as that by Warnicke, which cites Barton's admission that her prophecies were made up as evidence that she was 'an embarrassment to her Church'.[172] I have argued in this chapter that the notion that Barton was the creation of

---

168 PRO, SP 1/82, ff. 70r–71v (*L&P*, vii, no. 303).
169 Thomas Cranmer, *A Confutation of Unwritten Verities* in *The Remains of Thomas Cranmer*, ed. H. Jenkyns (Oxford, 1833), iv, 240–1; Morison, *Apomaxis calvmniarum*, T1r–V2v; Edward Hall, *Hall's Chronicle; containing the History of England*, ed. H. Ellis (London, 1809), 806–14; *The Acts and Monuments of John Foxe*, ed. J. Pratt (4th ed. London, 1877), v, 62–3; and Lambarde, *Perambulation*, T2v–T5r.
170 Morison, *Apomaxis calvmniarum*, T3v.
171 *Hall's Chronicle*, 814. This work was first published in 1548. There is no earlier record of the speech. Two other confessions are ascribed to Barton: London, PRO, SP 1/80, f. 142r–142v (*L&P*, vi, no. 1468 (7)); and PRO, SP 1/82, f. 87r (*L&P*, vii, no. 72 (2)). The former is a statement of her involvement with the Courtenay household. In the latter very brief confession, she takes full responsibility for her crimes.
172 Warnicke, *Women*, 68.

unscrupulous clerics is untenable. Elizabeth Barton's prophecies and visions reveal that in taking upon herself the role of political prophet she not only drew on traditions of popular political prophecy, but also followed the examples set by Bridget of Sweden and Catherine of Siena. However, by the time of her execution, her prophecies had been discredited, her reputation destroyed, and her followers dispersed, and under such circumstances it is not surprising that her influence was short-lived. While some women in Barton's immediate circle imitated her (her own sister is said to have collected the blood from Christ's side in a chalice and warned of the plagues which would come to the city of London;[173] and in response to Barton's prayers another female devotee was visited by an angel),[174] in the decades after her execution the closest parallels are once again found not in England but in central Europe, especially Spain and Italy. In these countries, in spite of the fact that they were sometimes persecuted by the Inquisition, *beatas* often held a great deal of control over religious and political leaders. Such holy women resemble Barton in that they too claimed the authority to give advice on matters relating to the public as well as the private arena; a number of them are known to have consciously emulated earlier female saints.[175]

Very few of these continental holy women were officially acknowledged to be saints. This must in part be due to what has been called the 'crisis of canonization' which the Catholic Church experienced in the sixty-five years between 1523 and 1588 – a period in which no Catholic saints at all were recognized, no doubt largely as a result of the criticisms levelled against the worship of saints by the Protestant reformers.[176] Peter Martyr Vermigli, for example, did not deny that 'Some women imbued with the gift of prophecy have taught the people in public, passing on to them those things which are revealed to them by God' on the grounds that 'divine things are not conferred in order to be hidden away, but so that they may promote the edification of the Church as a whole', but he advocated caution, 'it should not be deduced from this that that which God does in some particular case of privilege should be made by us a model of behaviour'.[177] Even when the Church did start making saints again, it gave the honour to only a very few

---

173 *Three Chapters*, ed. Wright, 18.

174 *Three Chapters*, ed. Wright, 17.

175 See, for example, María Vela y Cueto, discussed by M. Ortega Costa in 'Spanish Women in the Reformation' in *Women in Reformation and Counter-Reformation Europe: Public and Private Worlds*, ed. S. Marshall (Bloomington, 1989), 103–5. See also J. Bilinkoff, 'A Spanish Prophetess and her Patrons: the Case of María de Santo Domingo', *Sixteenth Century Journal* xxiii (1992), 21–34.

176 P. Burke, 'How to be a Counter-Reformation Saint' in *Religion and Society in Early Modern Europe 1500–1800*, ed. K. von Greyerz (London, 1984), 46.

177 Quoted by I. Maclean, *The Renaissance Notion of Woman: a Study in the Fortunes of Scholasticism and Medical Science in European Intellectual Life* (Cambridge, 1980), 21.

martyrs, despite the fact that so many Catholics died for their faith in the sixteenth century. As Merry Wiesner points out, the 'relative lack' of canonized women in the sixteenth century reflects the Church's bias towards roles such as that of the missionary, roles which largely excluded women.[178] The Counter-Reformation Church also canonized only a fraction of those individuals who claimed to experience ecstasies and revelations. Women visionaries in particular were subject to even closer scrutiny than had been the case at the end of the Middle Ages. Teresa of Avila (1515–1582), for example, seems to have been honoured as much for her reformation of the Carmelite order as for her mysticism. According to Wiesner, 'The version of Teresa which was presented for her canonization proceedings . . . was one which fitted her into the acceptable model of woman mystic and reformer, assuming a public role only when ordered to do so by her confessor or superior.'[179] The line which the visionary or prophet had to tread was an extremely fine one as the Inquisitions often accused such women of being too reliant on male confessors who encouraged them to fake their experiences and with whom they were sometimes suspected of having sexual relations.[180] Since these were exactly the sort of accusations levelled against Elizabeth Barton when she was publicly denounced, it is not perhaps surprising that there is no evidence that the Roman Church attempted to rescue her reputation. In Reformation England the patterns of female piety were rather different to those on the continent, as will be seen in the following chapters. Stories of fasting girls continued in the prodigy narratives of the sixteenth and early seventeenth centuries, but often only within a very generalized religious framework.[181] Although many Protestants, like the martyr Anne Askew (executed 1546), confident that they possessed the spirit of God, refused to be silenced by the laws of the land and defended their right to instruct others in the true faith, and, following the dissolution, some Catholics continued to see visions and experience union with God, most recusant women, such as Margaret Clitherow (executed 1586), seem to have confined their acts of rebellion to

---

[178] M.E. Wiesner, *Women and Gender in Early Modern Europe* (Cambridge, 1983), 198.

[179] Wiesner, *Women and Gender*, 199–200. Saint Teresa's mystical autobiography is translated as *The Life of Saint Teresa of Ávila by Herself*, trans. J.M. Cohen (Harmondsworth, 1957).

[180] W. Monter, 'Women and the Italian Inquisition' in *Women in the Middle Ages and the Renaissance: Literary and Historical Perspectives*, ed. M.B. Rose (Syracuse, 1986), 85.

[181] See, for example, George Hakewill's *An apologie or declaration of the power and providence of our God* (Oxford, 1635), OO4r-OO5r. Hakewill discusses some European examples from the previous hundred years, and concludes, 'truly me thinkes such wonderfull workes of God as these, should not passe by us without a marke set upon them, specially considering that the greatest and most notable part of the examples alleaged have beene of the Protestant Religion', *An apologie*, OO5r.

the household, converting family and friends, organizing devotions and harbouring priests.[182] To reiterate the point I made at the start, as a woman political prophet Barton is a unique figure: she is set apart not only from earlier English visionaries and from her contemporaries, but also from her successors by the active part which she played in the resistance to Henry VIII's reforms.

---

[182] For Askew, see Chapter Four below. For English recusant women, see M. Norman, 'Dame Gertrude More and the English Mystical Tradition', *Recusant History* xiii (1976), 196–211; Warnicke, *Women*, 164–85; M.B. Rowlands, 'Recusant Women 1560–1640' in *Women in English Society 1500–1800*, ed. M. Prior (London, 1985), 149–180; I. Grundy, 'Women's History? Writings by English Nuns' in *Women, Writing, History 1640–1740*, ed. I. Grundy and S. Wiseman (London, 1992), 126–38; Wiesner, *Women and Gender*, 195–203; Crawford, *Women and Religion*, 58–69; A. Hutchinson, 'Beyond the Margin: the Recusant Bridgettines' in *Studies in St Birgitta and the Brigittine Order*, ed. J. Hogg, Analecta Cartusiana 35: 19 (New York, 1993), ii, 267–84; and A. Hutchinson, 'Three (Recusant) Sisters' in *Vox Mystica: Essays on Medieval Mysticism*, ed. A.C. Bartlett (Cambridge, 1995), 147–158.

4

Serpents and Doves:
Anne Askew and Foxe's Godly Women

Behold, I send you forth as sheep in the midst of wolves: be ye therefore
wise as serpents, and harmless as doves.   (Matthew 10.16)

The Prophet and her Publisher

In 1546, in the last year of Henry VIII's reign, when the conservative faction
of the government had succeeded in regaining some of its control, the first
edition of *The first examinacyon of Anne Askewe, latelye martyred in
Smythfelde* was printed in Wesel (Germany) in a text which included an
introduction, conclusion and intertextual commentary written by the Protestant scholar, John Bale.[1] The false colophons, claiming that the tract had
been printed in Marburg in the land of Hessen, not only disguised the
publisher's whereabouts, but also indicated that he saw himself as a successor to William Tyndale. The following year the second part of this work,
The lattre examinacyon of Anne Askewe, was published in the same city.[2]
Bale's account of Askew's execution is a fitting conclusion to his

---

1   *The first examinacyon of Anne Askewe, latelye martyred in Smythfelde* (Wesel, 1546).
All references to *The first examinacyon* are to this edition unless otherwise stated.
Despite his conviction that the word of God should be taught in English, Bale originally
intended to publish a Latin version of the text for international circulation: *The first
examinacyon,* ♣5v. For a recent edition of both *The first examinacyon* and *The lattre
examinacyon* see: *The Examinations of Anne Askew*, ed. E.V. Beilin (Oxford, 1996).
Another account of part of Askew's examinations and execution was written by the
Protestant John Louthe, who was an eyewitness to some of the events: *Narratives of the
Days of the Reformation*, ed. J.G. Nichols, CS o.s. 77 (London, 1859), 39–47. The
fullest studies of Askew's text are E.V. Beilin, 'Anne Askew's Self-Portrait in the
Examinations' in *Silent but for the Word: Tudor Women as Patrons, Translators, and
Writers of Religious Works*, ed. M.P. Hannay (Kent OH, 1985), 77–91; E.V. Beilin,
Redeeming Eve: Women Writers of the English Renaissance (Princeton, 1987), 29–47;
E.V. Beilin, 'Anne Askew's Dialogue with Authority' in *Contending Kingdoms: His-
torical, Psychological, and Feminist Approaches to the Literature of Sixteenth-Century
England and France*, ed. M.R. Logan and P.L. Rudnytsky (Detroit, 1991), 313–22.
2   *The lattre examinacyon of Anne Askewe* (Wesel, 1547). All references to *The lattre
examinacyon* are to this edition unless otherwise stated.

commentary on *The lattre examinacyon*, with its fusion of historical event, hagiographic motif and apocalyptic imagery:

> Now to conclude with Anne Askewe as the argument of thys boke requyreth. In the yeare of our lord a M.D.XLVJ And in the monthe of Julye, at the prodygyouse procurement of Antichristes furyouse remnaunt, Gardyner, Bonner, and soch lyke, she suffered most cruell deathe in Smythfelde with her iij. faythfull companyons, Johan Lassels a gentylman whych had bene her instructour, Johan Adlam a tayler, and a prest so constaunt in the veryte agaynst the seyd Antichristes superstycyons as they, whose name at thys tyme I had not. Credyblye am I infourmed by dyuerse duche merchauntes whych were there present, that in the tyme of their sufferynges, the skye abhorrynge so wycked an acte, sodenlye altered coloure, and the cloudes from aboue gaue a thonder clappe. . . .[3]

Askew died for beliefs diametrically opposite to those of Elizabeth Barton, and she was perhaps as much a victim of what Annabel Patterson terms Henry VIII's 'persecuting temper' as she was a religious and political scapegoat.[4] Askew was a gentlewoman from Lincolnshire, married by her family to the son of a wealthy neighbour in the place of one of her sisters who had died before her wedding. She had first been arrested in June 1545, along with two others, but was acquitted when no witnesses appeared against her. In March 1546 she was rearrested under the Six Articles Act after a woman had reported her to the authorities for denying the real presence of Christ in the Sacrament of the Altar. Askew was examined by the heresy commissioners at Saddler's Hall and questioned by Sir Martin Bowes, the Lord Mayor, and Edmund Bonner, Bishop of London. She signed a confession of faith and was released, but two months later she was summonsed again along with her husband Thomas Kyme, whose violent opposition to her religious beliefs had originally forced her to leave her home and children. In the hope of obtaining a divorce, Askew had travelled to London (where she had family connections with the royal court, including a sister married to the steward of the Duke and Duchess of Suffolk), and was by now refusing to acknowledge the legitimacy of her relationship with Kyme. Her interrogators during her second examination before the King's

---

[3] *The lattre examinacyon*, I2v–I3r. Another witness of Askew's execution testified that he had heard 'a pleasant crackyng from heaven': *Narratives*, ed. Nichols, 44.

[4] A. Patterson, 'Sir John Oldcastle as Symbol of Reformation Historiography' in *Religion, Literature, and Politics in Post-Reformation England, 1540–1688*, ed. D.B. Hamilton and R. Strier (Cambridge, 1996), 12. For a romanticized history of Askew's life, see D. Wilson, *A Tudor Tapestry: Men, Women and Society in Reformation England* (London, 1972). According to an account written by Askew's nephew, she was forced into hiding but finally given up to the authorities by a close relative: Edward Ayscu, *A historie contayning the warres, treaties, marriages, between England and Scotland* (1607), V8r–V8v. For an alternative dating of Askew's examinations see *The Examinations*, ed. Beilin, xv–xxii.

Council included Stephen Gardiner, Bishop of Winchester; the Lord Chancellor, Thomas Wriothesly; and Sir William Paget, the King's principal secretary. On 28 June she was condemned as a relapsed heretic. In an attempt to force Askew to implicate her court associates, Wriothesly and Sir Richard Rich had her taken to the Tower, where they took the exceptional step of having her tortured and even turned the rack themselves. She was burned on 16 July. One of those executed alongside Askew, John Lascels, formerly in the service of Cromwell, was the leader of a religious group influenced by German theology and acted as her spiritual advisor; it was also said that he had disseminated prophecies against the King.[5]

The narrative of Askew's execution is interrupted by Bale's intrusive voice as he goes on to draw the readers' attention to the Scriptural significance of the crash in the sky which he understands to represent the voice of God. Bale explains that both prophecy and the Holy Spirit have been received in thunder. While the executioners believed the blast to vindicate their deeds, he reassures his readers that it offered Askew and her companions consolation in their suffering: when St Stephen died, only he and possibly a few disciples, but not the multitude who stoned him, saw the heavens open.[6] Bale comments that many people who witnessed the burning were converted as a result of it, and he observes that similar phenomena occurred at the Passion, causing the watching centurion and those with him to confess Christ to be the Son of God.[7] Many of his readers may also have been familiar with the legend that there was an earthquake at Wyclif's condemnation. The storm which marked the deaths of Askew, Lascels and the others is, then, a divine sign that these are true Christian martyrs. Bale interprets Askew's rendering of her interrogations as a Protestant saint's life, and defines his own authorial/editorial role as that of martyrologist, claiming that 'no lesse necessarye is that offyce now, though fewe men attempt it, nor no lesse profytable to the christen common wealth' than it was in the first centuries of Christianity.[8]

John Bale (1495–1563) was a former Carmelite friar who had embraced Protestantism in the 1530s; he went on to become Bishop of Ossory in the reign of Edward VI.[9] In the years immediately following his conversion,

---

5 *Narratives*, ed. Nichols, 302.

6 *The lattre examinacyon*, I5v; Acts 7.55–6.

7 *The lattre examinacyon*, I3r.

8 *The lattre examinacyon*, A2v. Bale is celebrated as the first Protestant martyrologist by: L.P. Fairfield, 'John Bale and the Development of Protestant Hagiography in England', *Journal of Ecclesiastical History* xxiv (1973), 145–60; and L.P. Fairfield, *John Bale: Mythmaker for the English Reformation* (West Lafayette, 1976). Cf. R.K. Kendall, *The Drama of Dissent: the Radical Poetics of Nonconformity, 1380–1590* (Chapel Hill N.C., 1986), 90–131.

9 For an overview of work on Bale, see W.T. Davies, 'A Bibliography of John Bale', *Proceedings and Papers of the Oxford Bibliographical Society* v (1936–1939), 201–79;

Bale turned from conventional hagiography and the histories of the Carmelite order which had previously occupied him to the writing of Protestant propagandist plays.[10] His *Kynge Johan* and *A comedy concernynge thre lawes* received the patronage of Thomas Cromwell, but following Cromwell's fall in 1540, Bale was forced to flee, first to Antwerp and then to Wesel. During his exile, Bale began publishing religious pamphlets, including *A brefe chronycle*, a reassessment of the Lollard knight John Oldcastle (first published 1544); a commentary on the Revelation of Saint John, *The image of bothe churches* (first published 1545–1546); and *The actes of Englysh votaryes*, a history of the English Church and monastic abuses (1546). The manuscripts of Askew's *Examinations* were smuggled out of the country and Bale organized the printing of the first part so that it came out within a year of her execution. After Edward VI's accession in 1547 he returned to England, only to go back into exile during Mary's reign, publishing his autobiographical account of his sufferings in 1553.[11] Recent studies have emphasized the nationalist impetus behind Bale's post-conversion works, which represent England as central to the European Reformation and seek to establish an indigenous martyrology.[12] Margaret Aston notes that Bale's entire historiographic project 'meant taking over enemy territory, and using enemy ammunition'.[13]

In his Protestant writings, Bale condemns hagiography and the veneration of saints as expressions of the idolatry of the corrupt Roman Church. On a number of occasions he opposes the example of Askew and her companions to saints like Thomas Becket, as well as to their contemporaries Thomas More and Elizabeth Barton, whose deaths, he claims, had been lauded by many conservatives as martyrdoms.[14] In *The image of bothe churches*, Bale follows Tyndale in condemning those false prophets and preachers who 'rayseth ye maydes of Ippeswhyce and of Kent to worke wonders and maruels',[15] and in his commentary on *The first examinacyon*,

P. Happé, 'Recent Studies in John Bale', *English Literary Renaissance*, xvii (1987), 103–13.

[10] For a modern edition of Bale's drama, see *The Complete Plays of John Bale*, ed. P. Happé, Tudor Interludes 4 and 5 (Cambridge, 1985–1986), i–ii.

[11] *The Vocacyon of Johan Bale*, ed. P. Happé and J.N. King, Medieval and Renaissance Texts and Studies 70 (Binghamton N.Y., 1990).

[12] See especially A. Hadfield, *Literature, Politics and National Identity: Reformation to Renaissance* (Cambridge, 1994), 51–80.

[13] M. Aston, *Lollards and Reformers: Images and Literacy in Late Medieval Religion* (London, 1984), 236.

[14] For the suggestion that the conservative faction in Henry VIII's court hoped that Askew's arrest would offer them an opportunity to reverse the gains made by the Protestants after Barton's execution, see J.K. McConica, *English Humanists and Reformation Politics under Henry VIII and Edward IV* (Oxford, 1965), 222.

[15] J. Bale, *The image of bothe churches after the moste wonderfull and heuenly reuelacion of Sainct John the euangelist* (Antwerp, 1548), ii, I5r. Compare the portrayal of the old

he stresses the contrast between the deaths of Askew and Lascels and 'the holye mayde of kent with Doctor Bockynge, though they wrought great wonders by their lyfe, yet apered non at their deathes',[16] going on to compare Askew and her 'condempned cumpanye' to 'these clowted, canonysed, solempnysed, sensed, mattensed, and massed martyrs' and posing the question, 'tell me by the Gospels tryall, whych of them seme most Christenlyke martyrs'.[17] Already, in both Askew's own accounts (which she claims she was inspired to write down by 'the secret mocyon of God')[18] and in Bale's commentaries, it is possible to see a change of emphasis in the understanding of prophecy, which while not entirely new, is nonetheless significant.

> Reformers had a particular affection for the prophets. They felt both inspired and justified by them in their own work of challenging established political and religious authorities, of speaking out in admonishment of emperors, kings, popes, and bishops. The myriad examples in Scripture and tradition of prophets going unappreciated in their own land offered, too, consolation when suffering persecution. Rejecting or ignoring Roman Catholic use of the prophets as examples of withdrawal into contemplation in order to receive a vision of the divine, Protestants followed them instead as models of hard-core evangelicals, going out and assailing those responsible for the depravity and corruption of the world.[19]

Thus, for Bale, the real prophets and saints are not the sensational miracle workers of the later Middle Ages, but those Christians who teach the word of God and are willing to give up their lives for the true faith. By the 1570s the meaning of prophecy had further evolved: Elizabeth I took action against the weekly Bible study meetings in the major towns, known as prophesyings, which she feared encouraged religious dissent.[20]

Bale's representation of Anne Askew has also to be understood in the

---

witch Idolatry, who demonstrates prophetic and supernatural abilities in Bale's *A comedy concernynge thre lawes*. On the rise of witchcraft trials and practices and their relationship with the religious crises in early modern England, see K.V. Thomas, *Religion and the Decline of Magic: Studies in Popular Beliefs in Sixteenth and Seventeenth Century England* (London, 1971), 435–583. On witchcraft generally, see also: B. P. Levack, *The Witch-hunt in Early Modern Europe* (2nd ed. London, 1995); C. Larner, *Witchcraft and Religion: the Politics of Popular Belief*, ed. A. Macfarlane (Oxford, 1984); D. Willis, *Malevolent Nurture: Witch-hunting and Maternal Power in Early Modern England* (Ithaca N.Y., 1995).

16 *The first examinacyon*, ♣5r.

17 *The lattre examinacyon*, A8r.

18 *The first examinacyon*, A1v.

19 J. Wojcik and R.J. Frontain, eds., *Poetic Prophecy in Western Literature* (London, 1984), 23.

20 H. Dobin, *Merlin's Disciples: Prophecy, Poetry, and Power in Renaissance England* (Stanford, 1990), 28.

context of his contribution to the English apocalyptic tradition.[21] Joachimism enjoyed a revival amongst Protestants and Catholics alike, and despite state legislation, popular political prophecies, such as those attributed to Merlin or the astrological prognostications of Nostradamus, were popular during the sixteenth century, especially in the late Tudor period, and continued to flourish right up to the mid-seventeenth century.[22] Early reformers and Protestants had, however, expressed their doubts about apocalyptic interpretations of Scriptural prophecy. John Wyclif had read the prophecies of the Book of Revelation allegorically rather than as a history of the world, and Erasmus even argued against its authenticity, reservations which were initially shared by Luther, and also by Zwingli and Calvin. William Tyndale and Robert Barnes also held back from interpreting Biblical prophecies in historical terms. Following the Augsburg Confession of 1530, radical millenarianism was widely condemned. Nonetheless Luther subsequently revised his opinion of Revelation, realizing it could be understood to validate the history of the Reformation. The text known as *Carion's Chronicle* is clearly influenced by apocalyptic thought: it draws on the Book of Daniel, the apocryphal Prophecy of Elias, as well as on astronomy and astrology and alludes to a number of non-scriptural prophecies; it was first published by Philip Melanchthon and several others in 1532, and printed in London in 1550.[23] Heinrich Bullinger's *A hundred sermons upon the Apocalyps of Jesu Christ* was published in English in 1561. John Foxe, John Knox and John Napier all wrote in this tradition, but the first major apocalyptic work by an English Protestant was Bale's *The image of bothe churches*, written between 1541 and 1547, and a key text in the English Reformation.[24] This commentary on the Apocalypse makes use

---

[21] See especially K.R. Firth, *The Apocalyptic Tradition in Reformation Britain 1530–1645* (Oxford, 1979); R. Bauckham, *Tudor Apocalypse. Sixteenth Century Apocalypticism, Millennarianism and the English Reformation: from John Bale to John Foxe and Thomas Brightman*, Courtenay Library of Reformation Classics 8 (Oxford, 1978); P. Christianson, *Reformers and Babylon: English Apocalyptic Visions from the Reformation to the Eve of the Civil War* (Toronto, 1978).

[22] See M. Reeves, *The Influence of Prophecy in the Later Middle Ages* (Oxford, 1969); Thomas, *Religion*, 113–50, 283–5, 289–432; B. Capp, *Astrology and the Popular Press: English Almanacs 1500–1800* (London, 1979); S.J. Tester, *A History of Western Astrology* (Woodbridge, 1987), 204–43; Dobin, *Merlin's Disciples*; S.L. Jansen, *Political Protest and Prophecy under Henry VIII* (Woodbridge, 1991).

[23] The English version mentions Askew's execution: J. Carion, *The thre bokes of cronicles* (1550), MM6r.

[24] On Bale's apocalyptic writings, see especially Baukham, *Tudor Apocalypse*, 70–3 and passim; Firth, *Apocalyptic Tradition*, 32–68; and Fairfield, *John Bale*. For Bale's influence on Foxe and others, see also J.F. Mozeley, *John Foxe and his Book* (London, 1940), 29–30 and 51; W. Haller, *Foxe's Book of Martyrs and the Elect Nation* (London, 1963), 58–72 and passim; V.N. Olsen, *John Foxe and the Elizabethan Church* (Berkeley, 1973), 39–45 and 74–5.

of the Book of Daniel, and shows the influence of Joachim of Fiore, as well as Wyclif, Luther and others.

In *The image of bothe churches*, Bale offers a historicist reading of the Biblical book which challenges orthodox medieval interpretations and explains the rise of Protestantism and its opposition to the Roman Church. According to Bale's Joachimist scheme, the history of the Church falls into seven periods from Christ's death to the end of the world – the first six stages mark a spiritual decline in the world. The Christian religion existed on earth in its purest form immediately after Christ's Ascension and Pentecost. Gradually, however, decay set in as it moved farther away from its early perfection. As the Roman Church expanded and evolved it became more and more corrupt. In the course of time, the True Church, in other words, those Christians whose beliefs and practices still reflected the purity of the Primitive Church, became peripheral to the Roman Church, and they often actively opposed it. As the Roman Church became increasingly rotten, so the opposition of the True Church strengthened. Joachim and Savoranola, for example, are described by Bale as 'godlye men' who, through prophecy and Scripture, had 'perceyued afore hande with Paule, the falle of fayth, the increase of errours, and that dyuerse shuld decline from ye truth'.[25] Bale does not predict the imminent arrival of the millennial kingdom, but he views the current time, the Reformation, as the sixth age when God chooses to reveal his secrets to His followers:

> Christe willed all faithfull belevers to searche the scriptures, to understande the prophecies, & to perceyue the mysteries of them. And for the perfourmaunce of his will therin, he hath sent in this age this peculiar aungell, besyde the common preachers, betokeninge these synguler learned men, whom nowe he hath endued with most highe knowlege.[26]

This age is a period of almost universal corruption as the established church has become entirely motivated by evil and, having abandoned altogether its spiritual role, is waging open warfare on the members of the True Church who have risen up, empowered by God, in opposition to it.

Even though the established English Church has broken with the Church in Rome, Bale believes that most of its leaders still harbour secret loyalties to the Pope, and thus it also is inherently corrupt (a point stressed in the *Examinations*); thus Bale often does not distinguish between the Roman Church and the established English Church in his satirical attacks. According to Bale's scheme, the Protestant Church represents the True Church militant. It is because Bale believes that this was directly descended from the Primitive Church that he seeks precedents from the early legends of the

---

[25] Bale, *The image of bothe churches*, i, P5v.
[26] Bale, *The image of bothe churches*, i, T5r.

saints for his portrayals of latter-day martyrs like Askew, whom he sees as the fulfillment of Biblical authority.

Bale understood apostleship to be the highest form of authorship, and, in *The image of bothe churches*, he likens himself in his state of enlightened exile to St John of Patmos. As Andrew Hadfield explains, Bale 'placed himself as one of the elect readers of the truth of the Bible in describing his commentary as a re-enactment of the Biblical moment of revealed prophecy'.[27] Bale's approach to reading Scripture, his conviction that his own interpretations are themselves both transparent and final, is typical of his commentary technique. The following sections will consider Bale's role as editor, before looking in some detail at the sometimes contradictory representation of Askew as prophet and martyr in the text of the *Examinations* and Bale's commentary, and finally comparing both the text and the commentary to Foxe's representation of sixteenth-century godly women in his *Acts and Monuments*.

John Bale as Editor

In 1548, the year after he had returned from his first period of exile and a year after the publication of *The lattre examinacyon*, Bale produced an edition of Elizabeth Tudor's prose translation of Marguerite d'Angoulême's 'Le miroir de l'âme pécheresse', a work which had originally been given to Catherine Parr by the 11-year-old princess as a New Year present on 31 December 1544.[28] Bale's version, entitled *A godly medytacyon of the christen sowle*, includes a lengthy dedicatory epistle and conclusion in which he interprets the text, much as he does in the commentary on the *Examinations*.[29] This edition is invaluable for what it reveals both about Bale's ideas about women, and about his editing processes.[30]

Marguerite d'Angoulême's 'Le miroir de l'âme pécheresse' was condemned by the Sorbonne in 1532, no doubt because of its Lutheran leanings.[31] The poem denigrates good works as a means of obtaining salvation,

---

[27] Hadfield, *Literature, Politics and National Identity*, 66.

[28] Oxford, Bodleian Library, MS Cherry 36. For photographic facsimiles, see *The Mirror of the Sinful Soul: a Prose Translation*, intro. P.W. Ames (London, 1897), 14; and *Elizabeth's Glass with 'The Glass of the Sinful Soul' (1544) by Elizabeth I and 'Epistle Dedicatory' & 'Conclusion' (1548) by John Bale*, intro. M. Shell (Lincoln NB, 1993).

[29] *A godly medytacyon of the christen sowle by the ryght vertuouse lady Elyzabeth* (Wesel, 1548).

[30] Bale's editing processes have previously been studied in relation to his version of the trial of Sir John Oldcastle, based largely on a pamphlet possibly written by Tyndale and published in 1530: Fairfield, 'John Bale', especially 151–4; Firth, *Apocalyptic Tradition*, 48–9; Patterson, 'Oldcastle'.

[31] For a full account of the original poem, Elizabeth's translation, and Bale's edition, see

emphasizing justification by faith. The speaking voice embraces death as a release for the soul which loves God from the prison of this life into an infinitely sweeter eternity. Elizabeth Tudor's translation describes the soul, traditionally feminine, achieving union with the Divine as daughter, sister and wife of the Lord. If the Virgin is Christ's corporeal mother, the loving soul is His spiritual mother, 'therfore withoute any feare will i take vpon me the name of a mother. Mother of God'.[32]

> She [the soul] poore, ignoraunte, and layme, doth fynde herselfe with the, riche, wise, and strong bycause thou hast written in her harte the rolle, of thy spirite, the holy word geuenge her true fayth to receyue it, wiche thinge made her to conccyue thy sonne: beleuinge hym to be god, man, sauyoure, and also the true remitter of all sinnes.[33]

For the Protestant mystic, the feminine soul is the vessel which has received the Spirit, the Word of God, or the gift of faith.

Bale's edition of this poem can be understood as a product of the royalist optimism surrounding the accession of Edward VI, which was celebrated by Protestants who anticipated a period of reforms. A.L. Prescott suggests that in publishing Elizabeth's translation, Bale is putting forward a case for Catherine Parr's continued role in the government following Henry VIII's death.[34] At any rate, Bale argues that a Christian commonwealth would benefit from adopting humanist principles of education, encourages Elizabeth in her scholarship, and prays that she may become 'a noryshynge mother to [God's] dere congregacyon'.[35] Bale describes the reaction of certain learned men to Elizabeth's poem, who rejoiced on beholding 'so moch vertu, faythe, scyence, & experyence of languages & letters, specyally in noble youth & femynyte'.[36] He attributes to Elizabeth not only the achievement of translating the poem (the style of which he nonetheless disparages as 'the worke of a woman'),[37] but also the pious sentence contained therein. The princess belongs to a tradition of 'godly mynded' Christian women in England which has existed since the conversion of the

---

A.L. Prescott, 'The Pearl of Valois and Elizabeth I: Marguerite de Navarre's *Miroir* and Tudor England' in *Silent*, ed. Hannay, 61–76. For an analysis of Bale's revisions of Elizabeth's text, based largely on linguistic and stylistic evidence, see S. Nevanlinna, 'The First Translation of a Young Princess: Holograph Manuscript Versus Printed Text' in *Proceedings from the Third Nordic Conference for English Studies, Hässelby, Sept. 25–27, 1986*, ed. I. Lindblad and M. Ljung, Stockholm Studies in English 73 (Stockholm, 1987), i, 243–56.

[32] MS Cherry 36, f. 17v.
[33] MS Cherry 36, f. 13v.
[34] Prescott, 'Pearl', 73.
[35] *A godly medytacyon*, B1v.
[36] *A godly medytacyon*, A7r–A7v.
[37] *A godly medytacyon*, E7v.

Britons. These women, who are characterized by their indomitable faith, great courage, wisdom and learning, have consistently opposed the Roman Church and its superstitions and idolatrous beliefs. Taking his examples from both legend and history, he seeks to explain the liberalizing tendencies of early Protestant thought which not only allowed but actually encouraged the education of women, particularly in knowledge of the Bible and religious matters generally. Such women, who have not always been born noble, are truly noble because they have striven to serve Christ. Bale gives Anne Askew as his most recent example, who 'as Christes myghty membre, hath strongly troden downe the head of the serpent, and gone hence with most noble vyctory ouer the pestyferouse seede of that vyperouse worme of Rome'.[38] Women, Bale believes, can be privileged recipients of God's grace and can fully possess the fruits of the Spirit.

It is unlikely that Bale, in producing his edition of Elizabeth Tudor's poem, was working from the autograph (and sole surviving) manuscript. Although Elizabeth asks Catherine Parr in her dedication not to show her translation to anyone lest they see its faults, other copies must have been in circulation in the royal court, and Bale's text may have been supplied to him by a member of Parr's own circle.[39] His editorial voice is intrusive and directive and he shows little respect for the authority of his source. He changes the original title which Elizabeth had given her poem from 'The glasse of the synnefull soule', and makes various alterations to the text itself: in addition to correcting the spelling, word order, grammar and punctuation and paragraph divisions, he substitutes synonyms one for another, and adds extra scriptural references to the margins.[40] The most substantive revisions are motivated by questions of religious doctrine: thus Bale stresses the Lutheranism of the text when he expands 'so that thou do conuerte my worke (wich is nothinge) in some good worke', into 'so that thu do conuerte my worke, whych is nothynge, into some good worke of thyne in me, whych is specyally faythe'.[41]

Bale does not reproduce in his edition the first item of the manuscript of the translation, Elizabeth's dedicatory letter to Catherine Parr, but replaces

[38] *A godly medytacyon*, F6v.

[39] For the suggestion that Catherine Parr was responsible for sending Bale the copy on which he based his edition, see R. Hughey, 'A Note on Queen Elizabeth's "Godly Meditation"', *The Library* 4th series xv (1934–1935), 238. I accept Nevanlinna's argument that Bale was working from a copy of Elizabeth's translation which the Princess had herself corrected, but not her contention that it was the Princess who gave Bale permission to edit and publish the work: Nevanlinna, 'First Translation', 243–56.

[40] Prescott notes that at some stage someone has also checked Elizabeth's translation next to a copy of 'Le Miroir' and made cursory corrections which Bale has incorporated into his edition: Prescott, 'Pearl', 72. For the suggestion that Catherine Parr was responsible for the verbal changes and corrections in Bale's edition, see Hughey, 'Note', 237–8.

[41] MS Cherry 36, f. 51v; *A godly medytacyon*, D8r.

A Godly Medytacy
on of the christen sowle, concer-
ninge a loue towardes God and
hys Christe, compyled in frenche by lady
Margarete quene of Nauerre, and apte-
ly tranflated into Englysh by the
ryght vertuouse lady Elyzabeth
doughter to our late fouerayne
Kynge Henri the.viij.

Inclita filia, fereniffimi olim Anglorum
Regis Henrici octaui Elizabeta, tam Græ
ce quam latine fœliciter in Chrifto
erudita.

Fig. 3. The Princess Elizabeth in apostolic pose. From John Bale's edition of her translation, *A godly medytacyon of the christen sowle* (1548). Oxford, Bodleian Library, Mal. 502 (2). Illustrated title page from part 2.

it with his own dedication, which he addresses to the Princess.[42] At the end of the text, someone, presumably Bale, has introduced a series of new items: verses from Ecclesiastes, which contrast the curse of a wicked woman to the blessing of a virtuous one, and which Bale asserts were 'added [by] my lady Helisabeth vnto the begynnynge and ende of her boke';[43] within the conclusion, verses of Scripture translated into Latin, Greek, French and Italian, which Bale attributes to the Princess, saying that she sent them to him;[44] and a metrical paraphrase of Psalm 13/14, attacking the corrupt evildoers who deny God and oppose the righteous, and 'touched afore of my lady Elizabeth' but actually of his own composition.[45] The woodcut which illustrates the beginning and end of Bale's edition [fig. 3] shows Elizabeth in apostolic pose kneeling before the figure of Christ. It is clear from Bale's dedicatory epistle and conclusion that he read Elizabeth's translation as a defence of Protestant belief and an attack on false Roman doctrine, and that he saw the Princess herself in much the same light as Anne Askew: as an exemplary Christian woman. The alterations which he made to his source reinforced his understanding of his material and his author.

In the case of his edition of the *Examinations*, Bale maintains that his editions are based on Askew's autograph manuscripts, which were 'sent abroade by her owne hande writynge'.[46] Bale is keen to stress the authenticity of the text. In his later discussion of the *Examinations* in his catalogue of English literature known as the *Summarium* (1548), he reiterates that 'she wrote this in her own hand and I illustrated it with preface and notes'.[47] One source of prohibited texts was German merchants travelling from England,[48] but Askew's text, like Elizabeth's poem, may have been obtained for him in the first place by a member of the royal court. It would seem that Askew's text was written at the request of Protestant sympathizers: the first part of *The lattre examinacyon* is addressed to 'a secrete frynde'.[49] Her

---

[42] The final item in MS Cherry 36, a prayer attributed to Elizabeth, is also not included in Bale's version, but it was certainly added long after Bale had published his edition: *Mirror*, intro. Ames, 9–10; F. Madan, *A Summary Catalogue of Western Manuscripts in the Bodleian Library at Oxford* (Oxford, 1895), iii, part 1, 79.

[43] *A godly medytacyon*, E6v.

[44] *A godly medytacyon*, F1r.

[45] *A godly medytacyon*, F7v. The metrical paraphrase of Psalm 13/14 appears wrongly numbered as Psalm 23 in Bale's *An expostulation or complaynte agaynste the blasphemyes of afranticke papyst of Hamshyre* (London, 1552); cf. D.S. Kastan, 'An Early English Metrical Psalm: Elizabeth's or John Bale's?' *Notes and Queries* n.s. xxi (1974), 404–5; and R. Zim, *English Metrical Psalms: Poetry and Prayer 1535–1601* (Cambridge, 1987), 220–1.

[46] *The first examinacyon*, ♣5r; cf. *The first examinacyon*, F1v.

[47] Quoted in translation by J.N. King, *English Reformation Literature: the Tudor Origins of the Protestant Tradition* (Princeton, 1982), 72.

[48] *The lattre examinacyon*, B3r.

[49] *The lattre examinacyon*, B3r.

supporters during her interrogations included her cousin Christopher Brittayn, a lawyer in the Inns of Court, a servant to Sir Anthony Denny, and the chronicler Edward Hall, but she also seems to have had associations with court aristocrats. Bishop Gardiner pressurized Askew to name members of her sect, specifically asking her about 'my ladye of Sothfolke, my ladye of Sussex, my ladye of Hertforde, my ladye Dennye, and my ladye fitzwyllyams'.[50] Bale praises these women for their virtue, which is 'more noble . . . for thus releuynge Christ and hys members, than for anye other acte, eyther yet degre of nobylyte'.[51] Eventually Askew acknowledged that two men who had given her money while she was in prison said they did so on behalf of Lady Hertford and Lady Denny, but claimed that for the most part she relied on her maid, who obtained money from apprentices.[52] Her examiners suspected that she was maintained by members of the Council, but even under torture she refused to speak.[53]

John Foxe and the recusant Robert Parsons suggest that Gardiner was trying to force Askew to incriminate Catherine Parr; certainly it was not long afterwards that the Queen herself came under threat of arrest.[54] In the last years of Henry's reign, Parr supported Latimer and Cranmer and gave encouragement to humanist scholarship, gathering around her a group of noble women who shared her intellectual sympathies.[55] According to Parsons, Askew was responsible for supplying Parr with heretical books.[56] Askew has also been linked to the Anabaptist Joan of Kent (executed 1550), who came from a family of rural craftsmen. She too was said to have smuggled Lollard books into the court. The recusant Robert Parsons describes her as Askew's 'dear sister, disciple, and handmayd'.[57] Following Henry's death, two of Askew's associates, Seymour's wife Anne, Countess of Hertford, and Catherine, Duchess of Suffolk, gave their support to Protestant writers and publishers,[58] and when Bale himself returned from exile he received the protection of Mary Fitzroy, Duchess of Richmond,

---

50 *The lattre examinacyon*, E8r–E8v.

51 *The lattre examinacyon*, F4r.

52 *The lattre examinacyon*, F2v–F3v.

53 *The lattre examinacyon*, F4v–F5r.

54 Foxe juxtaposes his account of Askew and the attack on Parr in the 1583 edition of the *Acts and Monuments*. Parsons claims that Askew admitted her connection with Parr: *Narratives*, ed. Nichols, 308.

55 See McConica, *English Humanists*, 200–34; W.P. Haugaard, 'Katherine Parr: the Religious Convictions of a Renaissance Queen', *Renaissance Quarterly* xxii (1969), 346–59; and J.N. King, 'Patronage and Piety: the Influence of Catherine Parr' in *Silent*, ed. Hannay, 43–60.

56 *Narratives*, ed. Nichols, 308.

57 *Narratives*, ed. Nichols, 309; cf. Miles Hogarde, *The displaying of the Protestantes* (1556), E7v. See also J. Davis, 'Joan of Kent, Lollardy and the English Reformation', *Journal of Ecclesiastical History* xxxiii (1983), 225–33.

58 King, *English Reformation Literature*, 103–13; and King, 'Patronage', 49–60.

patronage which may well have predated the Seymour Protectorate.[59] In addition to the two accounts of her interrogations by the ecclesiastical and secular authorities, the published material attributed to Anne Askew includes letters written by her to the Lord Chancellor, the King, and John Lascels; her confessions of faith; her prayer before her death; a translation of Psalm 54; and 'The Balade whyche Anne Askewe made and sange whan she was in Newgate' ('Lyke as the armed knyght / Appoynted to the fielde . . .'). The original manuscripts of the *Examinations* have not survived, and may have been in Bale's library when it was destroyed after he had to flee Ireland. Nor does it appear that the material was circulated in any other form: all subsequent published versions of the *Examinations*, even those which omit Bale's commentaries and prefatory and conclusory material, are descended from his original editions. While there is no good reason to doubt that Bale did base his versions on Askew's own accounts, the texts as we have them may well have been heavily revised.

Although it is impossible to know whether Bale was personally acquainted with Anne Askew, or how much he actually knew about her, it is evident that he had access to more information than he could have gleaned from her text. For example, he supplies additional biographical information, telling us about her family and the circumstances of her separation from her husband. One gloss elucidates an obscure point in the text, in which Askew avoids answering a question about her husband, and justifies her controversial desire to obtain a divorce.[60] It is important that the extent of the editorial changes Bale made to his texts should not be underestimated. Stephen Gardiner, in a letter to Seymour written in 1547, complained that the *Examinations* misrepresented the truth,[61] and as John Foxe pointed out, the account in the *Examinations* of the written statement which Askew signed during her first questioning does not agree with Bonner's record of it.[62] Although a number of critics have argued that the accounts of the examinations ascribed to Askew are stylistically distinct from Bale's comments,[63] it is difficult to judge the extent of his interpolations. L.P. Fairfield notes, for example, that Askew formulates her belief concerning the Eucharist as 'a mutuall pertycypacyon', words favoured elsewhere by Bale himself.[64] Elizabeth H. Hageman argues that the absence of the paraphrase of Psalm 54 and the Newgate ballad in Foxe's section on Askew in the *Acts and*

[59] King, *English Reformation Literature*, 72–3; King, 'Patronage', 51.
[60] *The lattre examinacyon*, B6v.
[61] *The Letters of Stephen Gardiner*, ed. J.A. Muller (Cambridge, 1933), 277–8.
[62] *The Acts and Monuments of John Foxe*, ed. J. Pratt (4th ed. London, 1877), v, 542–3.
[63] See, for example, Elizabeth H. Hageman's entry on Askew in *A Dictionary of British Women Writers*, ed. J. Todd (London, 1989), 17. The contrast is examined fully by Beilin in 'Self-Portrait', and *Redeeming Eve*, 29–47.
[64] Fairfield, *John Bale*, 134–5.

Monuments may indicate that she was not responsible for them.[65] The originality of the ballad can be questioned on other grounds: H.A. Mason has identified the final verses as being derived from Surrey's 'Ecclesiastes, Chapter Three'.[66] He suggests that Askew obtained Surrey's poem after her arrest, but if, as Emrys Jones has suggested, they were written during his final imprisonment between December 1546 and January 1547, Bale may have falsely attributed the ballad to Askew.[67] Bale's treatment of Elizabeth Tudor's translation and the problems surrounding the texts of the *Examinations* illustrate that Bale did not perceive the authorial text to be inviolable. It is entirely possible that Bale made quite radical, although almost entirely undetectable changes to Askew's autobiographical accounts. This caveat must be kept in mind in any reading of Askew's text.

Askew's Imitation of Christ

In his preface to *The Obedience of a Christian Man*, William Tyndale cites Christ's prophecies in John 20.21, John 15.20 and Matthew 10.16–21:

> We are called, not to dispute, as the pope's disciples do; but to die with Christ, that we may live with him; and to suffer with him, that we may reign with him. We be called unto a kingdom that must be won with suffering only, as a sick man winneth health. God is he that doth all things for us, and fighteth for us; and we do but suffer only. Christ saith, John. xx. 'As my Father sent me, so I send you;' and, John xv. 'If they persecute me, then shall they persecute you.' And Christ saith, Matt. x. 'I send you forth as sheep among wolves.' The sheep fight not; but the shepherd fighteth for them, and careth for them. 'Be harmless as doves, therefore,' saith Christ, 'and wise as serpents.' The doves imagine no defence, nor seek to avenge themselves. The serpent's wisdom is, to keep his head, and those parts wherein our life resteth. Christ is our head; and God's word is where in our life resteth. To cleave, therefore, fast unto Christ, and unto those promises which God hath made us, for his sake, is our wisdom. 'Beware of men,' saith he; 'for they shall deliver you up unto their councils, and shall scourge you; and ye shall be brought before rulers and kings for my sake. The brother shall betray, or deliver, the brother to death, and the father the son; and the children shall rise against father and mother, and put them to death.'[68]

Tyndale, who is described by Bale as one in whom 'the spirit of Elias was

---

65 *Dictionary*, ed. Todd, 17.

66 H.A. Mason, *Humanism and Poetry in the Early Tudor Period* (London, 1959), 243–4.

67 See *Henry Howard, Earl of Surrey: Poems*, ed. E. Jones (Oxford, 1964), 153. For the view that Askew imitated Surrey's poem, which may have been given to her by Anthony Denny, see S. Bridgen, 'Henry Howard, Earl of Surrey and the "Conjured League" ', *The Historical Journal* xxxvii (1994), 525.

68 W. Tyndale, *The Obedience of a Christian Man* in *Doctrinal Treatises and Introductions to Different Portions of the Holy Scripture*, ed. H. Walter (Cambridge, 1848), 137.

not at all asleep' and by Foxe as 'the Apostle of England',[69] finds in these verses Scriptural directions for the persecuted Christians. Writing about the French Protestants, Donald R. Kelley says that 'Christ was indeed "captain of martyrs" . . . in psychological terms the martyr was the very model of the true Christian, the true saint, and in the sixteenth century became a stereotype.'[70] Many English reformers, like the Lollards and other suppressed sects before and after them, found confirmation of their personal state of grace in the fact of their oppression and in their own perseverance.[71] Just as Christ's own life followed the divine plan for the salvation of humanity, fulfilling the Old Testament predictions concerning the coming of the Messiah, so the lives of the faithful would follow the ordained way leading to individual salvation which would entail suffering and possibly even martyrdom. Anne Askew represents her own afflictions in what Anne Hudson has called 'an apostolical tradition of persecution'.[72] John Bale, who likens himself to St Paul in his self-vindicatory *Vocacyon*, believes that Christ's words are fulfilled in the sufferings of Askew and her companions, who were 'reuyled, mocked, stocked, racked, execrated, condempned, and murthered'.[73]

According to the Gospels, Christ and His apostles were arrested not because they had committed any crime, but because the Jews plotted and brought false charges against them. They were faced with tempters, spies, deceivers and betrayers. Askew claims that she too has been treated unjustly and illegally, having been initially refused bail and then condemned without a jury.[74] Her interrogators are willing to use every possible means to trap her, including flattery, blackmail, threats and deception. When a priest sent to counsel her tries to elicit her beliefs concerning the sacrament of the altar,

[69] Quoted by P. Collinson, 'William Tyndale and the Course of the English Reformation', *Reformation* i (1996), 72.

[70] D.R. Kelley, *The Beginning of Ideology: Consciousness and Society in the French Reformation* (Cambridge, 1981), 121.

[71] See, for example, *The examinacion of master William Thorpe preste* (Antwerp, 1530). For a recent edition of part of the account in Oxford, Bodleian Library MS Rawlinson C.208, see *Two Wycliffite Texts: the Sermon of William Taylor 1406; the Testament of William Thorpe 1407*, ed. A. Hudson, EETS o.s. 301 (Oxford, 1993). For an analysis of the Thorpe text, see Kendall, *Drama*, 58–67 and passim; and also A. Hudson, 'William Thorpe and the Question of Authority' in *Christian Authority: Essays in honour of Henry Chadwick*, ed. G.R. Evans (Oxford, 1988), 127–37. For a Lollard sermon which links the persecutions of the times to Matthew 10.16, see *English Wycliffite Sermons*, ii, ed. P. Gradon (Oxford, 1988), no. 64, 52–3.

[72] A. Hudson, *The Premature Reformation: Wycliffite Texts and Lollard History* (Oxford, 1988), 222.

[73] *The lattre examinacyon*, B1r; cf. *The first examinacyon*, B3v.

[74] See P. McQuade, ' "Except that they had offended the Lawe": Gender and Jurisprudence in *The Examinations of Anne Askew*', *Literature and History* 3rd series iii.2 (1994), 1–14.

she refuses to answer, declaring, 'I perceyue ye come to tempte me',[75] while Bale compares the priest both to Satan tempting Christ in the wilderness and to Judas.[76] In the course of his elucidation, he also likens Bonner to Judas, Herod and Caiphas, noting that Bonner's attempts to trick Askew into heretical confessions mirror Satan's three temptations of Christ. Despite the cunning and guile of her interrogators, Askew always succeeds in outwitting them, appearing fearless and without worries. Christ's guidance to His followers on how they must react to their suffering, his paradoxical command to be as shrewd as a snake and as innocent as a dove, explains the apparently contradictory behaviour of Askew which causes her to be characterized by her opponents as both deceiver and fool, but by Bale as a martyr of the English Reformation.

Christ promises in John 14.26 that those who trust in Him will not have to face their persecutors alone and unaided, 'But that comforter which is the holy gost (whom my father will sende in my name) he shall teache you all thinges, and bringe all thinges to youre remembrauce whatsoever I have tolde you.'[77] The Spirit descends equally on both women and men, 'And on my servaunts, and on my honde maydens I will powre out of my sprete in those dayes, and they shall prophesye' (Acts 2.18).[78] As a divinely-inspired latter-day disciple, Askew spoke the words of Scripture, instructed listeners in matters of theology and doctrine, and adopted the tone and manner of Christ and His apostles. Her utterances are to be identified with the Spirit which speaks through her, and her self-assurance echoes that of Christ, who although brought as a lamb to the slaughter, an innocent unjustly accused and wrongly condemned, asserted his own authority as the Son of God, criticized His accusers and condemned their teaching. The first part of Askew's text opens abruptly:

> First Christofer dare examyned me at Sadlers hall, beynge one of the quest, and asked yf I ded not beleue that the sacrament hangynge ouer the aultre was the verye bodye of Christ realye. Then I demaunded thys questyon of hym, wherfore S. Steuen was stoned to deathe? And he sayd, he coulde not tell. Then I answered, that nomore wolde I assoyle hys vayne questyon . . . Secondly he sayd, that there was a woman, whych ded testyfye, that I shulde reade, how God was not in temples made with handes. Then I shewed hym the vij. and xvij. chaptre of the Apostles actes, what Steuen & Paule had sayd therin. Wherupon he asked me, how I toke those sentences? I answered, that I wolde not throwe pearles amonge swyne, for acornes were good ynough.[79]

Through a series of verbal manoeuvres, Askew establishes herself in a

---

75 *The first examinacyon*, B5v.
76 *The first examinacyon*, B4r.
77 *Tyndale's New Testament 1534*, ed. N.H. Wallis (Cambridge, 1938), 219.
78 *Tyndale's New Testament*, 235.
79 *The First examinacyon*, A1v–A2r.

position of power over her interrogator. From the start she evades giving direct answers, deflecting Christopher Dare's first question by asking him about St Stephen, and responding to the second by simply directing him to the Bible. When Dare asks her to interpret this text, she quotes another verse of Scripture, again without offering any gloss, but clearly implying that Dare is not worthy of an explanation. She refuses to allow him to dominate the situation by usurping the role of questioner and giving unpredictable and indirect answers, leaving him to work out for himself what she means. Throughout the first examination, Askew's shrewdness enables her to avoid condemning herself; her answers to the charges against her and to the questions of doctrine cannot be used against her because she has given nothing away. Indeed Askew seems to follow the example Christ himself set when he was brought before his accusers, by questioning her examiners, remaining silent or answering indirectly,[80] and again like Christ she was rebuked for her insolence and accused of speaking in parables.[81]

The issue of sex is foregrounded in Askew's text. At the end of her first examination, Askew was required to sign a document testifying to the orthodoxy of her faith in all points. Her execution of this act failed to please the Bishop:

> Then my lorde sate downe, and toke me the wrytynge to sett therto my hande, and I writte after thys maner, I Anne Askewe do beleue all maner thynges contayned in the faythe of the Catholyck church. Then because I ded adde vnto it, the Catholyck churche, he flonge into hys chambre in a great furye. With that, my cosyne Brittayne folowed hym, desyerynge hym for Gods sake to be good lorde vnto me.[82]

Askew follows Wyclif's definition of the True Church which contrasts the *congregatio predestinatorum*, made up of those saints already in heaven and the Christians who will reach it after their lives' ends, with the established Church on earth in which the predestined and those foreknown to damnation co-exist.[83] Although Wyclif asserted that an individual cannot discern her or his own state or that of another, Askew implies that she is among the predestined but her interrogators are not. Bonner's frustration is intensified by the sex of his opponent; thus her cousin attempts to alleviate

---

[80] Compare Christ's responses to his accusers in John 18.33–8, analysed by A.D. Nuttall, *Overheard by God: Fiction and Prayer in Herbert, Milton, Dante and St John* (London, 1980), 128–43.

[81] Bale notes that Askew is following Christ's example in speaking in parables: *The lattre examinacyon*, C1r.

[82] *The first examinacyon*, E6r–E6v.

[83] On Wycliffite and Lollard definitions of the church, see Hudson, *Premature Reformation*, 314–27.

his fury by contrasting Bonner's wisdom with her 'weake womannys wytt'.[84]

Askew was said to have come into conflict with her husband for her gospelling, that is for reading aloud from the Bible placed in the Church, and during her first examination she carried on her a copy of a book which her interrogators thought to be by Frith.[85] Throughout both her accounts, she claims for herself the roles of prophet, preacher and author, able to interpret God's word, to teach and to dispute with learned men on theological matters. In this respect she might remind us of Margery Kempe, whose strident voice was discussed in the second chapter. For example, in her account of her first hearing, Askew relates an encounter with sixty priests in Lincoln who boasted that they could refute her arguments about matters of religion.[86] As Askew sat reading in the Minster, the priests approached her in small groups but they did not have the courage to speak. Only one challenged her, but his words were of so little import that she could not remember them, and she thus succeeded in quelling her opponents. Likewise, during her first examination, one of her questioners rebuked Askew for quoting Scripture, citing St Paul's prohibitions on women speaking in Church and teaching. In a comparable situation, Kempe defended herself by arguing that her activities were legitimate because they did not take place in the pulpit. Askew's response is remarkably similar: with a self-confidence bordering on arrogance, she gives her own understanding of Paul's prohibitions and throws a question back:

> I answered hym, that I knewe Paules meanynge so well as he, whych is, j Corinthiorum xiiij. that a woman ought not to speake in the congregacyon by the waye of teachynge. And then I asked him, how manye women he had seane, go into the pulpett and preache.[87]

Askew believes that she has vindicated herself and reproaches the chancellor for victimizing 'poore women', even though she appears to undermine her argument later when she refuses to explicate another verse from the Bible on the grounds that it would go against the teaching of Paul for her to do so, especially in the presence of so many learned men.[88] She is reproached by a priest because she fails to answer a question according to 'the ordre of scoles' but remains undaunted, 'I tolde him, I was but a woman, & knewe not the course of scoles.'[89] Her examiners' attempts to force her to state her beliefs concerning transubstantiation unambiguously repeatedly

---

84 *The first examinacyon*, E6v.
85 On Askew's gospelling, see *Narratives*, ed. Nichols, 309.
86 *The first examinacyon*, D8v–E2r.
87 *The first examinacyon*, B2r.
88 *The first examinacyon*, D7v.
89 *The first examinacyon*, B6r.

fail because she refuses to commit herself on this issue, insisting that she believes 'as the scripture doth teache me'.[90] When the exasperated Bishop asks her why she has so few words, she turns the chancellor's pronouncement against women's speech against the Bishop himself, 'God hath geuen me the gyfte of knowlege, but not of vtteraunce. And Salomon sayth, that a woman of fewe wordes, is a gyfte of God.'[91] Like Kempe before her, Askew does not directly challenge the teaching of St Paul, but instead implicitly contrasts the true wisdom of the woman graced by God with the false intellectualism of her educated adversaries in order to undermine the stereotype of woman as unlearned and foolish. When Askew does finally state her beliefs, it is not because she has been persuaded to do so, but because she has decided to submit to her fate.

While the narrative describing Askew's trials is evidently carefully contrived, its structure is inevitably constrained by the formal nature of her examinations, which would have followed a prescribed format with certain questions being asked often in a certain order, and the dialogue form of the text reflects the ecclesiastical records of heresy trials.[92] Nonetheless, the centrality to Askew's text of her examinations and imprisonment mirrors the New Testament accounts of the trials of Christ and His disciples. Askew's narrative opens with a description of her examinations in front of the ecclesiastical inquisitors, focusing particularly on her questioning by the Bishop of London, and then moves on to her examinations before the King's Council at Greenwich. This structure parallels Christ's trials in front of both the religious and secular authorities, as Bale notes in his commentary.[93] It is followed by an extended account of Askew's suffering in the Tower of London where she was tortured on the rack, and Bale is quick to suggest similarities with the flogging and mocking of Christ which took place after His condemnation.[94] Paula McQuade argues that in her description of the sickness which afflicted her before she was sent to Newgate, Askew 'is purposefully attempting to shape her narrative upon an established literary model familiar both to her and to her potential Protestant readership through the biblical story of Saul of Tarsus, in which moments of profound psychological transformation are thematically marked by episodes of extreme physical suffering'.[95] Askew's letter to Henry VIII, a brief summary of her beliefs and plea for mercy, could be read as a fulfillment of Christ's prophecy that His apostles would witness to kings.

Some of the more diffuse elements of the *Examinations*, such as her two

---

[90] *The first examinacyon*, D3r.

[91] *The first examinacyon*, D5r.

[92] See A. Hudson, 'The Examination of Lollards', *Bulletin of the Institute of Historical Research* xlvi (1973), 145–59.

[93] *The first examinacyon*, E8r–E8v.

[94] *The lattre examinacyon*, F6r.

[95] McQuade, 'Gender and Jurisprudence', 9.

confessions of faith, or her answer to John Lascels' letter, make sense if they are viewed in the light of the textual conflict between the English Church and the Protestant reformers. Askew's unequivocal statements of her beliefs are clearly a response to the Catholic propaganda then in circulation which claimed that she had recanted, and which she acknowledges had come to Lascels' notice.[96] Letters of encouragement in adversity, such as her letter to Lascels, were not uncommon (Foxe prints numerous examples), and like the literature of consolation, they were in part inspired by the example of the epistles to the early churches sent by Paul during his imprisonment. Indeed Thomas More complained that the heretics began 'theyr pystles in suche apostolycall fashyon that a man wold wene yt were wryten from saynt Paule hymself'.[97] Poems and prayers such as Askew's were also popular in the early Reformation: Elizabeth I, for example, produced similar devotional works. In her final letters, confessions and prayers, Askew places her trust in God alone: like Christ in Gethsemane, she submits joyfully to God's will, despite neither seeking nor desiring death, and like Christ on the cross, she prays for forgiveness for those who have done violence upon her. Askew presents herself as steadfastly holding on to her faith against fearful odds right up to the end: in anticipation of her execution, she quotes the words for which Stephen was stoned, asserting that God is not found in things made by man and condemning those who resist the Holy Ghost (Acts 7.48 and 51).[98]

The Prophet as Martyr

Bale brings into his commentary on the *Examinations* the apocalyptic framework which he had developed in *The image of bothe churches*. According to Revelation 11, two witnesses will prophesy for 1,260 days, clothed in sackcloth. They will be armed with fantastic powers, and anyone who wishes to harm them will be devoured by the fire which comes from their mouths. After they have finished their testimony, they will be killed by the beast, and their bodies will lie in the streets while the people of the earth gloat over them. However, after three and a half days they will be resurrected and will ascend to heaven, while a severe earthquake will kill many. In *The image of bothe churches*, Bale interprets the Two Witnesses of Revelation, first as Moses and Christ, representing the Old and New

---

[96] Askew's opponents published her confession after her condemnation in order to justify their actions: *The lattre examinacyon*, G4r; *Letters and Papers, Foreign and Domestic, of the Reign of Henry VIII*, ed. J.S. Brewer, J. Gairdner and R.H. Brodie (Vaduz, 1965), xx, part 1, 391.

[97] Quoted by Hudson, *Premature Reformation*, 222.

[98] *The lattre examinacyon*, D3r.

Testaments, the Law and the Gospel, and then as members of the True Church who have risen up, empowered by God, in opposition to the corruption of the Synagogue of Satan.[99] He includes an extensive list of reformers and martyrs of the fifteenth and sixteenth centuries, including in it many English examples.

In Bale's analysis, the sackcloth worn by the Two Witnesses signifies their rejection of the self-aggrandizement and hypocrisy which he associates with the Roman Church and the established Church in England. There is no vanity in the dress or behaviour of these apostles, who refuse high office in law, government and religion, and concern themselves with living a life according to the will of God. They constantly attest the truth of God, revealing the mysteries of Scripture to the world. In their prophecies they condemn the covetous laws, hypocritical works and heretical doctrine of the ungodly. They are armed with the power of the word, not the power of men, which is expressed 'not in gloriouse wordes, fyne paynted termes, nor in perswasyble reasons of mans wytte, but in playne symple speakinge',[100] which cannot be known by the worldly wise and which is opposed to the 'crafty colours, subtle reasons, and deceytfull argumentes, vpon daungers doubtes, doctors, olde customes, & auctorite of fathers'[101] of their adversaries. When their office is finished, they will suffer unrelenting persecution. The bishops will overcome them not with Scripture but with their laws and traditions, and will hand them over to the secular authorities who will shed their innocent blood. This pattern of prophecy followed by persecution is repeated in each generation. The resurrection and ascension of the Two Witnesses signify that new Christians figuratively rise out of the ashes of their predecessors to declare the same message. The earthquake signifies the cruel persecutions of the Church which will follow their appearance.

Anne Askew is for Bale an example of the kind of martyr chosen and strengthened by God to withstand the unprecedented atrocities of the sixth, and current age. She is the fulfillment of Bale's ideal of the true Christian as portrayed in his commentary on the Two Witnesses. In Revelation 11 it is prophesied that after the deaths of the witnesses their bodies will lie on the streets. Bale understands this passage to foretell the condemnations of the true Christians as heretics and the slanderous accusations which will be aimed at them following their executions – they will never be revered as saints by the established Church. Bale believes these verses have been fulfilled in recent times when the bodies of many of those executed as heretics, such as Oldcastle, Sawtrey, Thorpe, Frith, Barnes and Tyndale, were not buried but either burned to ashes or left in the open to be eaten by birds. Bale almost certainly had the prophecy of the Two Witnesses in mind

---

99   Bale, *The image of bothe churches*, ii, B7v–C8v.
100 Bale, *The image of bothe churches*, ii, B5v–B6r.
101 Bale, *The image of bothe churches*, ii, B4v.

in his comparison of Askew's fate to that of Blandina, the Gallican martyr of the second century, for which his main source is Eusebius.[102] Eusebius records that Blandina's body was exhibited and scorned for six and a half days before being burned. Although Bale does not know what happened to Askew's ashes, Blandina's and those of her companions were thrown into the Rhône.[103]

In Bale's account of Anne Askew's death, he does not limit his narrative to the bare facts. Rather the supernatural dramatically intrudes in the form of the thunderous voice of God. Bale, who had been an orthodox hagiographer in his early career, clearly draws on medieval traditions in his representation of Askew.[104] The genre of the saint's life changed emphasis in response to theological developments in the Middle Ages: while the hagiographic tradition which centred on the entire life as an exemplum of complete devotion to God emerged in the later medieval period, that which focused on the death of the saint was widespread during the early persecutions of Christians.[105] In addition to comparing Askew's death to the passions of Christ and St Stephen, Bale emphasizes the similarities between Askew and the sufferings of the faithful in the primitive Church, before it became corrupted by the wickedness of the papacy.

Bale's commentary on Askew's text brings out parallels between her experiences and the legends of female martyrs like Katherine of Alexandria, Cecilia or Margaret of Antioch. Their stories are found in *The Golden Legend*, translated by Caxton at the end of the fifteenth century and still popular in Tudor England.[106] Certain patterns recur in the *vitae* of these women. The legend of St Katherine, for example, is set in the fourth century and tells of a noble and educated young virgin who protested in public against sacrificing to idols. After attempting to convert the Emperor through argument and persuasion, she successfully disputed with fifty pagan philosophers. Refusing to marry the Emperor because she said she was a bride of Christ, she endured terrible tortures: she was stripped and beaten with scorpions, locked up in a cell to starve for twelve days, threatened with a torture wheel (which broke before she could be injured) and eventually beheaded. Her example converted many, including the philosophers, the

---

102 *The first examinacyon,* ♣7r–*1v.
103 *The first examinacyon,* *1r.
104 For an overview of medieval saints' lives and legends, see R. Woolfe, 'Saints' Lives' in *Continuations and Beginnings: Studies in Old English Literature*, ed. E.G. Stanley (London, 1966), 37–66.
105 Woolf, 'Saints' Lives', 56.
106 See Jacobus de Voragine, *The Golden Legend*, trans. G. Ryan and H. Ripperger (Toronto, 1941), 351–4, 689–95, and 708–16; and *The legende named in latyn legenda aurea*, trans. W. Caxton (Westminster, 1483). The *Legend*'s popularity in the Tudor period is discussed by H.C. White, *Tudor Books of Saints and Martyrs* (Madison, 1963), 31–66.

Queen, the captain of the army, and two hundred soldiers. St Cecilia was a Roman martyr of the third century. Although betrothed to a pagan, she dedicated her virginity to God. She succeeded in convincing her husband that their marriage should not be consummated and both he and his brother became Christians. These two converts were later martyred and Cecilia was brought before the prefect. She too refused to sacrifice to false gods, and, again after disputing with her persecutor, was condemned to death. Like Katherine she was also responsible for many conversions. St Margaret of Antioch suffered for her faith after she refused to marry the prefect Olybrius. She had to endure not only the physical pain of racking and beatings but also psychological onslaught when bystanders, out of pity, tried to convince her to give up Christianity. In answer to her prayer that her spiritual enemy be made visible, the devil appeared to her as a dragon which she then succeeded in defeating.

Throughout their persecutions, Katherine, Cecilia and Margaret steadfastly hold their ground, answering their malignant opponents fearlessly, oblivious to their torments and embracing death, when it finally comes, joyously. In this respect, their martyrdoms bear a striking resemblance to the accounts of Askew's examinations, in particular the indefatigable perseverance of the saints in the face of verbal and psychological as well as physical assault. Bale even reports that Askew's execution converted one thousand people.[107] The woodcut of Anne Askew which introduces Bale's editions of her texts was probably designed by Bale himself [fig. 4].[108] Askew is portrayed as an evangelist holding a Bible, signifying her divine revelation, and what may be either a quill pen, signifying her writing, or a palm, the symbol of the martyr. Her radiance suggests that she fulfills the apocalyptic prophecy of the Woman Clothed with the Sun (Revelation 12.1). At the feet of this triumphant Protestant woman lies the papal dragon decked in its tiara. Yet her victorious stance over the monster is derived from the traditional iconography of St Margaret of Antioch (compare also the representation of St Katherine in fig. 1), and in his commentary, Bale notes a resemblance between Askew and St Cecilia because both bore the Gospel within their breasts, and the former 'neuer after ceased from the stodye therof, nor from godlye communycacyon & prayer, tyll she was clerlye by most cruell tormentes, taken from thys wretched worlde'.[109]

Bale's most extensive comparison is however with Blandina, a victim of the persecution of the Christians which took place in the reign of the

---

107 *The first examinacyon*, F3r.
108 See J.N. King, *Tudor Royal Iconography: Literature and Art in an Age of Religious Crisis* (Princeton, 1989), 207–9.
109 *The first examinacyon*, ♣7r.

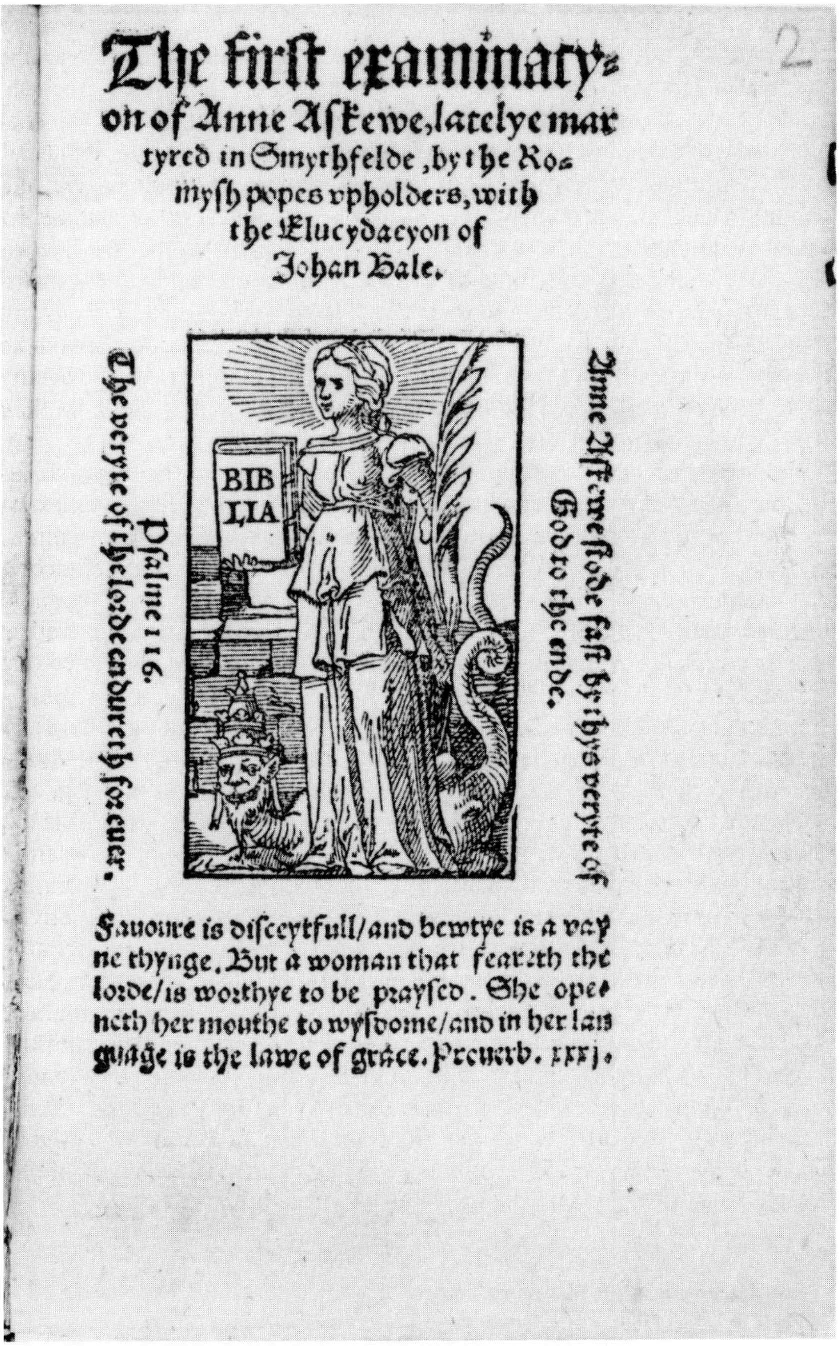

The first examinacy-
on of Anne Askewe, latelye mar
tyred in Smythfelde, by the Ro-
mysh popes vpholders, with
the Elucydacyon of
Johan Bale.

The verytye of the lorde endureth for euer.
Psalme 116.

Anne Askewe stode fast by thys verytye of
God to the ende.

Fauoure is disceytfull/and bewtye is a vay
ne thynge. But a woman that feareth the
lorde/is worthye to be praysed. She openeth her mouthe to wysdome/and in her lan
guage is the lawe of grace. Prouerb. xxxj.

Fig. 4. Anne Askew, holding a Bible and palm or quill, trampling the papal dragon underfoot. From John Bale's edition of *The first examinacyon of Anne Askewe* (1546). Oxford, Bodleian Library, 8ºC.46.Th.Seld (2). Illustrated title page from part 2.

Emperor Antonius Verus.[110] Blandina was tried and condemned, imprisoned and viciously tortured – scourged, forced into a burning seat, hung on a stake as food for wild beasts. She steadfastly confessed her faith and bravely refused to lie about her companions despite the torments which she was made to suffer. She was brought to the amphitheatre where attempts were made to force her to swear to idols, and when she would not submit, she was put in a net and thrown to a bull. According to Bale, both Blandina and Askew were known as the mother of martyrs. He says that the two women were imprisoned and tormented before their executions, and notices direct similarities in the incidentals of their lives. Both, for example, were given to wild beasts, but in Askew's case, he interprets the beasts figuratively as bishops and priests, and he suggests that the *Examinations* provides evidence enough that Askew, like Blandina, communed with Christ in prison. Both women, although they were deserted by some of those who were imprisoned with them, had three faithful companions in their sufferings. Blandina and Askew reacted to their persecutions in the same way: reproving their tormentors for their religious errors yet praying for them too, and rejoicing in their own afflictions. Bale believes that the two women exemplify identical virtues of bravery and steadfastness, and that the Holy Spirit operated in the same way in each of them. He maintains that both were young and tender by nature but made strong by the Spirit.

Bale, who had married after his conversion, rejected the ideal of virginity so exalted by the Roman Church. He spoke out in condemnation of celibacy and celebration of domestic life. It is no coincidence that he chose as his precedent for his portrayal of Askew a woman martyr and type of the Spouse of Christ who, in Eusebius's version, is not lauded as a virgin. Bale describes Askew as spiritually rather than physically undefined, 'A vyrgyne was she in that behalf, redemed from the earthe & folowynge the lambe, & hauynge in her fore head the fathers name written.'[111] Because Askew no longer lived with her husband, Bale stresses that she had lived a life of domestic piety and had been a dedicated wife and mother until her husband cast her out.[112] Nonetheless, Bale brings Askew closer still to Katherine, Margaret and Cecilia, who had suffered because they had dedicated their bodies to God, Katherine and Margaret having rejected their powerful suitors, by explaining that Askew was punished for her desire to be divorced from a cruel husband who tried to prevent her from serving God.[113] In emphasizing Askew's physical weakness, Bale echoes Eusebius, who tells how Blandina, physically small and weak, 'like a noble athlete received her strength in the

---

[110] Eusebius Pamphili, *Ecclesiastical History, Books 1–5*, trans. R.J. Deferrari, The Fathers of the Church 19 (Washington DC, 1953), 272–87.

[111] *The first examinacyon*, E5v.

[112] *The lattre examinacyon*, B7r.

[113] *The lattre examinacyon*, B7r–B7v.

confession, and her comfort and rest and release from the pain of what was happening to her was in saying, "I am a Christian woman and nothing wicked happens among us." '[114]

Askew's greatness does not come from her nobility or education, although Bale is careful to mention both her gentle birth and her learning, but from her faith and divinely-inspired wisdom. Persecuted for her refusal to believe the false doctrine and traditions of the established Church, her knowledge of the Bible offers her her only defence against the scholarship and wiles of the ecclesiastics, yet she is never defeated on this level. Bale opposes the conventional criticisms of women's education and preaching and defends Askew's utterance of Scripture by citing examples of women who spoke of God from the Bible and the Primitive Church, such as Mary, Elizabeth, the prophet Anna (Luke 2.36–8), the woman who blessed Christ's mother as he preached (Luke 11.27–8), the women who announced the appearance of the risen Christ (Matthew 28 and John 20), learned women from the time of St Jerome, and the legendary English saints Helena, Ursula and Hilda.[115] He argues that these women were knowledgeable in Scripture, and discusses Mary, not as a miraculous intercessor, but as the mother of Christ who 'retayned all, that was afterwarde written of hym'.[116] John King has shown that Reformation writers like Bale and his successors based their portrayal of the woman of faith on the biblical types of the Virtuous Woman of Proverbs, the Woman Clothed with the Sun, and the Five Wise Virgins.[117] The woodcut which illustrates Bale's edition of *The first examinacyon* has as its caption, 'Fauoure is disceytfull and bewtye is a vayne thynge. But a woman that feareth the lorde is worthye to be praysed. She openeth her mouthe to wysdome and in her language is the lawe of grace.'[118] Because women are physically weaker than men, it is Bale's contention that the martyrdom which Askew freely embraced is all the more remarkable: 'What a constancye was thys of a woman, frayle, tendre, yonge and most delycyouslye brought up? But that Christes sprete was myghtye in her who bad her be of good chere, for though the tyrauntes of thys worlde haue power to slee the bodye, yet haue they no power ouer the sowle.'[119]

Askew's martyrdom, like the deaths of the legendary saints Katherine, Margaret and Cecilia, is a triumph over physical pain and the powers of injustice. Because Bale is concerned not with Askew as an individual but as a type of the godly woman, he ignores anything in the text which might detract from his portrayal of her virtues. His commentary on Askew's

[114] Eusebius, *Ecclesiastical History*, 277.
[115] *The first examinacyon*, B2v–B3r.
[116] *The first examinacyon*, B2v.
[117] J. King, 'The Godly Woman in Elizabethan Iconography', *Renaissance Quarterly* xxxviii (1985), 41–84.
[118] *The first examinacyon*, ♣1r.
[119] *The lattre examinacyon*, D3v.

encounter with the priest sent to hear her confession illustrates the gulf between Askew's self-representation and Bale's interpretation of her character and actions.

> Then he [the priest] sayd, he wolde brynge one to me, for to shryue me. And I tolde hym, so that I myght haue one of these iij. . . . I was contented, bycause I knewe theme to be men of wysdome. As for yow or anye other, I wyll not dysprayse, bycause I knowe ye not. Then he sayd, I wolde not haue yow thynke, but that I or an other that shall be brought yow, shall be as honest as they . . . Then I answered by the saynge of Salomon. By commonynge with the wyse, I maye lerne wysdome, but by talkynge with a fole, I shall take skathe [injury].[120]

Only Askew's own associates are qualified to give her religious guidance. Implicit in the verses from Proverbs which constitute her refusal to be shriven by a priest of the established Church is a complete denial of his spiritual authority. Yet Bale is oblivious to the control which Askew has gained over the priest in this short exchange. Instead he describes her as the prey of a cunning aggressor, trying to lure her into participating in an impious Roman ritual: 'Se how thys aduersarye compaseth lyke a rauenynge lyon, to deuoure thys lambe.'[121]

Bale places such weight on Askew's femininity not only to demonstrate the power of the Spirit to transform even the weakest of people into an indomitable servant of God, but also to publicize the atrocities of the English Church and State against His people. In his commentary on Askew's racking, he vituperates Thomas Wriothsley and Richard Rich, who so cruelly gave themselves over to their raging fury: 'O Wrisleye and Riche ii. false christianes & blasphemouse apostataes from God. What chaplayne of the pope hath inchaunted yow, or what deuyll of helle bewytched yow, to execute upon a poore condempned woman, so prodygyouse a kynde of tyrannye?'[122] Throughout his writing, Bale consistently refuses to challenge the authority of the monarchy itself, but here he laments that a King's high counsellor and judge should have become a slave to the Antichrist. He dramatically envisages the Lord Chancellor casting off his gown as he takes upon himself the office of hangman and pulls the wheel of the rack. Whereas Askew herself minimizes her physical suffering and describes herself as continuing to reason calmly with her torturers, Bale portrays her as a powerless victim, 'lyke a lambe she laye styll without noyse of cryenge, and suffered your vttermost vyolence, tyll the synnowes of her armes were broken, and the strynges of her eys peryshed in her heade'.[123] It is impossible

---

120 *The first examinacyon*, B4v–B5r.
121 *The first examinacyon*, B5r.
122 *The lattre examinacyon*, F5v–F6r.
123 *The lattre examinacyon*, F6r–F6v.

that a mere gentlewoman, enfeebled by illness as she was at the time, a 'yonge, tendre, weake, and sycke woman', should so piously endure torments which not even the strongest man could withstand, unless it were with God's help.[124] Although his reading of Askew's text may seem naive and unconvincing in so far as he asks the reader to view this woman who so resolutely defended her faith despite suffering illness and torture as a pathetic victim, by directing the reader towards the illegalities in Askew's examinations and condemnation Bale is able to strengthen his attack on members of the government, figures like Wriothsley, Gardiner and Paget.

Bale's commentary on Askew's text obviously has a didactic intention. He frequently picks up on minor points in his source either to launch a satirical attack on the established Church, or to introduce his own long and complex doctrinal expositions, most often on the subject of the sacrament of the altar. There is also an oratorical element in Bale's elucidations, just as there was in much medieval hagiography. Bale chose Askew's account of her perseverance in adversity in order to encourage other Protestants, setting her up as an example of steadfast faith for others to emulate. Bale's edition of Askew's text is a work of propaganda, he is only interested in contemporary events in England in so far as they represent moments in his scheme of universal history, and in writing her life as a Protestant martyrology, he is concerned only with what is typical in her character and experiences. In contrast with his edition of Elizabeth Tudor's translation, which he published in what was a period of religious and political optimism for the reformers, he began work on the *Examinations* at a time when he, like many English Protestants, had been forced into exile. Under such circumstances it comes as no surprise that he is ultimately interested in Askew as 'an example of stronge sufferaunce . . . vnto all them that the lorde shall after lyke maner put forewarde in thys horryble furye of Antichrist, to the glorye of hys persecuted churche'.[125]

The Legacy of the Acts and Monuments

Bale's interest in Askew as an example of a godly Englishwoman continued after his publication of her *Examinations*: her story appears alongside other historical and legendary figures from Joseph of Arimathea and Helena the mother of Constantine to Cranmer and the Marian martyrs in his *Summarium* (a version of which was first published in 1548, the final much-expanded work appearing in 1557). Bale must have been writing this encyclopaedic account of writers in Britain from its earliest history until the present day at the same time as John Foxe (1517–1587) was working on his

---

124 *The lattre examinacyon*, F6v.
125*The first examinacyon*, *2r.

own major historiographic project. The two men had met in 1548 in the household of the Duchess of Richmond and were companions in Basle during the Marian exile. Bale was not only Foxe's mentor, but also the source of some of his information. Foxe incorporated Anne Askew's *Examinations* into both the Latin and English versions of his *Acts and Monuments*.[126]

In the introduction to her narrative in the 1563 edition (the first English edition), he impresses upon his audience the authenticity of Askew's story, echoing Bale's point that it was written not only at the request of some of her associates, but also for the benefit of the Christian community as a whole:

> Here next followeth . . . the true examinations of Anne Askew, which here thou shalt have, gentle reader, according as she wrote them with her own hand, at the instant desire of certain faithful men and women: by the which, if thou mark diligently the communications both of her and of her examiners, thou mayest easily perceive the tree by the fruit, and the man by his work.[127]

It is Foxe's contention that the godly testimony of Askew and the damning behaviour of her examiners speak for themselves. For the most part, Askew's text is reprinted intact (although some abridgments are made, and Askew's song which she was said to have composed in Newgate is not included), but Foxe omits Bale's elucidations altogether, and his own glosses on the text are much briefer than those of his predecessor. Nonetheless, he supplemented his account with Anne Askew's confession, taken from Bonner's diocesan records, drawing the reader's attention to inconsistencies between it and his principal source: according to Askew's text, she was arraigned and condemned before this confession was registered; and her signature on the document does not agree with her version of it.[128] Foxe, like Bale and like Askew herself, is keen to underline the illegality of the proceedings, although his addition of this material also reflects his general preoccupation with the bias and unreliability of official documents as evidence for his project as a whole. Foxe's commentary on Askew's racking, again like Bale's, condemns the behaviour of Wriothesley and

---

126 Cf. *The Acts and Monuments of John Foxe*, ed. J. Pratt (4th ed. London, 1877), v, 537–50. This is the final and most complete revision by Pratt of Stephen Cattley's eight-volume edition of the *Acts and Monuments* (London, 1836–1841), which used Foxe's 1583 edition as the copy text and collated the Latin and authoritative English versions. For a discussion of the faults of this edition, see W.W. Wooden, *John Foxe* (Boston, 1983), 111–12, 117–19. All references will be to the Cattley-Pratt edition unless otherwise stated, but have been checked where necessary against the 1563 and 1583 editions.

127 Foxe, *Acts and Monuments*, v, 537.

128 Foxe, *Acts and Monuments*, v, 542–3.

Rich, and he further exonerates Henry VIII, who is said to have been displeased when the lieutenant of the Tower reported what had occurred.[129]

In an elaboration of the torture scene which is partly dependent on Bale, Foxe depicts Askew's calm but unsubmissive resolution in the face of (graphically-described) intense physical suffering: 'And so, quietly and patiently praying unto the Lord, she abode their tyranny, till her bones and joints were almost plucked asunder, in such sort as she was carried away in a chair.'[130] This sort of portrayal is typical of the discourse of martyrdom which, as John R. Knott explains, 'typically show spiritual power triumphant over whatever physical punishment may be inflicted, through the heroic suffering of the persecuted Christian'.[131] Foxe also added his own conclusion which includes a fictionalized conversation between Askew and Shaxton, the Protestant bishop who preached at her execution.[132] This dialogue draws on information in Robert Crowley's *The confutation of .xiii. articles wherunto Nicholas Shaxton, late byshop subscribed* (1548).[133] Askew is described as being so crippled by her torture that she has to be carried to Smithfield and strung up at the stake to stop her from falling, but she steadfastly refuses Wriothesly's offer of a pardon nonetheless. Meanwhile the Chancellor and other officials are ridiculed for being scared of the gunpowder which had been set in the fire. No mention is made of the thunderclap to which Bale attributes so much significance. However, Foxe's publisher, John Daye, replaces Bale's illustration of Askew the evangelist, victorious over the papal dragon, with the woodcut of the execution which was first used for Crowley's text [fig. 5]. While Bale's woodblock may have been lost or destroyed, this new woodcut seems particularly appropriate to the *Acts and Monuments*, and appears to be based on Bale's account of the events at the execution: it shows Askew and her companions at the stake and surrounded by crowds as Shaxton preaches from his pulpit and lightning flashes in the sky.

The extent and exact nature of Bale's influence on Foxe has been much debated,[134] but K.R. Firth argues that he made a major contribution to the English Protestant apocalyptic tradition, 'If Bale was the bridge between the continent and England, Foxe was the farther shore.'[135] While an apocalyptic scheme is far less evident in Foxe's commentary on Anne Askew than in Bale's, the similarities between their works appear much clearer when viewed in their entirety. The full title of Foxe's 1563 work reads *Actes and*

---

[129] Foxe, *Acts and Monuments*, v, 547–8.

[130] Foxe, *Acts and Monuments*, v, 548.

[131] J.R. Knott, *Discourses of Martyrdom in English Literature, 1563–1694* (Cambridge, 1993), 9.

[132] Foxe, *Acts and Monuments*, v, 550.

[133] Cf. King, *English Reformation Literature*, 439–40; *The Examinations*, ed. Beilin, xxxv–xxxvi and liii–liv.

[134] See above, n. 24.

[135] Firth, *Apocalyptic Tradition*, 109.

¶ The order and maner of the burning of Anne Askew, Iohn Lacels,
Iohn Adams, Nicholas Belenian, with certayne of the Councell
sitting in Smithfield.

Fig. 5. The martyrdom of Anne Askew. From Robert Crowley's *Confutation of Nicholas Shaxton* (1548); later reprinted in John Foxe's *Acts and Monuments*. This illustration is from the 1583 edition of the *Acts and Monuments*. Oxford, Bodleian Library, F.3.2.Th., p. 1240.

Monuments of these latter and perillous dayes, touching matters of the Church, wherein are comprehended and described the great persecutions & horrible troubles, that haue bene wrought and practised by the Romishe Prelates, speciallye in this Realme of England and Scotlande, from the yeare of our Lorde a thousande, vnto the tyme nowe present. Foxe's view is postmillennialist: the year 1000 marks the release of the dragon from the pit, and for Foxe, as for Bale, the current age is one of corruption and persecution, in which the two churches are battling one against the other. While Foxe's focus is undoubtedly on Britain, and especially England, the extent to which he was constructing the history of an Elect Nation, as William Haller called it, is still debated.[136] Certainly Foxe is not limited by national boundaries any more than temporal ones. The interest in apocalypticism and prophecy which is apparent in this edition of the *Acts and Monuments* is more fully developed in the introductions, commentaries and conclusions of the 1583 version, and Foxe's final, incomplete work, the *Eicasmi*, is a commentary on Revelation.[137] Firth explains that Foxe looked to prophecy to provide 'an explanation for the function of martyrdom in the divine plan for human history'.[138]

In Foxe's 1563 text, Askew's story appears as one of the final episodes in the history of the reign of Henry VIII, and although it is followed by events in Edward VI's reign, it functions thematically as an introduction to Foxe's long section on the Marian martyrs. Foxe subsequently kept adding to this part of his work, because, as Firth puts it, he thought the persecutions during this period were 'one of the most horrible of the Church's sufferings under Anti-Christ'.[139] Mary's death and Elizabeth's accession confirmed to Foxe that God was on the side of the Protestants, that their suffering had been vindicated. The initial capital C from the preface to the *Acts and Monuments*, which in the first edition likens Elizabeth to Constantine as another Christian Emperor and himself to Eusebius, shows Elizabeth seated on the throne wielding a sword in her right hand, with the Pope lying at her feet with a serpent wrapped around him [fig. 6].[140] Foxe's stories of these later martyrs may be taken from disparate sources but are clearly often modelled on earlier narratives of the examinations and executions of those such as Thorpe, Oldcastle and Askew.[141] John R. Knott summarizes them thus:

---

136 For a summary, see Hadfield, *Literature, Politics and National Identity*, 57–9; see also R. Helgerson, *Forms of Nationhood: the Elizabethan Writing of England* (London, 1992), 254–68.

137 On Foxe's apocalypticism, see especially Haller, *Foxe's Martyrs*; Olson, *John Foxe*, 51–100; Bauckham, *Tudor Apocalypse*, 75–88; Firth, *Apocalyptic Tradition*, 69–110; Helgerson, *Nationhood*, 254–68.

138 Firth, *Apocalyptic Tradition*, 89.

139 Firth, *Apocalyptic Tradition*, 84.

140 Foxe, *Actes and Monuments* (1563), B1r. See King, *Tudor Iconography*, 154–5.

141 See Knott, *Discourses*, 33–83; cf. White, *Tudor Books*, 132–68.

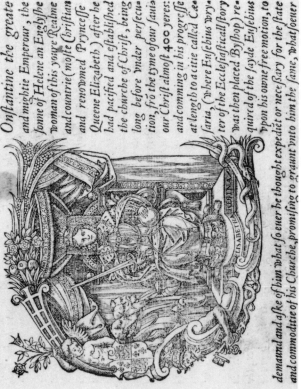

Onstantine the greate
and mightie Emperour, the
sonne of Helene an English
woman of this youre Realme
and countrie (moste Christian
and renowmed Pryncesse
Quene Elizabeth) after he
had pacified and established
the churche of Christ, being
long before vnder persecution, frō the tyme of our sauia
our Christ almost 400 yeres:
and comming in his progresse
at length to a citie called Cae-
saria, (where Eusebius wry-
ter of the Ecclesiasticall story
was then placed Byshop) required of the sayde Eusebius
vpon his owne free motion, to
demaund and aske of him what so euer he thought expedient or necessary for the state
and commoditie of his Churche, promising to graunt vnto him the same, whatsoeuer

Fig. 6. Elizabeth I as Constantine, wielding a sword and trampling the papal dragon underfoot. From John Foxe's *Acts and Monuments* (1563). Oxford, Bodleian Library, Douce F. Subt. 2, sig. Bj recto.

Vehemency in the defense of God's truth becomes a distinguishing characteristic of Foxe's martyrs. Confession assumes much greater importance as
protestant martyrs, through disputation with their examiners and often
through prison writings, give shape to their faith, and seek to communicate
it. Their *agon* includes suffering comparable to that of the early martyrs but
takes on a new dimension as they wield the sword of Scripture against
examiners testing them with crucial doctrinal questions that would determine
whether they were judged to have accepted the authority of the church.[142]

Helen C. White proposes that Askew represents 'a classic type' in the *Acts
and Monuments*, 'the woman martyr of high spirits and sharp tongue'.[143]
For example, in his relation of the fate of Lady Jane Grey he includes a
disputation between the martyr and Fecknam on the subjects of the duties
of a Christian man, the sacraments, and the nature of the church, which is
clearly reminiscent of Askew's autobiography. The exchange concludes
with Gray warning Fecknam that 'we shall never meet, except God turn
your heart; for I am assured, unless you repent and turn to God, you are in
an evil case'.[144] The voice with which she addresses her father's chaplain
in a letter urging him to return to the true faith is reminiscent of the prophetic
writings of the medieval women visionaries, 'Yea, when I consider these
things, I cannot but speak to thee, and cry out upon thee, thou seed of Satan,
and not of Judah, whom the devil hath deceived, the world hath beguiled,
and the desire of life subverted, and made thee of a christian an infidel.'[145]
The word of Scripture becomes the instrument with which she chastises the
priest for his apostasy.

Many of the Marian martyrs whose stories are recorded by Foxe were
not members of the aristocracy or gentility like Grey or Askew, but women
and men from the lower ranks of society. Their lack of formal education did
not prevent them from outmanoeuvring the secular and religious authorities.
One Alice Driver, the wife of a husbandman from Suffolk, condemned in
1558, silenced her opponents with her greater knowledge of Scripture, and
then taunted them:

'Have you no more to say? God be honoured! You be not able to resist the
Spirit of God in me, a poor woman. I was an honest poor man's daughter,

---

142 Knott, *Discourses*, 50.
143 White, *Tudor Books*, 149; see also R.M. Warnicke, *Women of the English Renaissance
and Reformation*, Contributions in Women's Studies 38 (Westport CT, 1983), 71–6.
For the view that the portrait of Anne Askew influenced subsequent portrayals of
Elizabeth I, and also Spenser's women of faith, see King, *English Reformation Literature*, 422 and 426. See also F. Sandler, '*The Faerie Queene*: An Elizabethan Apocalypse' in *The Apocalypse in English Renaissance Thought and Literature: Patterns,
Antecedents and Repercussions*, ed. C.A. Patrides and J. Wittreich (Manchester,
1984), 148–74.
144 Foxe, *Acts and Monuments*, vi, 417.
145 Foxe, *Acts and Monuments*, vi, 418–19.

never brought up in the university, as you have been, but I have driven the plough before my father many a time (I thank God): yet notwithstanding, in the defence of God's truth, and in the cause of my Master Christ, by his grace I will set my foot against the foot of any of you all, in the maintenance and defence of the same, and if I had a thousand lives, they should go for payment thereof.'[146]

Another woman, martyred in the same year in Exeter, and known only as Prest's wife, abandoned her Catholic husband and children, and found herself in trouble for speaking out against church rites and sacraments and proselytizing in the city. Foxe recounts that one gentlewoman who had spoken to her in prison told her own husband, 'that in her life she had never heard a woman (of so much simplicity to see) talk so godly, so perfectly, so sincerely, and so earnestly; insomuch, that if God were not with her, she could not speak such things, "to which I am not able to answer her," said she, "who can read, and she cannot" '.[147] Elizabeth Young, a woman arrested for smuggling books from the continent, was examined on thirteen different occasions, nine of which Foxe transcribes. She too disputed with learned doctors, and was so skilful in her arguments that one interrogator exclaimed, 'Twenty pounds, it is a man in a woman's clothes! twenty pounds, it is a man!'[148] Yet if Foxe dramatized the heroic suffering of these women, his praise was not always unambivalent, as his comments on the execution of four women at Canterbury reveal:

What heart will not lament the murdering mischief of these men, who for want of work do so wreak their tine [vexation] on silly poor women, whose weak imbecility the more strength it lacketh by natural imperfection, the more it ought to be helped, or at least pitied; and not oppressed of men that be stronger.[149]

While historians have contested the extent to which the apocalypticism of the seventeenth century was derived from his writings rather from than those of Thomas Brightman and others, the importance of the *Acts and Monuments* to the Elizabethans and subsequent generations cannot be denied.[150] It provided a supplement to Scripture and was kept next to the Bible in cathedrals and parish churches so that everyone could have access to it. Recent critics have proposed that Foxe's representation of women like Askew encouraged female readers to defend their faith and implicitly

---

146 Foxe, *Acts and Monuments*, viii, 495–6.
147 Foxe, *Acts and Monuments*, viii, 501.
148 Foxe, *Acts and Monuments*, viii, 539.
149 Foxe, *Acts and Monuments*, viii, 326.
150 See, for example, Haller, *Foxe's Martyrs*; Olson, *John Foxe*, 75–87; Bauckham, *Tudor Apocalypse*; Firth, *Apocalyptic Tradition*.

instructed them in behaviour appropriate to their religion and sex.[151] One Robert Glover is reported to have instructed his wife, 'Set before your eyes always the examples of such as behaved themselves boldly in God's cause, as Stephen, Peter, Paul, Daniel ... and in your days, Anne Askew, Laurence Saunders, John Bradford, with many other faithful witnesses of Christ.'[152] William Tyms, a curate burned at Smithfield in 1556, wrote to the women of his parish, thanking them for their kindness, likening them to Susannah, Judith, Esther, Nabal's wife, Rahab, and Mary Magdalen, and urging them to 'remember the blessed martyr Anne Askew in our time, and follow her example of constancy'.[153] Foxe followed Bale in portraying Askew as a godly woman, concluding,

> And thus the good Anne Askew, with these blessed martyrs, being troubled so many manner of ways, and having passed through so many torments, having now ended the long course of her agonies, being compassed in the flames of fire, as a blessed sacrifice unto God, she slept in the Lord A.D. 1546.[154]

Nonetheless, Askew, like the virgin martyrs of the Middle Ages, is represented here as an *exceptional* rather than a typical woman, 'a singular example of christian constancy for all men to follow'.

In the Reformation, as in the Middle Ages, the woman who assumed a public role could find herself in conflict with the established Church. Askew's characterization of herself as 'harmless as a dove, wise as a serpent' undermines the conventional portrayal of the pious Protestant woman as chaste, silent and obedient. It is drawn from Scripture and Reformation teaching which emphasizes that women and men are equal before God and that anyone can be transformed by the Spirit. As inspired prophet and preacher, Askew assumed the authority to denounce error and interpret the will of God. Refusing the submissive role traditionally allocated to women, she is portrayed in the *Examinations* as forthright in her beliefs, and steadfast in her faith. Yet Askew acknowledged her trust in certain male clerics of her sect while she lived, and after her death her text owed its publication and survival to others, who in creating a Protestant martyr, glossed over her powerful and independent personality.

---

151 Warnicke, *Women*, 75–6; R.H. Bainton, 'John Foxe and the Woman Martyrs' in *Women of the Reformation in France and England* (Minneapolis, 1973), 211–29; C. Levin, 'Women in *The Book of Martyrs* as Models of Behaviour in Tudor England', *International Journal of Women's Studies* iv (1981), 196–201; E. Macek, 'The Emergence of a Feminine Spirituality in *The Book of Martyrs*', *Sixteenth-Century Journal* xix (1988), 63–80.

152 Foxe, *Acts and Monuments*, vii, 388.

153 Foxe, *Acts and Monuments*, viii, 114.

154 Foxe, *Acts and Monuments*, v, 550.

5

Alpha and Omega:
Eleanor Davies, Civil War Prophet

I am Alpha and Omega, the beginning and the ending, saith the Lord,
which is, and which was, and which is to come, the Almighty.

(Revelation 1.8)

Turning the World Upside Down

In 1633, tracts by Lady Eleanor Davies which had been printed in Amsterdam and then smuggled back into England were publicly burnt by Archbishop Laud. Davies herself was brought before the High Commission: the charges laid against her included that she had dared to interpret Scripture ('which much unbeseemed her Sex') and that she had falsely claimed to have received prophetic revelation.[1] Davies was an aristocrat and moved in court circles, but her social rank was not sufficient protection from the State's powers of retribution for the publication of seditious texts, and she was heavily fined and imprisoned. A year after her release from the Gatehouse in 1635 she desecrated the altar of Lichfield Cathedral, an act of protest against the episcopacy which was met by a general outcry; according to her own account the people's outrage resembled that over the Gunpowder Plot.[2] Davies was arrested and, in a desperate attempt to control her rebellious behaviour (it was feared that she might attack other churches),[3] she was committed without trial to Bedlam. In 1638, for reasons which are not specified in the surviving documents, she was moved to the Tower.[4] During the 1640s Davies enjoyed much greater freedom even though she was imprisoned for debt and infringements of the publishing laws on at least two more occasions, and in 1651, the year before her death, she was again jailed for a short period.[5]

---

1 Eleanor Davies, *The blasphemous charge against her* (1649), B1r.
2 Eleanor Davies, *Bethlehem signifying the house of bread* (1652), A3r.
3 Davies, *Bethlehem*, A3r–A3v.
4 *Calendar of State Papers, Domestic Series* (London, 1856–1924), 1640–1641, 21.
5 *Historical Manuscripts Commission Sixth Report* (London, 1877), appendix, 197.

The gatehouse salutation, printed in 1646, vividly describes Davies'
tribulations during her incarceration in Bedlam, her Bethlehem:

> Bethlems Manger sometime the Throne, as its describ'd, where she did grone;
> a Feather-bed cald otherwise, some Dormix curtains wrought with eyes; their
> work both sides alike doth shew, full of holes, besides all eaten so; A Rug
> and Blankets thereon laid, a woful prisoner, the aforesaid, whose companions
> tedious hours, no better Church then prisoners towers.[6]

The text identifies these verses with the new song of Revelation 5.9, and it
carries the direction that they are to be sung 'To the Tune of Magnificat'.[7]
Davies depicts her imprisonment as the antithesis of the world's future
redemption; the poem finishes triumphantly with the promise, 'So Gates
and Prison Doors be no more shut, / The King of Glory comes, your souls
life up.'[8] Allusions to a mystical encounter (the first of a series) which
occurred on 28 July 1625, recur throughout her writings. The apocalyptic
warning which she heard, 'There is Nineteen years and an half to the
Judgement day, and be you as the meek Virgin', clearly recalls the angel
Gabriel's visitation (Luke 1.26–38).[9] In describing herself as the handmaiden of God, Davies alludes to the Virgin's song as well as to the
Pentecostal prophecy of Acts. 2.18.[10] The events which followed Davies'
calling, the movement of Parliament to Reading and Oxford in 1625 and
her expedition to Amsterdam in 1633 are figured as the journey of the magi
and the flight into Egypt.[11] Her sorrow over the destruction of her tracts
suggests the tears of the *Mater Dolorosa* which foretold the cleansing and
rebirth bought by the sacrifice on the cross.[12]

Tropes of the Virgin and the Woman Clothed with the Sun appear
alongside biblical food metaphors, taken, for example, from the Book of
Daniel, and eucharistic imagery (both potent and empowering symbols for
many medieval women mystics, as is illustrated by Elizabeth Barton's
visions) to represent both communication with God and unity with
fellow believers.[13] Prophecy is perceived by Davies as a divine gift to be

6 Eleanor Davies, *The Gatehouse salutation from* (1647), A2v–A3r.
7 Davies, *Gatehouse salutation*, A2r and A4r.
8 Davies, *Gatehouse salutation*, A4r.
9 Eleanor Davies, *The Lady Eleanor her appeal* (1646), B1v.
10 Eleanor Davies, *The Lady Eleanor, her appeale* (1641), B2r.
11 Eleanor Davies, *The everlasting gospel* (1649), A3r–A4v.
12 Davies, *The everlasting gospel*, B1r–B1v.
13 See, for example, C.W. Bynum, *Jesus as Mother: Studies in the Spirituality of the High Middle Ages*, Publications of the Center for Medieval and Renaissance Studies UCLA 16 (Berkeley, 1982) 256–8; R. Bell, *Holy Anorexia* (Chicago, 1985); C.W. Bynum, *Holy Feast and Holy Fast: the Religious Significance of Food to Medieval Women* (Berkeley, 1987); on the relationship between such imagery and the fasting body of sevententh-century woman prophets, see D. Purkiss, 'Producing the Voice, Consuming

individually consumed but also to be passed on and shared with others: 'The Burthen of God Word received from Angelicall hands, The blessed Sacrament or Seale, eaten of the Lords comming at hand, & therfore commanded to be publishd even proclaimd beyond Sea.'[14] Just as Christ predicted His death during the Last Supper, the Second Coming is revealed in these sacramental tracts.[15] The acceptance of her message brings the promise of Christ's return and of universal salvation:

> Likewise this Sacramentall book containing the mistery of his second comming shewed to be at hand: commands it to be taken and eaten up, being compared to a womans travill: That for joy of a man child forgets her former paine and anguish. Likewise when this booke to be re-prophecied. . . . Yee now therefore have Sorrow, but I will see you again, and your heart shall rejoyce.[16]

The cult of the Virgin Mary had emerged in the early Church and gained enormous popularity in the later Middle Ages.[17] Medieval theologians argued that as Eve is our first and natural mother, so her archetype, the Virgin Mary, is our second and spiritual mother. Eve's error caused the Fall, but Mary gave the world the Redeemer. As Queen in Heaven, Mary was intercessor for sinners, the embodiment of mercy. Reformers not only questioned the notion of the Immaculate Conception (according to which the Virgin was conceived free from sin) and thus undermined the idea that she was the source of Christ's purity as well as His flesh, but they also challenged the Virgin's role as co-redeemer. Melanchthon claimed she supplanted Christ, the sole intercessor, 'just as if he were not the Reconciler but only a terrible Judge, desirous of revenge'.[18] Davies, however, did not question the Virgin's unique perfection, and in understanding the salvation offered by Christ to be a prefiguration of universal salvation, she conflated the figures of Christ and the Virgin Mary in the Gospels as precursors of her own role as the true second Eve: 'And thus his wayes equale, as this most proper to be done by that Sex: a Woman being the occasion of the worlds woe and undoeing: Therefore this PLAISTER or PARDON by a

the Body: Women Prophets of the Seventeenth Century' in *Women, Writing, History 1640–1740*, ed. I. Grundy and S. Wiseman (London, 1992), 139–58.
14 Eleanor Davies, *Great Brittains visitation* (1645), E3v–E4r.
15 Eleanor Davies, *Apocalypsis Jesu Christi* (1644), D3v.
16 Davies, *Apocalypsis Jesu Christi*, D3v–D4r.
17 On the Virgin Mary, see H. Graef, *Mary: a History of Doctrine and Devotion* (London, 1963–1965), i–ii; R.R. Ruether, *Mary: the Feminine Face of the Church* (London, 1979); J. Irwin, ed., *Womanhood in Radical Protestantism: 1525–1675* (New York, 1979), 1–8; and M. Warner, *Alone of All Her Sex: the Myth and the Cult of the Virgin Mary* (London, 1990).
18 Quoted by Graef, *Mary*, ii, 16.

Womans hand.'[19] Just as John Bale metaphorically describes Anne Askew, who had borne two children, as a spiritual maiden, so Davies, the mother of three, identifies with the Blessed Virgin Mary. As the mother of all, Davies gives birth to the promise of salvation, and the fruit of the tree of life is offered to the whole of humanity and after the Judgement will bring universal redemption, 'Not unlike the tree of Knowledge, at first pleasant to Him, afterward all as bitter: Nevertheless when the houre past, like her Travell the Mother of all living, rememberd not at all.'[20]

If Eleanor Davies' prophetic message is in itself extraordinary, the means by which she communicated it is no less so. Davies published almost seventy pamphlets between 1625 and 1652 (the year of her death).[21] Although, after 1640, religious and political prophecies spoken or written by women gained a significant hold in the publishing market, the early date of her first tracts, as well as her prolificness, affirm her literary and historical importance.[22] Nonetheless, Davies, like Elizabeth Barton, has been marginalized, although for rather different reasons. While Davies may have had no discernible effect on contemporary politics, the fact that her pamphlets were banned, confiscated, used in evidence against her and destroyed is an indication in itself that they had been read and at least partially understood. Yet Davies has been ignored by literary critics and historians who dismiss her texts as obscure and unreadable, and, like Margery Kempe, she has been

---

[19] Eleanor Davies, *The restitvtion of reprobates* (1644), C1r–C1v.

[20] Eleanor Davies, *The second comming of Our Lord* (1645), C3v.

[21] See my bibliography; C.J. Hindle, *A Bibliography of the Printed Pamphlets and Broadsides of Lady Eleanor Douglas the Seventeenth-Century Prophetess* (Edinburgh, 1936); and E.S. Cope, *Handmaid of the Holy Spirit: Dame Eleanor Davies, Never Soe Mad a Ladie* (Ann Arbor, 1992), 169–72. It is certain that not all Davies' works have survived. Most notably, none of the original versions now exist of a suppressed tract published in Amsterdam in 1633, entitled in the later editions *Given to the Elector Prince Charles of the Rhyne*. Copies of the first edition of this tract were publicly destroyed by the censors. A reference to a work by Davies entitled *The appeal to the throne* is recorded in *CSPD* 1637–1638, 219. *The new proclamation* (1649) appears to have been published by Davies but was actually written by her daughter Lucy Hastings, Countess of Huntingdon. *Strange and wonderfull prophesies* (1649), a reprint of one of Davies' prophetic poems, is included in my bibliography but may not have been published by her. Two unpublished poems have also survived: 'Hand writeing. October 1633. Exaudi Deus. psalme. 55' (London, Public Records Office State Papers 16/248, f. 212r (*CSPD*, 1633–1634, 266)); and 'When hee was come to the other side of the contrye' (PRO SP 16/345, f. 200r (*CSPD*, 1636–1637, 414): an autograph and signed verse, dated Lichfield January 1636). Cope has identified another unpublished tract, 'Bathe Daughter of Babylondon', amongst the Hastings Manuscripts in the Huntington Library. Some of Davies' tracts are reprinted as parts of her later pamphlets. For a modern edition of a selection of her tracts, see *Prophetic Writings of Lady Eleanor Davies*, ed. E.S. Cope (Oxford, 1995).

[22] B. Nelson, 'Lady Eleanor Davies: the Prophet as Publisher', *Women's Studies International Forum* viii (1985), 403–9.

characterized as hysterical and eccentric.[23] Keith Thomas suggests that 'the modern reader, to whom most of her effusions appear incomprehensible, may well be tempted to agree that she was insane'.[24] However, more recent studies of Davies' life, like that by Roy Porter, have recognized the importance of factors like gender and the religious milieu in the cultural construction of madness,[25] while contemporary feminist critics, using a variety of critical approaches, have produced positive readings of her texts.[26] If women's texts are not to remain in obscurity, critical judgements which reject certain genres and styles as sub-literary must be questioned, and more positive responses to the complexities of such writing have to be encouraged. Davies herself attacked the 'arrogancy begetting incureable blindness' of those who judge her tracts to be nonsense, likening herself to Galileo who 'cared for none of these matters', implying a comparison between his scientific discoveries and her own spiritual revelations.[27] Her fragmented syntax and idiosyncratic punctuation can be understood as an attempt to create an authentic and esoteric prophetic voice for the writer or secretary of God. Esther S. Cope argues that Davies is deliberately obscure and that, in keeping with established classical and Christian traditions, the 'seemingly inscrutable message' of her tracts 'demonstrated graphically how the unbeliever could not understand the wisdom of the prophet'.[28] Her narrative-prophetic voice is neither unified or stable. She saw herself variously as the type of Daniel, St John of the Apocalypse, the Virgin, or

---

[23] The only book length study is Cope's recent biography, *Handmaid of the Holy Spirit*. Articles about Davies include S.W.G, 'Dougle Fooleries', *Bodleian Quarterly Record* vii (1932), 95–8; T. Spenser, 'The History of An Unfortunate Lady', *Harvard Studies and Notes in Philology and Literature* xx (1938), 43–59; *Biographical Dictionary of British Radicals in the Seventeenth Century*, ed. L. Greaves and R. Zaller (Brighton, 1982), i, 216–17; E.S. Cope, ' "Dame Eleanor Davies Never Soe Mad a Ladie" ', *Huntington Library Quarterly* i (1987), 133–44; M. Matchinske, 'Holy Hatred: Formations of the Gendered Subject in English Apocalyptic Writing, 1625–1651', *English Literary History* lx (1993), 349–77; T. Feroli, 'The Sexual Politics of Mourning in the Prophecies of Eleanor Davies', *Criticism* xxxvi (1994), 359–82.

[24] K.V. Thomas, *Religion and the Decline of Magic: Studies in Popular Beliefs in Sixteenth and Seventeenth Century England* (London, 1971), 137–8.

[25] R. Porter, 'The Prophetic Body: Lady Eleanor Davies and the Meanings of Madness', *Women's Writing*, i (1994), 51–63; cf. M. Mcdonald, *Mystical Bedlam: Madness, Anxiety, and Healing in Seventeenth-Century England* (Cambridge, 1981).

[26] See, for example, the recent study which appears as a critical appendix in *A Bibliographical Dictionary of English Women Writers 1580–1720*, ed. M. Bell, C. Parfitt and S. Shepherd (Hemel Hempstead, 1990), 250–7, and 243–4. For an analysis of Davies' style which applies the theories of Irigaray and Kristeva, see C. Berg and P. Berry, 'Spiritual Whoredom: an Essay on Female Prophets in the Seventeenth Century' in *1642: Literature and Power in the Seventeenth Century*, ed. F. Barker, J. Bernstein, J. Coombes, P. Hulme, J. Stone and J. Stratton (Colchester, 1981), 37–54.

[27] Eleanor Davies, *The restitution of prophecy* (1651), A3v.

[28] Cope, *Handmaid*, 4.

the Woman Clothed with the Sun, indirectly constructing her identities by metonymy. In all her tracts except for the first, she referred to herself in the third person, self-effacement reminiscent of Margery Kempe's use of 'þis creature'. This also bears comparison with the writings of other women prophets of her own time, such as Anna Trapnel who again uses the third person with reference to herself.[29] It is a strategy which potentially facilitates the dislocation of an authoritative and thus male voice from the female body. Davies, however, erases herself as subject only to place herself in the position of the object of her discourse; in fact, she emphasizes her own status as both woman and aristocrat and the uniqueness of her role as prophet.

Davies' tracts cannot easily be read linearly and in order to understand the complexity of meaning, intertextuality and historical and biographical context have to be painstakingly retrieved and reconstructed. The narrative shifts freely between allegory and biblical exegesis, classical mythology, contemporary politics and autobiography. Davies' use of the Bible in her writings is particularly problematic. As God's secretary, she confronted orthodox theology, for example by challenging translations of Scripture or by asserting the authenticity of the Apocrypha.[30] She assumed that her readers would be as familiar with the Bible as she was herself and often did not supply any references, or only gave the first few words of a quotation. She also drew on language and imagery common to many prophetic texts of the period but quite unfamiliar to the twentieth-century reader, interpreting the events of her age by popular symbolic systems such as anagrams, astrology, heraldry, numerology and the doctrine of signatures in which letters and syllables derive meaning from (mis)spelling and associative puns. Aware that her texts were often difficult to understand, she defended them on the grounds that they were so full of meaning, 'That should it be written at large a Chronicle or a booke as ample as those tables, of the Mapps of the World could I suppose not contain it.'[31] She believed that her own works were superior to those of scholars: claiming absolute authority in discerning the will of God, she drew attention to the absence of endless rhetorical figures in her writing,[32] asserting that her own interpretations were 'not with Froath filled up, or Interlarded with differing Opinions of others'.[33]

It is difficult to trace direct influences on Davies' thought. She was certainly educated: she appears to have been able to read and write Latin, although her knowledge of Greek and Latin may have been derived from a

---

[29] On subjectivity in the writings of the women prophets, see especially D. Purkiss, 'Producing the Voice'.

[30] See, for example, Eleanor Davies, *Of errors ioyned with Gods word* (1645) which corrects the errors of translation in *King James his divine prophecie* (1645).

[31] Eleanor Davies, *From the Lady Eleanor, her blessing* (1644), E2v.

[32] Davies, *From the Lady Eleanor*, A3v.

[33] Davies, *From the Lady Eleanor*, A2r.

polyglot Bible, and she was acquainted with some classical literature and the Church Fathers, as well as some contemporary thinkers who addressed the question of universalism, namely John Goodwin and Gerrard Winstanley.[34] Davies was convinced that the end of the world was imminent, originally claiming that it would occur in 1644, and then predicting that the earth would be destroyed in a catastrophic flood in 1656. Such ideas were of course widespread in the Civil War period, but in her interpretations of history Davies makes no allusions to Joachim or any later apocalyptic writers.[35] There is no evidence, either, that she was familiar with the ideas of her near contemporary Jakob Boehme who described a female spirit of Wisdom which is the likeness of God.[36] Despite holding unconventional beliefs about salvation and the Sabbath, attacking the authority and corruption of the English Church, and denouncing Arminianism, idolatry and the vices of the world, Davies was neither a Puritan nor a sectarian. The significance she placed on the feasts of the church calendar and on the sacrament suggests indeed tendencies in the opposite direction. There is no reason to think that she joined a religious congregation, and, apart from Goodman, the only cleric whom she mentions is the royalist, Dr James Sibbald.[37] Cope notes a strong vein of conservatism in Davies' beliefs, which can almost certainly be explained by her aristocratic status: 'Countering the potentially radical content of her prophecies was her apparent acceptance of existing institutions.'[38]

As is the case (to a greater or lesser extent) with the other women prophets studied in this book, the world in which Davies was living was in a state of flux. Religious and political prophetic activity intensified at the end of Elizabeth's reign with the threat of Spanish invasion and the succession crisis (the Union of the English and Scottish Crowns in 1603 was felt by

[34] On Davies' religious background and education, see Cope, *Handmaid*, 10–13; on Goodwin and Winstanley, see below.

[35] See K.R. Firth, *The Apocalyptic Tradition in Reformation Britain 1530–1645* (Oxford, 1979); R. Bauckham, *Tudor Apocalypse. Sixteenth Century Apocalypticism, Millennarianism and the English Reformation: from John Bale to John Foxe and Thomas Brightman*, Courtenay Library of Reformation Classics 8 (Oxford, 1978); P. Christianson, *Reformers and Babylon: English Apocalyptic Visions from the Reformation to the Eve of the Civil War* (Toronto, 1978); C. Hill, *The World Turned Upside Down: Radical Ideas During the English Revolution* (London, 1972).

[36] On Boehme, see N. Smith, *Perfection Proclaimed: Language and Literature in English Radical Religion 1640–1660* (Oxford, 1989), 185–225. For Boehme's influence on the visionary Jane Lead, a key member of the Philadelphian Society, see C.F. Smith, 'Jane Lead: the Feminist Mind and Art of a Seventeenth-Century Protestant Mystic' in *Women of Spirit: Female Leadership in the Jewish and Christian Traditions*, ed. R. Ruether and E. McLaughlin (New York, 1979), 183–203; and C.F. Smith, 'Jane Lead: Mysticism and the Woman Cloathed with the Sun' in *Shakespeare's Sisters: Feminist Essays on Women Poets*, ed. S.M. Gilbert and S. Gubar (Bloomington, 1979), 3–18.

[37] See Cope, *Handmaid*, 47, 96, 105 and 146.

[38] Cope, *Handmaid*, 166.

many to be the fulfilment of the prophecy of Merlin and Thomas of Erceldoune),[39] and prophetic rhetoric was central to political discourse during the Civil War and Interregnum. Dobin observes that 'English Society, despite the efforts of the church and state, consisted of a swelling cacophony of individual prophetic voices.'[40] The definition of prophecy extended to include the preaching of the word of God, and Puritans emphasized the importance of private spirituality, relying on the 'inner light' of individual inspiration, rather than authority and tradition, in order to interpret Scripture. Many people in the seventeenth century believed that through prophecy God communicated directly with His children. To be blessed with the gift of prophecy was an indication of salvation, a sign that an individual was one of the elect. Often prophecy combined interpretation of Scripture with 'experimental theology' in which knowledge of God was perceived through the experience of the regenerate.[41] Nigel Smith has attempted to distinguish Eleanor Davies from the sectarian prophets, arguing that her exegetical predictions reflect instead the classical notion of the *vates* who foretells the future in an inspired vision, and focuses on God's plan for mankind rather than private experience of the Divine.[42] Certainly Davies perceived herself as a Christian soothsayer, comparing her own predictions about the death of Buckingham to the warning given to Julius Caesar to beware the ides of March.[43] However, although her writings are not confessional and do not contain extended self-examination, Davies does represent her prophecy as an extension of her own identity, describing it as 'this Babe, or little Booke',[44] and as this chapter will illustrate, her prophecies have an allegorical content and reveal a concern with the working of God in her own life, bringing her closer than is sometimes recognized to other more frequently studied prophets of the seventeenth century.

Following a tradition of female prophecy which had emerged at various times in the preceding centuries and was seen in many European heretical and radical religious groups such as the Anabaptists,[45] increasing numbers

---

[39] H. Dobin, *Merlin's Disciples: Prophecy, Poetry, and Power in Renaissance England* (Stanford, 1990), 105–15.
[40] Dobin, *Merlin's Disciples*, 33.
[41] Smith, *Perfection Proclaimed*, 26–7.
[42] Smith, *Perfection Proclaimed*, 32; cf. P. Mack, *Visionary Women: Ecstatic Prophecy in Seventeenth-Century England* (Berkeley, 1992), 91; and Cope, *Handmaid*, 13.
[43] Eleanor Davies, *The revelation interpreted* (1646), A3r–A3v.
[44] Davies, *Apocalypsis Jesu Christi*, D2r.
[45] See, for example, the account of a sixteenth-century Anabaptist woman in Strasbourg, whose revelations were published by a male spiritualist, in M.E. Wiesner, 'Nuns, Wives, and Mothers: Women and the Reformation in Germany' in *Women in Reformation and Counter-Reformation Europe*, ed. S. Marshall (Bloomington, 1989), 16. See also M.E. Wiesner, *Women and Gender in Early Modern Europe* (Cambridge, 1993), 203–10.

of women between the 1640s and 1660s spoke out publicly on religio-political issues, and sometimes their words were written down and put into print.[46] In *The resurrection of the witnesses*, published in 1648, the Fifth Monarchist Mary Cary argued that 'Every Saint in a sense, may be said to be a Prophet, For they are Prophets to whom God discovers his secrets: and there is no true saints, but the secrets of God are discovered to them', going on to say that 'when the Lord hath revealed himself unto the soul and discovered his secrets to it . . . the soul cannot choose but declare them to others . . . yet he that speaketh to edification, exhortation and consolation, though with much weaknesse, doth as truly prophesie as he that hath greatest abilities'.[47] While Eleanor Davies did not even argue for the ordination of women, in some sects women became empowered as leaders, instructors and preachers: Cary, for example, saw herself in the role of minister, and Katherine Chidley organized Leveller protests during the trials of their leader John Lilburne, writing and presenting the women's petitions and manifestos.[48] Yet, as Phyllis Mack points out, even the Fifth Monarchists, a sect in which women played an active part, 'insisted on a distinction not only between preaching and prophesying but between prophesying as a leader of the church and as a "mere" vessel of God'.[49] Despite claiming that women could prophesy, Mary Cary denied her own agency, calling herself 'a very weake, and unworthy instrument' and likening herself to 'a pencill or pen.'[50] A decade and a half later, the Quaker Margaret Fell still recognized the necessity of challenging St Paul's prohibitions of women's speech, citing Scriptural examples of women acting as God's messengers and arguing that Paul was only addressing churches in confusion: 'And what is all this to Womens Speaking? that have the Everlasting Gospel to preach, and upon whom the Promise of the Lord is fulfilled, and his Spirit poured upon them according to his Word.'[51]

---

[46] On women prophets as writers, see E. Hobby, *Virtue of Necessity: English Women's Writing 1649–88* (London, 1988), 26–53; P. Mack, 'Women as Prophets During the English Civil War', *Feminist Studies* viii (1982), 19–45; S. Wiseman, 'Unsilent Instruments and the Devil's Cushions: Authority in Seventeenth-Century Women's Prophetic Discourse' in *New Feminist Discourses: Critical Essays on Theories and Texts*, ed. I. Armstrong (London, 1992), 176–96; Mack, *Visionary Women*, especially 87–124; and Purkiss, 'Producing the Voice', 139–58. For an anthology which includes extracts of some of these writings, see *Her Own Life: Autobiographical Writings of Seventeenth-Century Englishwomen*, ed. E. Graham, H. Hinds, E. Hobby and H. Wilcox (London, 1989).

[47] Mary Cary, *The resurrection of the witnesses* (1648), F1r–F2r.

[48] I. Gentles, 'London Levellers in the English Revolution: the Chidleys and their Circle', *Journal of Ecclesiastical History* xxix (1978), 292–4.

[49] Mack, *Visionary Women*, 107.

[50] Mary Cary, *The little horn's doom and downfall* (1651), A8r.

[51] Margaret Fell, *Women's speaking justified* (1666), A4v; for other defences, see Hobby, *Virtue of Necessity*, 43–4.

The whole range of women's prophetic experience (apocalyptic, political or apolitical, mystical and visionary) demonstrated in the preceding centuries was revived in the seventeenth century. Mary Cary, like Davies, believed that the book of Daniel was about to be fulfilled, urging the saints to take up arms in order to bring about the New Jerusalem, although, unlike Davies, her utopian vision of a Godly Commonwealth had radical social and religious implications. Opposition to the Protectorate was expressed by another Fifth Monarchist woman, Anna Trapnel, whose very public trances and fastings, like those of her predecessor, the Baptist, Sarah Wight, resemble the ecstacies and torments of Elizabeth Barton: for example, Wight's body, like Barton's, became the site of the triumph of good over evil, when she was healed from experiencing the pains of damnation, 'walking daily in the midst of fire and brimstone, as one in Hell, already'.[52] One of Trapnel's tracts, a self-justificatory account of her trial, also has parallels with both Margery Kempe's *Book* and Anne Askew's *Examinations* – once more the woman filled with the spirit of God, imitates Christ and his Apostles and outmanoeuvres her persecutors. Trapnel, who was accused of witchcraft, was twice arrested for travelling and preaching around the country. She was regarded with suspicion, much as Kempe and Askew were, because she was not accompanied by a husband, and defended herself, saying 'Then having no hinderance, why may not I go where I please, if the Lord so will?'[53] Some religious writings by women urge withdrawal from worldly concerns, such as An Collins's work in verse, *Divine songs and meditacions* (1653), written 'for the benifit, and comfort of others, Cheifly for those Christians who are of disconsolat Spirits, who may perceive herein, the Faithfullnesse, Love, & Tender Compassionatnesse of God to his people'.[54] Reminiscent in certain respects of parts of *The Book of Margery Kempe*, this collection of poems and songs interweaves autobiographical narrative with contemporary and biblical history. Confined to the house by a debilitating illness, Collins was converted from her state of ignorance and found a vocation in poetry.[55] She urges others to withdraw not only from political involvement, but also from marriage and family life, in order to experience a mystical union with the true spouse, Christ.[56]

An Collins may well have published her own texts (although very little is known about her life, beyond what she herself reveals), but even after

---

52 See Henry Jessey, *The exceeding riches off grace advanced* (1647), B5r; cf. B.R. Dailey, 'The Visitation of Sarah Wight: Holy Carnival and the Revolution of the Saints in Civil War London', *Church History* lv (1986), 438–55.

53 *Anna Trapnel's report and plea* (1654), d1v.

54 An Collins, *Divine songs and meditacions* (1653), A2v.

55 Collins, *Divine songs*, A3r.

56 See, for example, Collins' 'A Song expressing their happinesse who have Communion with Christ' in *Divine songs*, C6v–D1r.

1640 when more women were organizing the printing of their tracts on private presses, Eleanor Davies was exceptional because of the extent to which she thought, spoke and acted independently. Some women prophets, like Elizabeth Poole who was expelled from the Baptists after opposing the General Council's intention to execute the King, were not authorized by their churches. Others, such as Trapnel, were encouraged to have their prophecies written down by members of their congregations. Whereas Davies acted in defiance of both her husbands, many women remained subject to the guidance of men, whether their spouses or their church leaders. In 1647, for example, Henry Jessey published an account of the experiences of Sarah Wight; and in 1654, Arise Evans edited and published Elinor Channel's prophecy as *A message from God (by a dumb woman)*, imposing his own royalist interpretation on it. Mary Cary's *The little horn's doom and downfall* was mediated by introductions by three men, Hugh Peter, Henry Jessey and Christopher Feake, all of whom betrayed their anxiety about the sex of the writer. These women were not, however, simply the instruments of various religious and political camps: Mack notes that not only did they 'display an understanding of the economic and political issues of the time; they also turned visionary language into a form of political resistance'.[57]

Despite her assurance that she herself was Elijah promised in the Last Age, Eleanor Davies may not have had the support of a religious group, but she did not completely ignore the existence of other contemporary prophets. In one tract, she includes a marginal reference to the prophetess Grace Cary, a Bristol widow whose bloody visions of the King's fate would seem to confirm her own revelations,[58] and, in another, she published some prophetic letters written by her second husband.[59] But as an aristocrat, Davies does stand apart from her Civil War successors, many of whom were sectarians and from the lower ranks of society; Anna Trapnel, for example, was the daughter of a shipwright. Davies' wealth, education and social prominence are all factors which may have contributed to her early access to print culture. Her example illustrates that social rank was no more of a bar to the adoption of a prophetic voice than formal education or lack of it, and that women of a wide range of religious persuasions might hear God's calling. She is an exceptional figure, not only because she found her vocation at such an early date, or because she operated independently of any religious sect or movement, but also because of her unusual status as publisher as well as writer of her works, and because of her personal theology, which I discuss further in the next sections. Although parallels can be drawn between Eleanor Davies' prophesying and that of her male

---

[57] Mack, *Visionary Women*, 119.

[58] *Given to the Elector* (1651), A3r; on Grace Cary, see Cope, *Handmaid*, 36–7.

[59] Eleanor Davies, *The new Jerusalem at hand* (1649).

contemporaries, her voice can be distinguished as feminine because of the extent to which it is constructed through tropes – for example, images of the Eucharist, virginity and childbirth – which, although certainly not exclusive to women's prophecy, are not only gendered female, but which also have specific resonances for women. In the final section I argue that Eleanor Davies' universalism is distinct from that of other prophets such as Gerrard Winstanley because it has a particular relevance to this specifically feminine prophetic voice. It was noted in the second chapter that earlier women visionaries like Margery Kempe and Julian of Norwich also expressed anxiety about the doctrine of eternal damnation, and suggested that the implied universalism of the latter's theology is related to her extended exploration of the metaphor of a maternal Christ and sublimation of the concept of mercy (often perceived as feminine). Similarly, Eleanor Davies' vision of universal salvation and her construction of God as feminine are connected: Davies herself becomes 'a Woman by whom death came to be the Messenger of Life'.[60]

Prophesying and Publishing

In Davies' first pamphlet, *A warning to the dragon and all his angels*, political developments in Europe were interpreted as a fulfilment of Daniel 7–12 and the prophecies of Revelation. Davies found scriptural evidence for a periodization of Christian history which culminated in a final age of Roman profanity and the now imminent Judgement, a time when the age of martyrdom is ended. The four beasts of Daniel 7 represent the four kingdoms: the lion of Judah; the devouring bear of the Roman Empire; the beast, half leopard and half lion, which stands for the division of the Empire; and the horned papal Anti-Christ. Davies approved of her country's intervention in the Thirty Years War; James was 'our Prince of Great Britaine and Ireland, that fights and contends with the Enemies of the Lord'.[61] The pamphlet was dedicated to 'THE GREAT PRINCE, the King of Great BRITAINE, FRANCE, and IRELAND, Defender of the Faith', and included prayers for Charles I and Henrietta Maria.[62] However in later tracts, Davies denounced the Stuart monarchy which had ignored her 1625 tract and prohibited her later publications, forcing her to take flight abroad like the adolescent Joseph.[63] Subsequently, she revised her allegory: Michael no

---

60 Davies, *From the Lady Eleanor*, E2r.
61 Eleanor Davies, *A warning to the dragon and all his angels* (1625), H3r. For Bale's periodization of Christian history, see above, Chapter Four.
62 Davies, *A warning to the dragon*, B1r and a2v.
63 Davies, *The Lady Eleanor, her appeale* (1641), A2r.

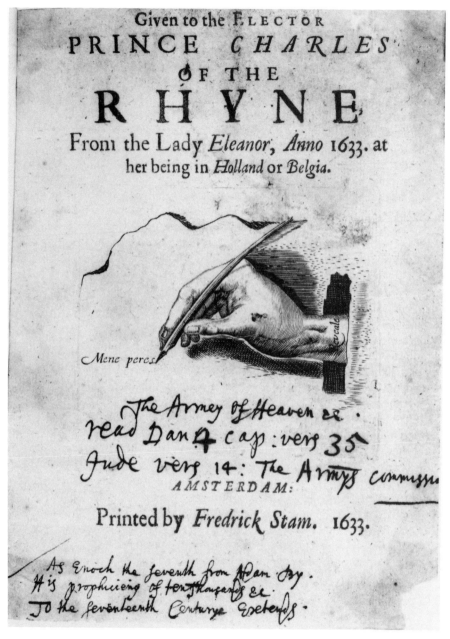

Fig. 7. The writing on the wall, a warning to Charles I. From Eleanor Davies'
Given to the Elector Prince Charles of the Rhyne (1648). Oxford,
Worcester College Library, BB x 6. Illustrated title page.

longer signified a heroic Protestant king but England itself.[64] Similarly, Davies brought out new editions of 'To Sion most belov'd I sing', which caused an outcry when it was first published because it compared Charles I to the Old Testament king Belshazzar, in which she reinterpreted her prophetic poem in the light of developments in the political situation in the British Isles and Europe.[65] Some of these editions are illustrated by a picture of the hand of God writing on the wall (Daniel 5) [fig. 7]. One conclusion which can be drawn from the existence of the two tracts *Prophetia de die* (1644) and *A prophesie of the last day* (1645), which have substantially the same content, is that the former tract, which is in Latin, was specifically intended for foreign distribution; certainly Davies believed that her prophecies were of significance to the whole world.[66] Nonetheless, she jealously controlled their publication: at the end of a tract entitled *Samsons legacie* (1643) appears the command 'None offer without Priviledge, to Reprint These.'[67] She may not have always been successful. On 25 August 1649, Theodore Jennings printed yet another edition of 'To Sion most belov'd I sing' as *Strange and wonderful prophesies*. However, although Davies did not organize this publication, she does not seem to have opposed it.[68]

Davies' first tract, *A warning to the dragon and all his angels*, was published without a license, possibly by the London printer Bernard Alsop. It was not perceived to be dangerous by the authorities and no attempt was made to suppress it.[69] Davies did not publish any more prophecies until eight years later when she travelled to the continent on the pretence of accompanying her second husband Archibald Douglas to the spa. In fact she had planned the journey in order to organize the printing of tracts which included another interpretation of Daniel, a broadside attack on her brother's accusers (Mervin Touchet, Earl of Castlehaven, had been executed for sodomy and rape in 1631), and the song 'To Sion most belov'd I sing'.[70] She explained her reasons for her journey thus:

> Constrained for printing to go into Holland . . . pretending in her husbands behalf the Spaw obtained a Licence, since none for printing to be had here,

---

64 Davies, *The Lady Eleanor, her appeale* (1641), B3r.
65 Eleanor Davies, *Amend, amend; Gods kingdome is at hand* (1643); *Given to the Elector Prince Charles of the Rhyne from the Lady Eleanor* (1648) and *Given to the Elector* (1651); and *Strange and wonderful prophesies*.
66 Davies claimed that she was not only given 'the Burthen' of prophecy, but also commanded by God to publish abroad: *Great Brittains visitation*, E3v–E4r.
67 Eleanor Davies, *Samsons legacie* (1643), D4v.
68 At least one copy of Davies' *Strange and wonderful prophesies* has additions added to the printed text in Davies' handwriting; see Hindle, *Bibliography*, 26.
69 Davies brought her tract to the attention of the censors by presenting a copy to Archbishop Abbot: Eleanor Davies, *The Lady Eleanor her appeal* (1646), B2r.
70 Eleanor Davies, *All the kings of the earth shall prayse thee* (Amsterdam, 1633); *Amend, amend; Given to the Elector*; and *Woe to the house* (Amsterdam, 1633).

inquisition and hold such, among them imprisoned about it formerly, till afterward all as free, Cum Privilegio out of date become.[71]

Although Eleanor Davies was viewed by some as a seer, and even consulted about the Queen's first pregnancy by a royal servant and then by Henrietta Maria herself, in the years between 1625 and 1633, she had encountered hostility, scepticism and opposition from both her first and second husbands and also from the royal household because of her predictions, especially her prognostication about Buckingham's death and the personal warnings which she had given to the King.[72] John Davies and Archibald Douglas successively attempted to restrain her activities by burning her manuscripts. Presumably Eleanor Davies could not get her prophecies printed in England, but in Amsterdam she was able to employ J.F. Stam. She evidently feared the consequences of her actions as she sought the protection of Elizabeth of Bohemia, who wrote to Charles I on her behalf.[73] Elizabeth's intervention was unsuccessful and after returning to England Davies was arrested. In defiance of the court she refused to offer any submission or acknowledge her offence.[74] Her sentence was severe: she was fined £3,000 and imprisoned, and her books were burnt in St Paul's Churchyard.

The events of the trial and imprisonment in 1633 recur throughout Davies' writings. She was charged with compiling seditious or 'fanatical' prophecies, with smuggling them abroad and having them printed, and with disseminating them in England.[75] The Court of the High Commission, led in 1633 by Archbishop Laud, took the opportunity of the trial to attack her prophetic role. In full, her condemnation read that

> she took upon her (which much unbeseemed here Sex) not only to interpret the Scriptures, and withal the most intricate and hard places of the Prophet Daniel, but also to be a Prophetess, falsely pretending to have received certain Revelations from God.[76]

At the trial Laud burnt her pamphlet and scorned her warning that 1644 was to be the year of judgement, and one of the commissioners is said to have ridiculed the anagram which she made of her name, 'ELEANOR AUDELEY:

---

[71] Eleanor Davies, *The everlasting gospel* (1649), A4v–B1r.

[72] See Eleanor Davies, *The Lady Eleanor her appeal* (1646), B3v–D2r.

[73] This letter, dated 12/22 September 1633, is quoted in the *CSPD* Addenda 1625–1649, 458.

[74] *CSPD*, 1634–1635, 176.

[75] Eleanor Davies, *The blasphemous charge against her* (1649), B1r–B1v; the description of her prophecies as 'fanatical' is quoted in *CSPD*, 1633–1634, 480.

[76] Davies, *The blasphemous charge*, B1r. Davies' account of the charges against her is largely confirmed by a letter from one Nicholas to Captain John Pennington, dated 28 October 1633. A description of the contents of this letter is given in the *CSPD*, 1633–1634, 260–1.

REVEALE O DANIEL', by presenting her with another, 'DAME ELEANOR DAVIES, NEVER SO MAD A LADIE'.[77] Davies waged a long-running vendetta against Laud for his part in this trial. When he was beheaded she saw this as punishment for his scepticism and the fulfilment of her first prophetic message: 'in truth his own fatal hour, those years of Nineteen and a half, reaching to his Execution Moneth and Year, Anno 44. January, when parted head and body'.[78]

After her arrest in 1633, Davies petitioned the King to license the banned pamphlets.[79] She personified her interpretations of the Book of Daniel and Revelation as the Two Witnesses of Revelation who had been murdered (the tracts torn apart and burned), but which would be resurrected by the printing press:

> The B: BEAST ascended out of the Bottomlesse pitt: having seven Heads, &c. seven Yeares, viz. making Warre hath overcome, and killed them: Bookes sealed by the Prophets. By the Bishop of Lambeth horned like the Lambe, harted like a Wolfe, are condemned to be burned at Pauls-Crosse, where our Lord crucified &c. This is the third Day, that their dead Bodies shrowded in loose sheets of paper. Lye in the streets of the Great Citie, &c. more cruell and hard harted, then other tongues and Nations, who will not suffer them so to be buried. If your Highnesse please to speake the word the spirit of life will enter into them they will stand upon their feet, &c.[80]

Davies' apocalyptic imagery places her firmly in the apocalyptic tradition: the violent suppression of her tracts 'unto a senceless, saltless age sent' is described in terms of an assault 'by merciless, desperate men'.[81] Much later, in a pamphlet entitled *Hells destruction* (1652), she likened herself to the persecuted saints described in Revelation 2.10. She interpreted her arrest on 17 July 1646 for non-payment of a debt as a sign of the imminence of the end of the world, giving her experience both current and cosmic significance by associating it with the Civil War massacres which she believed to have been presaged by the appearance in 1572 of a new star in Cassiopeia.[82] In a passage reminiscent of John Bale's description of the thunder which roared as Anne Askew was martyred in the fire at Smithfield, she described a terrible storm which broke out after she had been locked in a damp and rat-infested cell in Woodstreet Compter: 'That Night till day break, the Heavens without intermission flashing out Lightnings, as Noon-

---

77 Peter Heylyn, *Cyprianus Anglicus* (1668), 266.
78 Davies, *The everlasting gospel*, B1v.
79 Eleanor Davies, *To the Kings most excellent majesty: the humble petition* (1648); and *As not unknowne, . . . this petition* (1645); cf. *CSPD*, 1633–1634, 346.
80 Davies, *As not unknowne*; and *Historical Manuscripts Commission Sixth Report*, appendix, 197.
81 Eleanor Davies, *Apocalyps, chap. 11. Its accomplishment* (1648), A1v.
82 Eleanor Davies, *Hells destruction* (1651), B3v–B4r.

day; The Element like a Casemate standing open, without Thunder at all, or any Rain, those continued fireworks notwithstanding.'[83] The unnatural storm was a supernatural indication of the injustice of Davies' imprisonment.

In her tracts of the 1640s and early 1650s, Davies expressed her anger at religious and political abuses, claiming that these were not the times for the 'flattering Pencil, or falsifying Pen', and demanding that neither sex be inhibited from unsheathing the two-edged sword of the spirit of prophecy.[84] Her phallic metaphor has a subversive force: woman can also claim the power which she believes was previously accessible only to men. The overturning of the limitations of gender had important implications for Davies. The production of her tracts was an independent endeavour – whereas the works of many other women prophets were transmitted by male editors and writers, Davies, often in the face of enormous difficulties, organized for herself the printing and distribution of her works. The vivid account of her imprisonment in *Hells destruction* incidentally reveals the extent to which she was concerned with overseeing the printing of her tracts: Davies had owed £60 to her printer Thomas Paine, and in order to facilitate her arrest, Paine had lured her to his shop by telling her that he had lost the copy text of one of her tracts.[85] Davies was also concerned that the word of God spoken through her should be accurately transmitted. A number of her works exist in multiple editions and issues, some containing quite minute corrections. The collection of Eleanor Davies' tracts in the Folger Shakespeare Library, which may originally have come from her daughter's library, includes a large number of pamphlets with corrections, additions and cancellations in the hand of the author.[86] Elaine Hobby's examination of

---

[83] Davies, *Hell's destruction*, B2v.

[84] Eleanor Davies, *The bill of excommunication* (1649), D4r.

[85] Davies, *Hells destruction*, B1r–B2v. Only one of Davies' tracts names Paine as the printer: Eleanor Davies, *Prophetia de die* (*Excudebat Tho. Paine*, 1644). However Paine's printer's device appears in a number of Davies' texts in or before 1646: *From the Lady Eleanor*; *The restitvtion of reprobates*; *For the blessed feast of Easter* (1646); and *The revelation interpreted* (1646). For Paine's device, see the title-page border which Paine is recorded as using: R.B. McKerrow and F.S. Ferguson, *Title-page Borders used in England and Scotland 1485–1640* (London, 1632), 172–3 (and cf. no. 214). The central portion of the sill with *fleur de lis* (25 mm by 45 mm) occurs as his device on the title-page of *Prophetia de die* (1644). It is possible that Paine was responsible for all or most of Davies' tracts (with the exception of the first) published in England until her arrest at his printing house brought their business relationship to an end. Paine, a London-based printer, was associated with radical sectarianism (printing, for example, Thomas Killcop's *Seekers svpplyed* in 1646), and it is therefore not surprising that Davies should have chosen to use his press; see the list of his publications in P.G. Morrison, *Index of Printers, Publishers and Booksellers in Donald Wing's Short-Title Catalogue* (Charlottesville VA, 1955). The printers of Davies' tracts after 1646 have not been identified.

[86] I have had access to microfilms of the Folger's collection of Davies' tracts.

several copies of *Elijah the Tishbite's supplication* (1650) reveals that Davies transcribed identical corrections into each.[87] Sometimes such handwritten corrections formed the basis of new issues or editions.[88]

Davies demanded that those in power should read and act upon her prophecies. Her early tracts were dedicated to Elizabeth of Bohemia and to Prince Charles of the Rhine, and she presented or sent manuscripts and pamphlets to Archbishop Abbot, Charles I, General Fairfax and Oliver Cromwell, and wrote petitions and appeals to Parliament. Her belief in the singularity of her role as prophet lent an urgency to her insistence that she be listened to. In one of her last tracts, *The appearance* (1650), she claimed the authority of Christ to deliver the promise of the imminent arrival of the Son of Man. She reinterpreted Christ's invitation (in Mark 4.23 and elsewhere), 'If any man have ears to hear, let him hear' as an open threat, 'He that hath an ear (to wit) on pain or peril of his head.'[89] Even Parliament had no right to ignore her message:

> Proclaiming no other then the Supreme Order or Authority, their unlimitted Commission: The Spirit after absent so long, now (as it were) stands knocking at the door: whereof these the sum or substance of no inferior consequence: A greater then the Conquerer, Parliaments Prerogative not exempted.[90]

The Conqueror was Oliver Cromwell, whom Eleanor Davies identified with the rider on the white horse of Revelation 6.2.[91] The message proclaimed was that of The Book of Revelation 2.26–8: those who hold on until the arrival of the Son of God will rule with a rod of iron, able to dash nations to pieces and they will see their enemies, smashed like pottery, or, in Davies' evocative and intensely personal phrase, 'scattered, suddenly a Printers Press like'.[92]

In the 1640s changes in the political situation in England had resulted in a free press ('*Cum Privelegio* out of date become'): the Star Chamber and High Commission were abolished by the Long Parliament, removing the controls on printing which these courts had previously exercised.[93] Successive attempts to reintroduce restrictions failed to re-establish an effective censorship system. Many texts which would previously have been suppressed, including an unprecedented number by women, could now be

---

87 Hobby, *Virtue of Necessity*, 28.
88 Cf. the notes to no. 46 in Hindle, *Bibliography*, 29; Hindle draws attention to the fact that Davies' hand corrections in the first issue of *The benediction* (1651: Oxford, Bodleian Library, 12 1336(5)) are incorporated into the later editions.
89 Eleanor Davies, *The appearance* (1650), A2r.
90 Davies, *The appearance*, A2r–A2v.
91 Cf. Davies, *The benediction* (1651), A2r.
92 Davies, *The appearance*, A2v.
93 D. Thomas, *A Long Time Burning: the History of Literary Censorship in England* (London, 1969), 12–13.

published.[94] Davies was freer than previously to publish her tracts. None-theless, right up to her death in 1652, Davies' prophecies continued to be viewed with suspicion by those in power. Only one text, that published by Theodore Jennings, carried an imprimatur.[95] According to a note made by Thomason, the fragmented tract *A prophesie of the last day* was seized at the press on 17 January 1644.[96] In *Her appeal from the court to the camp* (1649), addressed to General Fairfax, Davies attempted to counter doubts about her authenticity by requesting that some of the faithful be sent to test her spirit of prophecy.[97] In *Before the Lords second coming* she argues that it is no wonder that so many were charged with abusing toleration and liberty of conscience when 'higher Powers express no better use made of theirs, then by leasing and scoffing to abuse the Holy Ghosts long-suffering'.[98] She was angered by Parliament's introduction of new legisla-tion for licensing the press in June 1643. In November of that year she published a tract which lamented the fact that sermons and dedications were authorized daily while her own texts remained unlicensed. Echoing the words of Christ recorded in Matthew 26.11, she pleaded: 'Preaching ye have alway, and may hear them when ye please, and their large Dedicatories and Volumns may License them daily: But the little Book, The Spirit of Prophesie, Not alway that.'[99] Davies attacked those texts which were licensed:

> Fictions of fresh edition, University Excrements daily, whereby oppressing Shops and Presses with them: overflowing too shameful, whilest Close-Stools set to sale, lined through with Scriptures old and new: When Turks, lest Gods name therein, refrain to set their foot on a leaf of Paper, whose Alcoran Mahomets the false Prophets, Cum Privilegio, &c.[100]

Her satire is reminiscent of Thomas Nashe's description of the 'purgations

---

94 For an extensive bibliography of women in print, 1649–1688, see Hobby, *Virtue of Necessity*, 228–45.

95 Davies, *Strange and wonderful prophecies*, A1r.

96 This fragment is recorded as *I am the first, and the last* (*Short-Title Catalogue 1641–1700*, compiled D. Wing (New York, 1972–1988), D1996; Hindle, *Bibliography*, 13): London, British Library, Thomason Collection E25(4).

97 Eleanor Davies, *Her appeal from the court to the camp* (1649), π1v.

98 Eleanor Davies, *Before the Lords second coming* (1650), B3r.

99 Eleanor Davies, *The star to the wise* (1643), C1v.

100 Davies, *The restitution of prophecy*, D2r. In *Areopagitica*, Milton criticized 'all the sermons, all the lectures preached, printed, vended in such numbers and such volumes as have now well nigh made all other books unsaleable': *Complete Poems and Major Prose*, ed. M.Y. Hughes (New York, 1957), 737. A translation of the Koran was first printed by Wynkyn de Worde in the early sixteenth century; it was republished in 1649.

and vomits wrapt vppe in waste paper' infecting St Paul's Churchyard and the 'goose gyblets or stinking garbage' sold by stationers and booksellers.[101]

In defiance of the Parliamentary Order of 1643, Milton published without a licence his controversial *The Doctrine and Discipline of Divorce*, following it in 1644 with his *Areopagitica*, in which he wrote that the book censored before publication was in worse condition than 'a peccant soul, should be to stand before a jury ere it be born to the world and undergo yet in darkness the judgment of Rhadamanth and his colleagues'.[102] Davies depicted her prophecy as a child in danger, developing a comparison between the difficult publication of her pamphlets and the birth and circumcision of Christ:

> THis Babe, object to their scorn, for speaking the truth, informing of things future, notwithstanding thus difficult to be fathered or licensed. That incission to the quick, hath under gone; without their Benediction, in these plain Swathe-bands, though commended unto thy hands.[103]

In describing licensing as fathering, Davies implies that it should be a protective process of patronage.[104] However, her own texts, like Christ himself, have no earthly father. Davies wrote and published with divine rather than worldly authority; she needed no other sponsor than God.

The Prophetic Mission – Restitution and Salvation

It was not only as writer and publisher that Eleanor Davies entered the public sphere and transgressed the norms of feminine activity. Davies believed that her behaviour could have prophetic significance: for the prophet, the messenger of a God whose words are deeds, words without deeds were meaningless.[105] In 1636 Eleanor Davies entered Lichfield Cathedral, sat on the Bishop's throne and declared that she was Primate and Metropolitan, and then, pouring tar over the altar, told worshippers 'that she had sprinkled holie water upon the same against their Communion there next'.[106] Prior to this attack, she had sent the Bishop a book entitled *The appeal to the throne*

---

101 *The Works of Thomas Nashe*, ed. R.B. McKerrow, rev. F.P. Wilson (Oxford, 1966), i, 239.

102 John Milton, *Complete Poems and Major Prose*, 725.

103 Davies, *The restitution of prophecy*, A2r.

104 The *OED* does not give any examples of the verb 'father' being applied to the licensing of texts, although it does cite the noun, as 'one who exercises protecting care ... with reference to patronage of literature'. As a verb, 'father' can have the meaning 'to ascribe (something) to (a person) as his production or work': *OED* s.v. 'father'.

105 See the opening lines of Davies' tract, *And without proving what we say* (1648), A1r.

106 PRO SP 16/380, ff. 138v–139r (*CSPD*, 1637–1638, 219).

(no copies of which now exist).[107] Such behaviour was not unique to Davies. The Ranter Abiezer Coppe was to find justification for his own rebellious and subversive actions in the Old Testament stories of the outlandish behaviour of the prophet Ezekiel:[108] Coppe would eat and drink with gypsies, 'putting my hand in their bosomes, loving the she-Gipsies dearly', as a challenge to conventional morality.[109] Davies also realized that a powerful statement could be made by provocative and symbolic gestures. She explained that she had been driven to her act by the erection of a giant crucifix in the Cathedral, 'exposed to the view of all to kneel before it: like as in Golgatha that Fridays dismal Day bowed the knee: Then his humble Servants also. Which Goliah portray'd with the Crown of Thorns', and by the installation of a purple woollen altar hanging which obscured the Ten Commandments on the wall.[110] Davies saw her spectacular attack on these profane objects as the fulfilment in the Last Age of Exodus 32.20, in which Moses destroyed the golden calf worshipped by the Israelites.[111] She claimed a divine authority for actions which empowered her as a woman, but also resulted in her confinement in Bedlam. As has been seen already in the case of Elizabeth Barton, manifestations of divine inspiration could be interpreted by hostile witnesses and authorities as indications of diabolic possession or madness. In the seventeenth century, women like Anna Trapnel were also suspected of witchcraft, and it may have been Davies' position in society which protected her from such an accusation.[112]

Although many refused to accept that Davies was divinely inspired she did have sympathizers and followers. Two friends, Marie Noble and Susan Walker, joined her protest at Lichfield. Before the attack on the altar, they caused a series of disturbances inside the Cathedral by claiming the right to sit in the seats reserved for the wives of the Cathedral dignitaries. Davies' companions defended her act of destruction and defiance, saying that she had merely 'done her conscience'.[113] Despite his opposition to his wife's political activities, Archibald Douglas also had prophetic powers and wrote in a similar style.[114] According to Davies, he was filled with the spirit of God, and she also claimed that he was the illegitimate son of James I and as Charles' elder brother the rightful heir to the Kingdom.[115] Davies was

---

[107] PRO SP 16/380, f. 138v (*CSPD*, 1637–1638, 219).

[108] Cf. Smith, *Perfection Proclaimed*, 54–66.

[109] *A Collection of Ranter Writings from the Seventeenth Century*, ed. N. Smith (London, 1983), 106.

[110] Davies, *Bethlehem*, A2r(missigned B2r)–A2v.

[111] Davies, *Bethlehem*, B2v.

[112] For a discussion of the accusations against Anna Trapnel, see Hobby, *Virtue of Necessity*, 34.

[113] *CSPD*, 1637–1638, 219.

[114] *CSPD*, 1637–1638, 554.

[115] Davies, *The new Jerusalem at hand*, B2r.

supported throughout her troubles by her daughter Lucy Hastings, Countess of Huntingdon, who petitioned the courts on her mother's behalf,[116] and who also wrote a letter in support of Davies' interpretations of Scripture which the latter published.[117] Davies described her daughter, who had suffered 'such dishonour' on her behalf, as her 'Copartner' and 'sole support under the Almighty'.[118] After the sudden death of Lucy Hastings' nineteen-year-old son Henry, Davies wrote a consolatory tract likening her grieving daughter to the tragic city of Zion which is portrayed as a mourning mother in the Second Book of Esdras.[119] After Davies' death, her daughter and another grandson protested that she had been defamed in recent publications, and they succeeded in having passages concerning her removed from the continuation of Baker's *Chronicle*.[120] Theophilus, Earl of Huntingdon, said that evaluations of his grandmother as mad or deluded by the devil were 'barbarous' considering her noble extraction.[121]

Davies' own concern with her aristocratic rank seems to be directly connected with her prophetic mission of the 1640s and early 1650s. Davies called herself

> ELEANOR AUDELEY, handmayden of the most high GOD of Heaven, this Booke brought forth by Her, fifth Daughter of GEORGE, Lord of CASTLEHAVEN, Lord AVDLEY, and Tuitchet. NO inferior PEERE of this Land, in Ireland the fifth EARLE.[122]

Her father's line was as exalted, as worthy of honour as that of David.[123] 'Je le Tien', the motto of the first Earl of Castlehaven, is read as an allusion to the Book of Revelation 2.25–8: Davies presents herself as the one who holds on until the End and thus overcomes her enemies.[124] However, as she herself

---

116 Davies was not released from her imprisonment in the Tower until 1640 after her daughter and son-in-law succeeded, after much petitioning, in obtaining custody of her: *CSPD*, 1640–1641, 21.

117 Lucy Hastings, *The new proclamation, in answer*.

118 Davies, *From the Lady Eleanor*, E3v. On the significance of the relationship between mothers and their children in women's prophetic texts, see Mack, *Visionary Women*, 92–3.

119 Eleanor Davies, *Sions lamentation* (1649); and 2 Esdras 10.

120 A. Fraser, *The Weaker Vessel: Woman's Lot in Seventeenth-Century England* (London,1989), 282.

121 Fraser, *Weaker Vessel*, 283.

122 Davies, *The Lady Eleanor, her appeale* (1641), B2r.

123 Cf. her near contemporary, Lady Clifford: it has been argued that the 'Great Picture' commissioned by Anne Clifford reflects her success in her legal struggle to be recognized as the rightful heir to her father's estates. The centre panel depicts Anne Clifford surrounded by her family. In the right-hand panel 'The dimunitive portraits of her two husbands hang behind Clifford . . . almost as trophies of her past': *Her Own Life*, ed. Graham et al., 35.

124 Eleanor Davies, *Je le tien. The general restitvtion* (1646), F3v.

observes, her family name had recently been brought into disrepute:[125] in 1631, her brother, Mervin Touchet, Lord Audeley and Earl of Castlehaven, was indicted for sodomy and also for abetting the rape of his wife Anne Stanley by a former servant, Giles Broadway.[126] The case shocked and fascinated the country: a series of tracts describing Touchet's behaviour was published throughout the seventeenth century.[127] The London public were horrified and fascinated by his crimes. Touchet, the head of an aristocratic household, had disgraced his family by his immorality, perverting the marriage vow, and bringing dishonour on his wife. Natural order had been overturned, because by rewarding his favourites with land and money and marrying them into the family, Touchet deprived his children of their inheritance and honour – he had even encouraged one former servant to become the lover of his son's twelve-year-old wife. Although Archibald Douglas and Touchet's other sisters petitioned for his release,[128] the government was insistent that justice should be seen to be done and the King himself intervened in the case. The legal system was used to purge the household, a microcosm of the national body politic, which had become corrupted. From his condemned cell Touchet sent Eleanor Davies a letter which reflected her own language:

> Reveale O Daniel, I send thee 1631. farwells with thanks for thy letter and advice. But I am bound for Nineveh: And having bidden Tarshish farewell. Not fearing death, I doe not desire life.[129]

Alluding to Jonah 1–3, Touchet implicitly acknowledges that he has not followed God. He identifies his former self with Jonah, who sailed to Tarshish to hide from the Lord, was thrown overboard during the storm and swallowed by a great fish. He perceives his death to be a divine message, comparable to Jonah's warning to the Ninevites of their imminent destruction. Subsequently Davies tried to restore her brother's good name, publishing four tracts in his vindication,[130] and developing arguments which had

---

[125] Davies, *The Lady Eleanor, her appeale* (1641), B2r–B2v.

[126] See *Cobbett's Complete Collection of State Trials and Proceedings for High Treason and Other Crimes and Misdemeanors* (London, 1809–1828), iii, 401–26; also see B. Breasted, 'Comus and the Castlehaven Scandal', *Milton Studies* iii (1971), 201–24; C. Bingham, 'Seventeenth-Century Attitudes toward Deviant Sex', *Journal of Interdisciplinary History* i (1971), 447–72; T. Feroli, 'Sodomy and Female Authority: the Castlehaven Scandal and Eleanor Davies's *The Resitution of Prophecy* (1651)', *Women's Studies* xxiv (1994), 31–49.

[127] *The arraignement and conviction of Mervin Lord Avdley* (1643); *The trial of the Lord Audley* (1679); *The tryal and condemnation of Mervin, Lord Audley* (1699).

[128] *CSPD*, 1631–1632, 26 and 38.

[129] Eleanor Davies, *The word of God* (1644), a2v.

[130] Davies, *Woe to the house; The word of God; The crying charge* (1649); *The restitution of prophecy*.

been made in the trial itself, for example by pointing out the injustice of allowing a wife to be her husband's accuser.[131] She explained her brother's execution as an indictment of the world's sinfulness. In a tract entitled *Woe to the House*, Touchet's household is likened to the vineyard of the Lord of Isaiah 5 which would only yield bad fruit.[132] The Lord will judge those who reject God's laws and they will be destroyed. Charles I is Ahab and Anne Stanley and her sister Elizabeth are Jezebel, plotting for their own gain. Whereas, according to the prosecution at Touchet's trial, the Earl had been unstable in his belief, saying 'he was constant in no religion, but in the morning would be a Papist, in the afternoone a Protestant',[133] Davies claimed that his family had rebelled against his attempts to reform their Catholicism.[134] Davies argued that Anne Stanley was an adulteress who wanted to inherit Touchet's wealth, while his brother Fernando, a Catholic, had conspired against him out of malice.[135] Touchet himself was an innocent, another Isaac:

> The sonne of old ancient Abraham also: The house of Audeley no obscure one, though one much envied, and such a one then come of no Sodome seed, but like Isaack rather sacrificed, who as he suffered for the misdemenors of an unrulie houshold sufferd by him, laying on him their faults, so had the honour to have this added.[136]

Touchet is also portrayed as the figure of Christ, martyred by a blinded nation. Davies reports that on being granted execution by beheading as a last-minute mitigation of his sentence, Touchet replied that 'he should esteem that Haulter which should draw HIM to Heaven before a collor of pearle or the like. And for the Gallows likewise that shold bring him to his Saviour and Redeemer that dispised not the crosse for him.'[137] For his sacrifice Touchet received the reward of the saints: 'the honor having to be the first entred into the joy of his Lord'.[138]

Davies contrasted her brother's situation with that of the King, whose misrule of his household directly threatened the nation as a whole. Interpreting the Parable of the Ten Talents (Luke 19.11–27), Davies likened Touchet to the servant who invested his talent wisely and was given charge of ten cities.[139] Charles, the bad steward of the Kingdom, was the servant who buried his talent and had it taken from him. The execution of Davies'

---

131 Davies, *The crying charge*, A2r; cf. *Cobbett's Trials*, iii, 402.

132 Davies, *Woe to the house*.

133 *The arraignement and conviction*, B1v.

134 Davies, *The crying charge*, A3v.

135 Cf. Davies, *The word of God*, B1r–B1v.

136 Davies, *The word of God*, A3r–A3v.

137 Davies, *The word of God*, a1r.

138 Davies, *The crying charge*, A3v–A4r.

139 Davies, *The word of God*, A2r–A3v.

brother seems to have signalled the beginning of her prophetic mission to expose the perversion of Charles I's rule. *The crying charge*, the third tract concerning her brother, was published by Davies in 1649. It was dedicated to the High Court of Justice appointed for the trial of the King.[140] Motivated by a desire for vengeance and with the clear aim of dissuading the court from leniency, she emphasizes in the opening lines both the injustice of Touchet's trial and the lack of mercy shown.[141] Soon afterwards Davies was to cite her own persecution and imprisonment as further evidence of the disorder of the nation: in *Hells destruction* she claimed that her imprisonment for debt in 1647 went against the very principles of justice and equity.[142] In 1649 Davies also brought out a number of tracts describing her trial of 1633, one of which included a dedication to the imprisoned Charles I warning him that he must first seek forgiveness from her 'if so be you expect to finde Mercy in this world or the other'.[143]

Another tract concerned with injustices both to and by her family was written about Davies' royalist nephew John Stawell, who had been imprisoned after the surrender of Exeter in 1646.[144] Stawell had refused to take the national covenant and negative oath and was accused of treason. He was not brought to trial for four years and remained in prison until 1650. Meanwhile his land was confiscated by the state. Stawell repeatedly protested that the proceedings against him were not being conducted legally. Davies held Stawell partly responsible for her own misfortunes, petitioning parliament with a claim for his lands,[145] but his experiences actually reflected her own because during her long imprisonments, she too had been deprived of her estates. Davies had experienced her first mystical summons to prophecy at Englefield House. This manor was seized after the trial of 1633. During her imprisonment in the Gatehouse, Englefield was sold to John Paulet, the Marquis of Winchester. She also lost her manor and rectory at Pirton. Her husband's sale of this property was challenged by Davies, with the support of her daughter, and she unceasingly campaigned for the return of both it and Englefield, which together comprised her jointure, or (as she called them) her 'widow's mites', and she found herself in conflict with the crown itself over this matter.[146] Davies addressed *And without proving what we say* to the judges who, in 1648, after a long and complex legal debate, issued a writ of *amoveas manus* which commanded the return of the Pirton estates into her possession. The *amoveas manus* could literally

---

[140] Davies, *The crying charge*, A1v.
[141] Davies, *The crying charge*, A1v.
[142] Davies, *Hells destruction*, A4v–B1r.
[143] Davies, *The blasphemous charge*, A1v.
[144] Eleanor Davies, *The Lady Eleanor Douglas, dowager, her iubilees plea* (1650).
[145] Cope, *Handmaid*, 154.
[146] Davies, *The appearance*, B2v–B3r; and *Historical Manuscripts Commission Fifth Report* (London, 1876), appendix, 25 and 49–50.

'remove [the King's] hands' from a property if it could be shown that the owner had been wrongly dispossessed, for example, if the property had been confiscated when the owner had been unjustly convicted of a criminal offence.[147] Davies reminded the judges in her court case that they stood in the place of the Judges of Heaven – the Father, Son and Holy Ghost. She ominously warned anyone who might try in future to deprive her of her property of the fate of Basing House, John Paulet's family seat, which was destroyed in 1645.[148] God's mysterious vengeance would pursue those who persecuted His chosen messengers and the time would come soon for the judgement in Heaven of those who perpetrated injustice on earth.

Davies aimed to expose the failure of the English legal system to measure up to divine standards of justice; she called for a reformation of the law courts on the lines of the Reformation of the church.[149] *And without proving what we say*, with its description of her struggle to win back her property at Pirton, follows on from *The writ of restitution*, a vivid courtroom allegory, in which she stated one of the most exceptional aspects of her radical theology – her belief in universal salvation. Davies warns reprobates of the imminent Judgement, but balances her threats with the assurance that the punishment of sinners will be finite:

> ANd before the great and dreadfull day of the Lords comming: When sent that Prophet which for a signe of it, foreshewing what Plagues with; He will smite them, and truly never greater knowne, then at this very time: So take this into consideration, as probable as other things, before they came to passe; For Mercy, and Judgements going together, in these last dayes reveal'd. . . . Shall cansell that oppinion of old, of Hell to be a place or prison without redemption, as it stands not intruth well with Equitie, where mercy is so immeasurable for the offence of our first deceived parents; Who knew not what they did: That for their cause, so many without compassion, and commisseration, utterly should be undon & cast away, whereas SODOM for so few, their sakes had been spair'd when prest, shall not the Judge of all the world doe right?[150]

The disobedience of Eve and Adam is the result of their deception by the serpent and their own ignorance; their culpability is limited and, according to the principles of equity, humanity's sentence will be mitigated. Maintaining a traditional juridical framework, Davies rejects orthodox interpretations of the Last Judgement in which justice takes precedence over mercy: divine vengeance will be terrible, but tempered with the supreme virtue of compassion.

The allegory of *The writ of restitution* centres on an appeal to the court

---

147 Cf. *Dictionary of English Law*, comp. Earl Jowett, C. Walsh and J. Burke (London, 1977) for all definitions of legal terms.

148 Davies, *And without proving what we say*, A3r.

149 Eleanor Davies, *Ezekiel, cap. 2.* (1647), C2r–C2v.

150 Davies, *The restitvtion of reprobates*, A2r–A3r.

by tenants evicted from their property by officers of the law who had acted on a *supersedeas* which set aside the *amoveas manus*. The judge presiding over the proceedings, with whom Davies herself identifies, represents divine justice. The tenants are humanity, deprived of paradise and everlasting life. The *amoveas manus* is the promise of universal salvation (described elsewhere as an 'olive leaf');[151] the *supersedeas* is the orthodox doctrine of hell and damnation. The legal officers represent Eve, Adam and the serpent, who together deprived humanity of its rightful inheritance; but they also signify the theologians and churchmen who, through their 'evil' reading of Scripture, have eternally condemned part of God's creation. The judge, charging the officers with acting in contempt of court in seizing the estate, announces that the *amoveas manus* stands good. A writ of restitution is then issued to return paradise to the whole of humanity.

Davies' allegory is reminiscent of George Herbert's devotional sonnet 'Redemption', in which a tenant 'not thriving' is granted a new lease by his 'rich Lord', the crucified Christ.[152] The identification of divine justice and the common law was expressed in many sermons and other types of literature.[153] In his *The Araignement of Mr. Persecution*, the religious agitator Richard Overton, writing under the pseudonym Yongue Martin Mar-priest, voiced contemporary dissatisfaction with the Prebysterian parliament.[154] Claiming liberty of conscience as a natural right, he denounced intolerance: in a trial before the judge Lord Parliament, the prisoner Mr Persecution, unsuccessfully defended by Sir John Presbyter and his father Sir Symon Synod (personifying the Westminster Assembly of Divines), was found guilty of treason. Davies moves fluidly between theological debate and accounts of her own experiences of injustice: in arguing for universal salvation, she satirizes the courts which had dealt with her appeals for the return of her property and recognition of her rights. The officers in *The writ of restitution* have historical as well as allegorical referents: Pomfret and Massingale were sheriff and undersheriff of Hertfordshire, and the 'honest poor Solicitor J: Rand', was Davies' agent at Pirton.[155] The accusations levelled against the fictional legal officers reflect widespread criticisms of the Chancery courts, which, like the High Commission, had been seen to be very much in the control of the Stuarts.

Universalist beliefs were attributed to heretics in the late sixteenth

---

151 Davies, *Je le tien*, F2v.
152 George Herbert, 'Redemption', lines 1–14: *The Works of George Herbert*, ed. F.E. Hutchinson (Oxford, 1953), 40; see M.C. Schoenfeldt, *Prayer and Power: George Herbert and Renaissance Courtship* (Chicago, 1991), 79–82.
153 See C.B. Herrup, *The Common Peace: Participation and the Criminal Law in Seventeenth-Century England* (Cambridge, 1987), 194.
154 Richard Overton, *The Araignement of Mr. Persecution*, reprinted in *Tracts on Liberty in the Puritan Revolution 1638–1647*, ed. W. Haller (New York, 1934), iii, 205–56.
155 Eleanor Davies, *The writ of restitution* (1648), A4r; Cope, *Handmaid*, 137 and n. 76.

century, and the doctrine of eternal damnation was openly challenged by a number of religious groups in the seventeenth.[156] Davies' religious ideas developed from her own reading of the Bible (in both the Geneva and King James versions),[157] but she was also influenced by the teachings of some radicals, preachers and pamphleteers. The Coleman Street cleric John Goodwin distinguished between general redemption and universal salvation, rejecting the possibility that Christ died for reprobates, and contending:

> That such Intentions and Desires in God, and in Christ, which are real and cordial, may yet very possibly never take place, or be fulfilled . . . God may intend the Salvation of all Men by the Death of Christ, and yet all Men not be saved.[158]

Although Goodwin's major defence of general redemption, *Redemption Redeemed*, was not published until 1651, Davies may have been familiar with his arguments from listening to his sermons, and although she did not agree with his conclusions, she cited his interpretation of the chasm which separates Lazarus from the rich man in Hades (Luke 16.26) as a 'void space of time'.[159]

More significantly, however, Davies was acquainted with Gerrard Winstanley. After experiencing a trance late in 1648, Winstanley convinced others to join him in digging the commons at St George's Hill and then Cobham, proclaiming his revelation of a utopian society in which property would be held in common and wage labour would be abolished:[160]

> WHen this universall law of equity rises up in every man and woman, then none shall lay claim to any creature, and say, This is mine, and that is yours, This is my work, that is yours; but every one shall put to their hands to till the earth, and bring up cattle, and the blessing of the earth shall be common to all; when a man hath need of any corn or cattle, take from the next store-house he meets with.[161]

Although both Davies and Winstanley were concerned that equity should prevail, conventional aristocratic ideas concerning hierarchy and property were entrenched in the former's mind, and she cannot be said to have shared Winstanley's vision. In 1650, after the Diggers were driven from Cobham, she employed them on her estate in Pirton. The Ranter Lawrence Clarkson

---

156 C. Hill, 'The Religion of Gerrard Winstanley', *Past and Present* supplement v (1978), 11–12; cf. D.P. Walker, *The Decline of Hell: Seventeenth-Century Discussions of Eternal Torment* (Chicago, 1964).

157 Cope, *Handmaid*, 5.

158 John Goodwin, *Redemption redeemed* (1651), KKK1v.

159 Eleanor Davies, *The mystery of general redemption* (1647), D1r. For an account of Goodwin's gathered church, see E.S. More, 'Congregationalism and the Social Order: John Goodwin's Gathered Church, 1640–60', *Journal of Ecclesiastical History* xxxviii (1997), 210–235.

160 Cf. Hill, 'Religion', 20ff.

161 Gerrard Winstanley, *The new law of righteousnes* (1649), D2r.

seems to have criticized Winstanley and his companions for abandoning their revolutionary project and accepting this compromise of their ideals.[162] Winstanley himself accused Eleanor Davies of exploiting her position of economic power:

> Againe, you said in Purton Barne, that you were the prophettesse Melchisedecke, which is a high assumption. You might as well call yourself The christ, for you sett yourself in the chare of the Allmightie god. Melchisedecke ys king of rightesness and prince of peace, Now if you be that divine power soe called, Then I say what meanes the lowing of the oxen and the bleating of the shep? What's the reason that divers men calle upon you for money, which you truly owe them, and you either putt them off by long delays, or els makes them spend 10 tymes more to it in suites of law, whereas you have estate sufficient that you might pay all (which is king of rightesnes) and setle them and your self in Peace (which is prince of peace), If your bussines were ordered by you with Melchisedeck's spirit.[163]

Yet, despite their different values, Winstanley's apocalyptic language and millenarianism at times resemble Davies' writings: in *Fire in the Bush*, he interprets the four beasts which the prophet Daniel describes rising out of the sea (Daniel 7.3ff) as the clergy, the power of kings, the law, and buying and selling.[164] Significantly, Winstanley also rejected the doctrine of eternal damnation, claiming in *The Mysterie of God* (1648) and *The saints paradice* (1648) that every soul will be saved.[165] He claimed that hellfire would burn for a long time, but was not everlasting.[166] Davies came to the same conclusion, arguing that in the original Greek, the lake of sulphur of Revelation 14.11 does not burn eternally but rather 'for Ages and FARTHER'.[167]

Although some of her beliefs were fairly widespread in her time, Davies argued that her prophetic knowledge was unique, placing her above preachers like Goodwin and the 'schoole-men' responsible for distinguishing between sufficient grace which renders salvation possible, and efficient grace, which effects salvation, on the grounds that it is only she who takes the argument to its final stage by claiming Christ's suffering to have been 'alsufficient'.[168] She insisted that the belief that there is no restoration from

---

[162] See the introduction to Winstanley's *The Law of Freedom and Other Writings*, ed. C. Hill (Cambridge, 1982), 31–2.

[163] Winstanley's letter to Eleanor Davies is edited by P.H. Hardacre, 'Gerrard Winstanley in 1650', *Huntington Library Quarterly* xxii (1959), 345–9; this quotation appears on 348.

[164] Winstanley, *The Law of Freedom*, 233ff.

[165] Hill, 'Religion', 5.

[166] Hill, 'Religion', 5.

[167] Davies, *Je le tien*, C3v; and also *The mystery of general redemption*, B1r.

[168] Davies, *The restitvtion of reprobates*, E1v–E2r; cf. Goodwin, *Redemption redeemed*, KKK1r.

the second death was one of the three great heresies of the Church.[169] The others were transubstantiation and the denial of the spirit of prophecy in the post-biblical era. Davies believed that the Reformation had not gone far enough and wished to see a much more intense purge of Roman Catholic errors from the Protestant creed. The fundamentalist and primitivist drive of the Protestant theologians, which challenged non-Scriptural beliefs incorporated into the pre-Reformation Church, had failed to question the dogmas and doctrines developed in the teachings of many of the early Church Fathers, in particular St Augustine. At the same time, other Christian philosophers, such as the early third-century universalist Origen, continued to be denounced as heretics.[170] The refusal to listen to the spirit had blinded people to the reality of universal salvation. Davies compared herself to Lazarus, while the primates of the English Church were like the rich man and his brothers who ignored the Law and the message of the Prophets.[171] She warns her enemies that they will have to pay for their lack of mercy 'till the debt discharged, every farthing accompted for'.[172]

Davies' interpretation of the fall and redemption allowed her to assert the absolute goodness of the omnipotent Creator. She also entertained the notion of the *felix culpa*: the idea that the fall had resulted in a greater good, the increased happiness of the reprobates who are rescued from hell:

> Their future estate of Blisse, and Restitution, a Thousand times happie in the End, that shall see GOD; Though a thousand Yeeres, or Times: punishment to indure, in that hot BATH or BOYLING Lake for the purging of their boyles and soares to be cleansed of them. . . .[173]

While denying the existence of a separate purgatory, she argued that hell has a cleansing function, making souls perfect. Eleanor Davies asserted that Judas,[174] the Jewish race,[175] and even Lucifer would be saved.[176] Eleanor Davies' prophecies offered election to all and transformed the mark of Cain into the mark of the Lamb's forgiveness.[177] The promise of universal salvation is the ultimate act of grace and the final vindication of God's justice; this is the good wine kept until last.[178]

---

169 Davies, *Je le tien*, B3v–B4r.
170 For Davies' defence of Origen, see, for example, *The mystery of general redemption*, D1v.
171 Davies, *Je le tien*, D2r–D2v; and Luke 16.19–31.
172 Davies, *Je le tien*, D4r.
173 Davies, *The restitvtion of reprobates*, D1v.
174 Davies, *The restitvtion of reprobates*, B4v.
175 Davies, *The restitvtion of reprobates*, C2v.
176 Davies, *Je le tien*, D1r.
177 Davies, *The restitvtion of reprobates*, C2v.
178 Davies, *The mystery of general redemption*, A1v.

Feminine Authority

Unlike Elizabeth Barton, who in terms of the extent of her political involvement can be seen as her predecessor in the tradition of women's prophecy in England, Davies not only spoke, acted and wrote, but also directly challenged gendered power relations. She insisted that in the eyes of God, women are equal to men. As justification for her calling, she cited Acts 2.17–18: 'Former things are come to passe, and new things I declare vnto you; no age so weake, not sex excusing; when the Lord shall send and will put his words in their Mouth. He powreth out his Spirit vpon his hand-maidens . . .'[179] Yet in locating herself specifically in a *scriptural* (rather than classical or even Protestant) tradition of prophecy, perceiving herself as the heir not to Deborah, but to Daniel and John of the Apocalypse, and as a new Moses, Ezekiel or Elijah, she was faced with the difficulty that the antecedents whom she chose for herself were male. The phenomenon of God's words being uttered through a woman was potentially problematic, because, even though as a conduit her relationship to her prophecy was one of passivity, she became vicariously empowered by the voice speaking through her. In writing in the third person, Davies did not efface her own subjective position as a woman; on the contrary she reconstructed God, and thus authority, as female. In her first tract, *A warning to the dragon*, Davies assimilates conventional maternal imagery with that of the Woman Clothed with the Sun of Revelation 12, one of the types of the Godly Woman found in much Protestant iconography and a figure often understood to signify the Church persecuted by the forces of the Antichrist.[180] Describing the tribulations of the current age, she likens Christ's constancy to a mother who will not forget the thirst of her new-born son, 'her sucking childe'.[181] The Lamb will nourish and comfort His children, making their bodies in His own likeness (see Isaiah 49.14–15 and 66.11–13).[182] The faithful can console themselves in their trials with the promise of future happiness: 'Persecutions are but like the Trauell of a Woman, who hath sorrow because her houre is come, but as soone as shee is delivered of the Childe, shee remembreth no more the anguish, for ioy a man-childe is borne into the world.'[183] The End is imminent, and the faithful will be saved by He whom the grave was no more able to contain 'then the wombe can keepe backe a sonne at the time of perfection'.[184] Churchmen, 'our Over-seers', who

---

[179] Davies, *A warning to the dragon*, A3v–A4r.
[180] Davies, *A warning to the dragon*, G2v–G3r.
[181] Davies, *A warning to the dragon*, G2v.
[182] Davies, *A warning to the dragon*, G2v–G3r.
[183] Davies, *A warning to the dragon*, G2v.
[184] Davies, *A warning to the dragon*, G4r.

refused to receive her prophetic message and were thus unprepared for Judgement, are likened to women who, immune to the pangs of birth, continue to sleep whilst their babies choke.[185]

In Davies' writing the persecution which accompanied her prophesying is represented as the pain and difficulty of childbearing.[186] Twenty-four years after her prophetic calling, Davies described herself as 'a sufferer so many years for; no less then the burthen of his word to Great Britain (Anno Dom.) 1625'.[187] *The everlasting gospel* proclaims her mystical experience of 1625 as the rebirth of the spirit of prophecy; her account is headed, 'The Holy Gospel, According to the Evangelist, By the Lady ELEANOR'.[188] The production of her prophecies, fathered by God and not man, is troped as the nativity. At times Davies' self-representation recalls the sort of *imitatio Mariae* found in Margery Kempe's affective mirroring of the life of the Mother of God. For Davies and others, the Virgin Mary was the figuration of the type of the woman prophet because she offered a female model of powerful, autonomous, God-inspired behaviour. Anna Trapnel also described herself as the handmaiden of God and bride of Christ, and reports of women who announced that they were pregnant with the Christ of the Second Coming caused unease in this period.[189] Davies, as Protestant, identified with the Virgin in her role as Mother of Christ, rather than as a miracle-working saint.

In *The restitution of prophecy* Davies created a complex feminine identity from the figures of the Wise Virgins (Matthew 25.1–13), the Bride of the Lamb (Revelation 21.2 and 9 and 22.17) and the Virgin Mary; the first two being types which, along with the Woman Clothed with the Sun, were associated in traditional Marian iconography,[190] while the metonym which I discussed earlier in this chapter (p. 137) of her prophecy as the infant Christ 'difficult to be fathered', allowed her to explore her own role as the mother of God, the woman who, in bearing Christ, was more than a mere conduit or physical vessel.[191] The preface to the tract is dated 25 December (the main text is dated Candlemas, the Feast of the Virgin's Purification); the location of its production is the Fleet prison, which although not a stable is 'a place like restles'.[192] In this preface, Davies' metonymy is particularly

---

185 Davies, *Ezekiel, cap. 2.*, A3v–A4r.
186 For other examples of maternal imagery in the writings of seventeenth-century women prophets, see Hobby, *Virtue of Necessity*, 42, and Mack, *Visionary Women*, 114–15; and in writings by men, see Smith, *Perfection Proclaimed*, 58, 60–1, 65, 81.
187 Davies, *Her appeal from the court of the camp*, 1v–2r.
188 Davies, *The everlasting gospel*, A2r.
189 Berg and Berry, 'Spiritual Whoredom', 50–1.
190 Davies, *The restitution of prophecy*, B1v–B3r; cf. J.N. King, 'The Godly Woman in Elizabethan Iconography', *Renaissance Quarterly* xxxviii (1985), 50.
191 Davies, *The restitution of prophecy*, A2r–A3v.
192 Davies, *The restitution of prophecy*, A2v.

fluid and unsettling. Alluding to the Parable of the Narrow and the Wide Gates (Matthew 7.13–14), she opposes the Fleet and its prison to the 'passage of Inns', both Inns of Court and drinking houses. Taking her exegesis further, she also opposes the 'straits of the Virgins-Womb' passed by sailors to a welcome haven (the road to life, and an allusion to the Virgin as patron of seafarers) to the broad way (which she defines as 'Ebrieties', the route to destruction, but which also, in an extraordinary nexus of meanings, refers to the servant, Giles Broadway, whose testimony that he had raped Anne Stanley condemned her brother).[193] She identifies with the Virgin Mary herself, but also tropes her pamphlet as the Virgin's body, implicitly inviting the believing reader to enter the womb itself (in other words, her book) as the source of everlasting life.

Although, some reformers argued that the Virgin Mary's status was unjustified because many of the stories about her did not appear in Scripture, they were often less concerned with doctrinal issues than with the way in which Mary was worshipped. Yet while veneration of images of the Virgin and saints was suppressed in the course of the Reformation, John King argues that 'traditional iconography often survived iconoclastic attacks, albeit in a "desanctified" form that altered or disguised its relationship to medieval prototypes'.[194] Elizabeth I, who as an unmarried queen regent could be thought to have transgressed the boundaries of expected feminine behaviour, had adapted traditional images of the Virgin in her own iconography.[195] Elizabeth's self-presentation was politically motivated: as virgin, a mother only to her subjects, she was a woman to be honoured and adored. Retrospective accounts of her reign often incorporated such imagery: Eleanor Davies described the Queen's death on the Feast of the Virgin's Annunciation as 'The Bridegroom Sun and his Virgin Spouse, parting the hours ushering the Obsequies'.[196]

The status of the Virgin Mary in the seventeenth century was, however, problematized because of the role played by Mariolatry in the European Counter-Reformation.[197] Devotion to Mary had been recommended by the Council of Trent (1545–1563). Fraternities and Sodalities were founded in

[193] Davies, *The restitution of prophecy*, A2v–A3r.
[194] King, 'Godly Woman', 52; also see M. Aston, *England's Iconoclasts* (Oxford, 1988), i.
[195] C. Levin, 'Power, Politics, and Sexuality: Images of Elizabeth I' in *The Politics of Gender in Early Modern Europe*, ed. J.R. Brink, A.P. Coudert and M.C. Horowitz, Sixteenth Century Essays and Studies 12 (Kirksville MO, 1989), 97; H. Hackett, *Virgin Mother, Maiden Queen: Elizabeth I and the Cult of the Virgin Mary* (London, 1995); cf. also L.A. Montrose, ' "Shaping Fantasies": Figurations of Gender and Power in Elizabethan Culture' in *Representing the English Renaissance*, ed. S. Greenblatt (Berkeley, 1988), 31–64.
[196] Davies, *The restitution of prophecy*, B4r.
[197] See E. Veevers, *Images of Love and Religion: Queen Henrietta Maria and Court Entertainment* (Cambridge, 1989), especially 92–109.

her honour. Throughout the sixteenth and early seventeenth centuries Marian books were secretly distributed in England. After Charles I's marriage to Henrietta Maria, daughter of Henry IV of France, a neoplatonic cult of the Virgin Mary became established at the royal court. In 1630 priests from the Catholic missionary order of the Capuchins came to serve the Queen, and in 1632 a chapel dedicated to the Virgin was built in the grounds of her palace at Somerset House. An Arch-Confraternity of the Rosary was established which held religious ceremonies and processions in public. Courtly writers identified Henrietta Maria with the Mother of God, an idealization of Beauty and virtue which inspired love, and thus love of God.[198] As E. Veevers says,

> For Catholics, the Queen's roles, of mediatrix, mother, and bride must have seemed to parallel those of Mary. As mother and bride she won Charles to mercy and love; as intercessor on behalf of her Catholic subjects she protected the Catholic faith in England.[199]

Veevers' study demonstrates that Henrietta Maria's religious devotion was integral to her public roles as patron of court culture and political intercessor and peacemaker, but amongst Puritans, Henrietta Maria became increasingly unpopular.

Criticism was directed not only at the public display of Catholicism in the royal household, but also at the whole culture of the court. Eleanor Davies may well have voiced popular opinion when she condemned Catholic forms of worship, associating them with the spectacle and theatricality of the masque:

> [Priests] acting (in their Copes, I might say, party coloured fooles Coates) like painted Peacocks, the part of HECUBA, the franticke Troyan Wiues and POLLIXINA; Such pompe and gaudinesse of Masking garments, being fitter for the Theator then the Temple, the state thereof requiring rather Mourners with all their BACCUS Savage Ceremonies, apish and affected Fashions, No Vice on a Stage, with senselesse jests to moue the vulgars laughter, good folkes ashamed; So rediculous without vnderstanding babbling like Parrots or Children, a Tongue they know not; yet no Babes or Children in Mallice, Pyping with out distinction; Pricketh not this the hearts of the hearers, twanging vpon a Harpe, Instead of an Egge, asking a Scorpion; and saying Amen to any Pater-Noster.[200]

Seven years later, William Prynne was punished after attacking the stage

---

198 Veevers, *Images of Love*, especially 103–109.
199 Veevers, *Images of Love*, 103; cf. also D. Clarke, 'The Iconography of the Blush: Marian Literature of the 1630s' in *Voicing Women: Gender and Sexuality in Early Modern Writing*, ed. K. Chedgzoy, M. Hansen and S. Trill (Keele, 1996), 111–28.
200 Davies, *A warning to the dragon*, K4r–K4v.

and the Queen more overtly in his *Histriomastix*. Henrietta Maria's cult of love was widely perceived as morally corrupting, an excuse for licentious and immoral behaviour, while the Queen's intervention in political affairs was thought to have seduced the monarchy and rendered it powerless. Davies likens Charles to the demon-possessed man bound in fetters (Luke 8.27–33),[201] and to Samson brought into thraldom by a blind love.[202] Yet although Davies described the Queen's Mariolatry as profanity, 'as free with her impostures to communicate our Heavenly Saviours homage to Idol blocks',[203] she ignored Puritan objections that by worshipping Mary, womankind is exalted over Christ.[204] Instead she implied that the wrong Virgin was venerated by Henrietta Maria and her circle – Davies herself was the true Virgin, entrusted with God's word. The year of Davies' own prophetic calling was that of the royal couple's 'unhappy Nupitals' and of Charles I's coronation. This was the year of the jubilee, of remission of sins, but the King, who was 'matched with a Yoak-fellow, and could not come', refused to listen to her message.[205]

In perceiving the Virgin as a type of the prophet, Davies encountered the difficulty of describing her without having recourse to iconolatry. In the 1630s, representations of the Virgin had been the subject of debate between Puritans and Catholics, the former objecting to the hyperbole used by the latter to describe her sublime beauty and transcendental virtue, and in particular to the transference into the religious sphere of politically-charged sensual and courtly language associated with Henrietta Maria's cult of love.[206] Davies' strategies for avoiding this conflict can be seen in her description of a visitation from an angel which occurred on 24 September 1634 in the Gatehouse Prison:

> Full Moon the ever-lasting Lamp, prisoners fire and candle, who from the Angel sent thither the Holy Ghost, that by the space of an hour, the Bed his throne rested thereon, from his mouth for a farewel received a salute; and for another farewel, that had on his right hand an Amber glove, left such an odoriferous scent when he was gone, all oyled with Amber-greece, the Spirit thereof proceeding from the Leather, so far beyond expression, as it were invisible food, like when as said, Cause thy belly to eat, and fill thy bowels.[207]

---

201 Davies, *For the most honorable states sitting at White-Hall* (1649), A4r–A4v.

202 Davies, *Samson legacie*, B1v.

203 Davies, *The restitution of prophecy*, B3v.

204 Cf. the Puritan objection to Catholics who 'make to your selfe a She Saviour, I meane a Woman' in N. N., *Maria triumphans. Being a discourse, wherein the B Virgin Mary is defended* (St Omer, 1635), D10r.

205 Davies, *The restitution of prophecy*, B3r–B3v.

206 Clarke, 'Iconography of the Blush', 111–28.

207 Eleanor Davies, *Ezekiel the prophet explained* (1647), A3r–A3v; for another account of 'The Misterie of God open in the Angels hand', see *Great Brittains visitation*, E3v.

The Annunciation provided many visionaries with a model of ecstatic submission to God's will or prophetic inspiration: St Teresa of Avila, whose autobiography was translated into English in 1611, described the sweet pain of rapture which she felt when she was stabbed by a spear held by an angel.[208] However, metaphors of dying, melting and wounding, conventionally appropriated from the language of love to describe the ecstasy of encountering the Divine, are completely absent from Davies' text. Davies' angel is almost certainly Gabriel, who appeared not only to announce the conceptions of John the Baptist and Christ (Luke 1.11–20 and 26–38), but also to explain Daniel's visions (Daniel 8.162–6; 9.21–7). The glove signifies that Davies is a bride of Christ; elsewhere in her exposition of the Five Foolish Virgins, she warns that those who are asleep when the bridegroom returns are unworthy of the 'oderissrous [sic] marriage gloves'.[209] The seed of the divine word that is sown in her is the Holy Spirit: conventionally represented as a scent, it penetrates without piercing and lingers after the visitation. Yet while Davies' status as the Virgin is implicit in the appearance and salutation of the angel, as well as in the presence of the moon (a Marian attribute), her visitation differs significantly from traditional depictions of the Annunciation, such as that by Fra Angelica, in which the Virgin sits bathed in light, in a porch in a garden.[210] Davies' subjective position allows her to remain absent from her account, and thus to avoid completely the iconographic problems inherent in describing the Mother of God. While the angel's perfumed glove suggests his rank in the court of heaven,[211] Davies' unexalted position is emphasized. Some Catholic literature of the period dwelt on the traditional association of the Virgin with a garden, which carried with it profane secular connotations of Venus' bower of love, but Davies' visitation occurs in the austerity of her prison cell.[212] The contrast of the light of the moon with that of a candle emphasizes her own lowliness, and may also carry with it an implicit criticism of the use of candles in Catholic devotion.[213]

While emulation of the Old Testament prophets was not uncommon in the Civil War years, and tropes of the Virgin and the Woman Clothed with the Sun recur in women's visionary literature throughout the century, Eleanor Davies went beyond the limits of many in her radical reconstruction

---

[208] *The Lyf of the Mother Teresa of Jesus*, English Recusant Literature 1558–1640 212 (Antwerp, 1611; reproduced Ilkley, 1974); cf. Warner, *Alone of All Her Sex*, 299–300.

[209] Davies, *The restitution of prophecy*, B2v.

[210] *The Annunciation*, c.1430–1432, Museo del Prado, Madrid.

[211] For an allusion to the use of ambergris to perfume courtiers' gloves, see William Davenant's 'Madagscar', lines 391–6: *The Shorter Poems, and Songs from the Plays and Masques*, ed. A.M. Gibbs (Oxford, 1972), 20.

[212] On the garden image in Catholic literature of the 1630s, see Veevers, *Images of Love*, 128–31.

[213] On the controversy over the use of candles, see Veevers, *Images of Love*, 143–4.

of God. In *The appearance or presence of the son of man* (1650) Davies depicts the herald of Judgement described in Revelation 1 as a female deity:

> She whose Throne heaven, earth her footstool from the un-created, saying, I am A. and O. first and last, both beginning and ending, by whom all things were done: Not without her anything done or made; Trinity in Unity, of Manhood the head: Who of Death have the Keys and Hell: Then the Queen of the South a greater, born of a greater not of Women: Melea, by Interpretation, Queen of Peace, or She-councellor . . . she his Executor, Made like unto the Son of God, the ancient of days likeness: owner of that Title of Tythes. . . . Even the Lord upon her right hand, wounding even Kings in the day of his wrath . . . such headships of the Church of such no more.[214]

In the image of the female herald the concepts of the Judge and the Redeemer are combined. The herald is the Executor – She carries out the Divine purpose after Christ's death upon the cross according to His command. She is able to wound even kings, but She also holds the keys to Death and Hell; She has the power to raise the dead and to release condemned souls.[215] This female power is greater than the leaders of Church and State. She is Father, Son and Holy Ghost. This vision empowers Davies to extricate herself from male authority, human and divine. She becomes her own authority:

> Imprimis, first and for most saying I am A. and O. alias, Da: and Do: by her first and last marriage so subscribes . . .[216]

She identifies the feminized power which licensed her tracts with her own voice: 'Da' and 'Do' are abbreviations of her married surnames Davies and Douglas. Going further than any of the earlier visionaries and prophets studied in this book, Davies depicted herself as the Herald of Judgement uttering the words of God, the secrets reserved for the end of time, and thus she not only sanctified but actually deified herself; she became one with the Trinity.

---

[214] Davies, *The appearance*, A4r–A4v.

[215] Cf. Davies, *Je le tien*, F1v in which the keys also signify the power to release reprobates from hell.

[216] Davies, *The appearance*, A4v.

Epilogue

This book has looked at a number of women prophets who wrote, or had their books written, in late medieval and early modern England. While I argue that prophecy, which has its roots in Hebrew traditions, classical antiquity and various pagan cultures, had long had particular associations with women, and was both widespread and diverse in its manifestations in Western Christendom, the subjects of this study have also been located in their specific religio-political contexts. Where appropriate, similarities and differences between them have been suggested, and certain themes traced, such as the roles of male transcribers and editors in shaping their texts. These women, like their male counterparts, emulated biblical and Christian precedents of either sex (the lives of the Old Testament prophets, as well as Christ and his Apostles and later Christian saints). Nonetheless their surviving writings are haunted by preoccupations with authorization, mediation, effacement and validation because, despite their differing historical, religious and social backgrounds, they all were vulnerable to hostility, policing or persecution when they ventured to act, speak or write. Even though they were empowered by the belief that as individuals they were inspired by God, and to varying extents gathered around themselves groups of followers who shared their beliefs and sometimes even imitated their examples, the long term influence of the women in this study was often limited. The public character of the prophet was fluid: hailed as a saint or Christian witness one moment, without enduring and effective support she might gain the notoriety of a reprobate, lunatic, devil or witch the next. An examination of the posthumous reputations of Margery Kempe, Elizabeth Barton, Anne Askew and Eleanor Davies illustrates what Germaine Greer refers to as 'the transcience [sic] of female fame'.[1]

Although *The Book of Margery Kempe* is now established in the literary canon, for centuries it seems to have virtually disappeared from sight. The library of Cecily, Duchess of York (died 1495) reflects the daily reading of an educated and devout aristocrat; it included works by Hilton and Mechtild of Hackeborn, a life of Catherine of Siena, the *Revelations* of St Bridget and *The Mirrour of the Blessed Lyf of Jesu Christ*, as well as the *Legenda aurea* and a book known as *De infantia Salvatoris*, yet there is no record that she possessed a copy of *The Book of Margery Kempe*.[2] It is impossible

---

1 Quoted by E. Showalter, *A Literature of their Own: from Charlotte Bronte to Doris Lessing* (London, 1988), 12; see also G. Greer, *Slip-Shod Sibyls: Recognition, Rejection and the Woman Poet* (London, 1995), xi–xxiv.

2 C.A.J. Armstrong, 'The Piety of Cicely, Duchess of York: a Study in Late Medieval

to say if the book found its way into the hands of either pious laypeople or priests, or if it was circulated amongst the libraries of religious institutions. All that is known is that the extant manuscript of *The Book of Margery Kempe* was once part of the library at Mountgrace Priory in North Yorkshire. The circulation of some of the works of the vernacular mystical writers seems to have been restricted at the end of the fifteenth century, often because of their theological complexity.[3] Although Kempe's book may well have slipped into obscurity purely by chance, it is also possible that it was deliberately kept out of lay hands, but for rather different reasons.

The fifteenth- and sixteenth-century annotations on the extant manuscript of the book allow speculation about the early reception of Margery Kempe's text. One of the readers of the manuscript, a Carthusian monk, noticed with apparent approval an affinity between Kempe's ecstasies and those of two of his contemporaries at Mountgrace, the writers and contemplatives Richard Methley and John Norton.[4] Yet in *The Book of Margery Kempe*'s first appearance in print (published by Wynkyn de Worde in 1501 or thereabouts), which took the form of a series of extracts,[5] Kempe is presented as a passive contemplative, willing to listen to and accept the instructions which Christ, through His Grace, has chosen to give her.[6] Her role is undemonstrative and receptive: she is guided towards private

Culture' in *For Hilaire Belloc: Essays in honour of his seventy-second birthday*, ed. D. Woodruff (London, 1942), 79 and 82–8. On women's book ownership in the later Middle Ages, see C.M. Meale, ' ". . . alle the bokes that I haue of latyn, englisch, and frensch": Laywomen and their Books in Late Medieval England' in *Women and Literature in Britain, 1150–1500*, ed. C.M. Meale, Cambridge Studies in Medieval Literature 17 (Cambridge, 1993), 128–58.

3   While works by Hilton and Rolle were printed by Wynkyn de Worde, circulation of *The Cloud of Unknowing*, for example, seems to have been mainly restricted to a Carthusian audience: see G.R. Keiser, 'The Mystics and the Early English Printers: the Economics of Devotionalism' in *The Medieval Mystical Tradition in England*, ed. M. Glasscoe, Exeter Symposium 4 (Cambridge, 1987), 24; and M.G. Sargent, 'The Transmission by the English Carthusians of some Late Medieval Spiritual Writings', *Journal of Ecclesiastical History* xxvii (1976), 225–40.

4   For a description of the annotations, see *The Book of Margery Kempe*, ed. S.B. Meech and H.E. Allen, EETS 212 (Oxford, 1940), xxxv–xliv; and S.E. Holbrook, 'Margery Kempe and Wynkyn de Worde' in *Medieval Mystical Tradition*, ed. Glasscoe, Exeter Symposium 4, 35–8. For an account of Norton and Methley, see K. Lochrie, *Margery Kempe and Translations of the Flesh* (Philadelphia, 1991), 206–35.

5   This text is reproduced in *Book of Margery Kempe*, 353–7; see also xlvi–xlviii; and Holbrook, 'Margery Kempe', 27–46. The non-survival of early manuscripts of Julian of Norwich's *Revelations* makes it difficult to guess at the dissemination of the texts, although a manuscript does survive which is datable to *c.*1500 and which includes extracts from the long text alongside a compilation from Hilton's *Scale of Perfection: A Book of the Showings to the Anchoress Julian of Norwich*, ed. E. Colledge and J. Walsh (Toronto, 1978), i, 9–10.

6   One of the extracts of teaching is actually taken from a speech made by the Blessed Virgin Mary but no indication of this is given in the new context: *Book of Margery Kempe*, xlvi.

devotions and directed to commune silently with God through patient endurance, tears of compassion, and pious thoughts and prayers. The compiler gives no information about Kempe's life, and also excludes descriptions of her visions, her sensory mystical experiences and her often violent physical responses to her revelations, and Christ's voice as it addresses her loses its 'homeliness' or intimacy. George R. Keiser describes these extracts as 'the Dicts and Sayings of Christ to Margery Kempe'.[7] The printed extracts, in isolating Kempe's contemplations from her very active life in the world, could be taken as an indication that the compiler felt uneasy about her extreme religious enthusiasm. As Sue Ellen Holbrook points out, the extractor 'left behind all that is radical, enthusiastic, feminist, particular, potentially heretical and historical'.[8]

If the contents of *The Book of Margery Kempe* were considered unsuitable for general circulation without major abridgement, Wynkyn de Worde's decision to print the extracts may be taken as evidence that neither Kempe's name nor her book had been completely forgotten after her death. De Worde printed the text with an eye to economic considerations and must have had a specific readership in mind. The success of this piece is suggested by the fact that it was reprinted in the middle of the sixteenth century, when it appeared alongside a series of short treatises and extracts from other mystical works including *The Song of Angels* (possibly written by Hilton), devout works and translations written by the author of *The Cloud of Unknowing* or one of his disciples, and a short life of St Catherine of Siena.[9] All of these texts emphasize private, inner meditation. Although there evidently existed a market for texts such as those about Barton's life and revelations which described the more physical and emotional aspects of women's spirituality, Keiser argues that short compilation texts were not only cheaper and easier to print than large books, but they were also more popular. The publication of a compilation of extracts from *The Book of Margery Kempe* thus reflects aspects of contemporary taste in pious literature at the turn of the sixteenth century.[10]

It is entirely possible that Margery Kempe's reputation survived into the sixteenth century amongst the Bridgittine nuns at Syon, and that consequently the publication of her work was aimed at them in the first instance.[11] As was seen in the second chapter, Kempe had a special devotion to St Bridget and had some connections with the Abbey which she visited on her return from her pilgrimage in Eastern Europe. The nuns of Syon may well

---

7   Keiser, 'Mystics', 17.
8   Holbrook, 'Margery Kempe', 35.
9   Pepwell's version was reprinted at the beginning of this century in *The Cell of Self-Knowledge: Seven Early English Mystical Treatises Printed by Henry Pepwell in 1521*, ed. E.G. Gardner (London, 1910).
10 Keiser, 'Mystics', 16–17.
11 Holbrook, 'Margery Kempe', 42.

have been aware of the writings of a woman who had defended their own patron saint during a period of controversy. Significantly, there were also nuns of Syon in Elizabeth Barton's circle, and the existence of the printed extracts of her book indicated that Kempe's fame continued into the decades immediately prior to Barton's first visions. These factors lend weight to Hope Emily Allen's suggestion that the experiences of Margery Kempe and those of Elizabeth Barton are linked by a tradition of feminine piety and prophecy in England which was derived in part from the example of St Bridget.[12] As Allen observes, 'even where most imitative, Margery Kempe of Lynn was evidently to some extent a precursor'.[13]

If Margery Kempe may have had a more long term influence than is generally recognized, the same can hardly be said for Barton. However, despite the Protestant campaign to sully her memory, there are indications that many Catholics, in the reign of Mary and thereafter, still remembered her as a truly virtuous woman. In *The workes of Sir Thomas More*, first published in 1557, William Rastell omitted a letter from More to Cromwell which Rastell certainly must have seen.[14] It was written immediately after More discovered that his name was to be included in the indictment against Barton and her associates and gave a very circumspect account of his involvement with her. In it More describes Barton as 'lewde', a word which by 1500 could mean not only 'unlearned' or 'foolish', but also 'lascivious' and 'unchaste'.[15] It is not entirely clear which senses More intended to invoke, but his ambiguity is significant in itself as it reflects his general ambivalence about the nun. More explained to Cromwell that Barton's early miracles and prophecies had been uncontentious, but that after Christmas 1532 she had come more to his notice. He decided to meet her and was impressed by her humility and discernment, but later wrote to her advising her not to meddle in political matters.[16] More insisted to Cromwell that he had acted judiciously throughout, refusing to listen to talk of Barton's political revelations, admonishing others for their credulity, and recognizing that he could not be sure of her authenticity until she had been properly investigated by those in authority. He even praised Cromwell for bringing to light 'suche detestable ypocrisie'.[17]

The early recusants, who wished to portray More's circle as united in their beliefs, would certainly have been concerned that More's approbation of Barton's exposure would be seen to imply that he had deserted John

---

[12] *Book of Margery Kempe*, lxviii.

[13] *Book of Margery Kempe*, lxviii.

[14] *The workes of Sir Thomas More*, ed. William Rastell (1557); cf. *The Correspondence of Sir Thomas More*, ed. E.F. Rogers (Princeton, 1947), 480.

[15] *MED*, s.v. 'leued'; *OED*, s.v. 'lewd'.

[16] *Correspondence*, ed. Rogers, 466. More transcribed his letter to Barton in his letter to Cromwell, but Rogers prints it separately, 465–6.

[17] *Correspondence*, ed. Rogers, 486–8.

Fisher, who had failed in his attempt to defend his relations with the Maid – thus Rastell's decision to exclude this particular piece of correspondence. Editing two other letters on the subject, written on 5 March 1534 to the King and to Cromwell, Rastell also replaced More's phrase, 'wykked woman', with 'nunne' so that no evidence of More's criticisms of her remained.[18] In his life of Thomas More, Nicholas Harpsfield quoted the letter to Cromwell of 5 March and made the same substitution, and both he and William Roper depicted Barton as a woman reputed for piety, neither repeating any part of Thomas More's later reassessment.[19] The recusants of the later decades of the century were more dogmatic in their beliefs and outspoken in their opinions. In 1585 Nicholas Sanders asserted that More had diligently questioned Barton and found no indication of fanaticism.[20]

Some seventeenth-century historians continued to remember Elizabeth Barton positively. In 1655, Thomas Bayly, a Royalist and a Catholic, published a life of Fisher based on that by Richard Hall.[21] According to this version, Barton foresaw not only that Mary would eventually reign, but also that Henry VIII would find no comfort in the wives who succeeded Katherine of Aragon and that, because he had deprived the Catholic Church of so many children, his own offspring would die without issue. Bayly also asserted that Barton believed that Henry himself would die without consolation and that his infamy would last until the end of the world. In claiming that Barton had foretold that the heresy which Henry VIII had introduced into England would lead to national turmoil, Bayly no doubt intended to imply that she had effectively predicted not only the persecutions of the Catholics in the second half of the sixteenth century, but also the crises of the Stuart reign and the Civil War itself. Of course this tradition of Barton's life was not necessarily the dominant one, even in Catholic circles. Although Alan Neame has suggested that in the reign of Mary there was a movement for her canonization, there is very little evidence in support of the idea.[22] In Elizabeth's reign, the exiled Franciscan historian Thomas Bourchier wrongly claimed that two of Barton's associates also attainted of treason, the Observants Rich and Risby, were tortured and executed in 1537

---

18 *Workes*, ed. Rastell, XX4r–XX5r; cf. *Correspondence*, ed. Rogers, 489 and 500; and J.K. McConica, 'The Recusant Tradition of Sir Thomas More' in *Essential Articles for the Study of Thomas More*, ed. R.S. Sylvester and G.P. Marc'hadour (Hamden CT, 1977), 139–40.
19 Nicholas Harpsfield, *The life and death of Sir Thomas More*, ed. E.V. Hitchcock, intro. R.W. Chambers, EETS o.s. 186 (London, 1932), 155–64; and William Roper, *The Lyfe of Sir Thomas Moore*, ed. E.V. Hitchcock, EETS o.s. 197 (London, 1935), 59–71.
20 Nicholas Sanders, *De origine progressu schismatis Anglicani* (Cologne, 1585), K2v.
21 Thomas Bayly, *The life and death of that renowned John Fisher Bishop of Rochester* (1655), K3r–K5v.
22 A. Neame, *The Holy Maid of Kent: the Life of Elizabeth Barton, 1506–1534* (London, 1971), 351.

after they had refused the Oath of Supremacy.[23] Richard Rex has suggested that this account may be a distortion of an 'authentic tradition' in so far as it is just plausible that those condemned alongside Barton (and presumably therefore even Barton herself) refused an offer of mercy in exchange for taking the Oath of Succession.[24] Nonetheless the fact that Bourchier makes no mention of Rich's and Risby's involvement with Barton is highly indicative: if Barton or her other supporters had made such a stance it would surely have been recorded in the English martyrologies. Even John Hall, the writer of the sixteenth-century life of Bishop Fisher, remained uncertain of her authenticity because he said he had heard diverse opinions expressed by people of 'right good fame and estimacion'.[25]

While confusion about Barton's authenticity can be found even amongst the writings of recusant hagiographers, it is clear that throughout its early history, Anne Askew's text was used by Protestant editors and publishers as political and religious propaganda. *The first examinacyon* probably did not reach England before the death of Henry VIII, which may well explain why so many copies have survived: under the more liberal Seymour administration the press was temporarily released from censorship.[26] John Bale's publication of Askew's texts was designed not only as a response to contemporary portrayals of Barton as a Catholic martyr, but also, according to John King, as an attack on Stephen Gardiner and the conservative counsellors involved in the whole affair, as is evidenced by an exchange of letters between Bishop Gardiner and Seymour in which the former demanded the suppression of the *Examinations*.[27] Gardiner complained that the *Examinations* had been publicly sold at Winchester, 'some with leaves unglued, where Master Paget was spoken of; and some with leaves glued'.[28] Gardiner claimed that he opposed dissent, heresy and the circulation of

---

[23] Thomas Bourchier, *Historia ecclesiastica de martyrio fratrvm ordinis divi Francisci* (Paris, 1582), B3v-B6r.

[24] R. Rex, 'The Execution of the Holy Maid of Kent', *Bulletin of the Institute of Historical Research* lxiv (1991), 219–20. Rex finds evidence for the suggestion that Edward Bocking was also executed for refusing the Oath of Succession in Richard Morison's claim that Bocking was the only other doctor to die besides Fisher and More. However, it seems more probable that Morison was attempting to defame Fisher and More by associating them with such a notorious figure as the Holy Maid's confessor than that he 'in effect conceded that Bocking was killed for much the same reasons as Fisher and More' (220).

[25] Richard Hall, *Vie du bienheureux martyr Jean Fisher*, ed. Fr. van Ortoy (Brussels, 1893), 247.

[26] On censorship and the Six Articles Act, see D. Loades, *Politics, Censorship and the English Reformation* (London, 1991), 131–47. On freedom of the press under the Seymour administration, see J.N. King, *English Reformation Literature: the Tudor Origins of the Protestant Tradition* (Princeton, 1982), 76–121.

[27] King, *English Reformation Literature*, 78–80.

[28] Quoted by King, *English Reformation Literature*, 79. See also *The Examinations*, ed. Beilin, xiv–liii.

unauthorized books, but more personal issues were at stake. A deliberate attempt was being made to discredit Gardiner in his own diocese, and the glued pages concealed an attack made by Bale in his commentary on William Paget, now a prominent figure in Seymour's government. In his letters, Gardiner tried to justify his role in Askew's trial, and condemned Bale because he 'would have Anne Askew, blasphemously denying the presence of Christes natural body, to be taken for a saint'.[29] The controversy continued in the following years. In addition to the separate publications of the two volumes in 1546 and 1547, Askew's texts were reprinted three times in the middle of the sixteenth century, and the passages referring to Paget were omitted in some of these editions.

After Somerset's deposition Askew's autobiography was not reprinted until the reign of Elizabeth, but it was of course its incorporation into Foxe's *Acts and Monuments* alongside the narratives of other godly women that ensured its survival in the ensuing centuries. Not surprisingly, Askew became the object of Catholic condemnation: the Jesuit Robert Parsons, for example, derided her as unfeminine because he had 'left the company of her husband, maister Kyme, to gad up and downe the countrey a ghospelling and ghossipinge where she might, and ought not';[30] while Miles Hogarde recorded that she defied those who came to offer her a pardon with 'opprobrious names' and made the sign of the gallows to the preacher at her execution.[31] Yet even within the Puritan tradition, Askew's reputation was not entirely secure, and her literary fate can be compared to that of her patron, Catherine, Duchess of Suffolk, whose flight from the persecution of Bonner and Gardiner became the subject of both a play and a song. The broadside ballad, 'I am a woman poore and blinde', which came out in a number of editions over a period of some seventy years during the seventeenth century, replaces the calm, rational and disputatious heroine of Askew's own testimonial with an image of feminine passivity and suffering. In this popular account of her death, the historical circumstances of her martyrdom are omitted, as are her doctrinal arguments, and, in King's words, she is reduced to a 'scarcely humanized embodiment of faith'.[32]

Unlike Barton, Eleanor Davies died with her reputation as a prophet intact, but in the long term their fates were not entirely dissimilar. Just as

---

29 *The Letters of Stephen Gardiner*, ed. J.A. Muller (Cambridge, 1933), 277–8.

30 *Narratives of the Days of the Reformation*, ed. J.G. Nichols, CS o.s. 77 (London, 1859), 309.

31 Miles Hogarde, *The displaying of the Protestantes* (1556), E7v.

32 King, *English Reformation Literature*, 444; cf. T. Watt, *Cheap Print and Popular Piety, 1550–1640* (Cambridge, 1991), 90–6; and J. Wiltenburg, *Disorderly Women and Female Power in the Street Literature of Early Modern England and Germany* (Charlottesville, 1992), 198.

Barton's predictions were used in the seventeenth century to provide a prophetic explanation of or justification for subsequent political developments, so Davies' message of universal salvation was reinterpreted after her death as a prognostication of the re-establishment of the monarchy (a rather ironic transformation given her attacks on Charles I).[33] On the whole, however, Davies seems to have been forgotten by all except her family and a few antiquarians, no doubt largely because she was not seen as a representative of a larger religious movement, and, like Anne Askew, her life was also reinscribed. In her epitaph, the substance of which is attributed in the 1670 continuation of Baker's *Chronicle* to Peter DuMoulin, Davies was represented as a paragon:

> Learned above her sex,
> Meek below her rank,
> Than most people greater
> Because more humble,
> In eminent beauty She possessed a lofty mind,
> In pleasing affability, singular modesty:
> In a woman's body a man's spirit,
> In most adverse circumstances a serene mind,
> In a wicked age unshaken piety and uprightness.[34]

In the same way as her unorthodox prophecies were given a more acceptable meaning after her death, so her transgressive behaviour was omitted from this conventional and inappropriate portrayal of feminine virtue.

The parallels between the fates of Anne Askew and Eleanor Davies can be taken even further. Anne Askew's reputation was not only kept alive in Foxe's *Acts and Monuments* and the broadside ballad, but also in the treatise entitled *An Essay to Revive the Ancient Education of Gentlewomen*, published in 1673, and written by Bathsua Makin, tutor to Charles I's daughter Elizabeth. As proof of the advantages of allowing women access to learning, Makin cites the example of Elizabeth I, going on to state that women were actually responsible for bringing about the Reformation:

> Mrs. Anne Askew, a person famous for learning and piety, so seasoned the Queen and ladies at Court, by her precepts and example, and after sealed her profession with her book, that the seed of reformation seemed to be sowed by her hand.[35]

For Makin, Askew was exemplary, not only as a leading figure in the Reformation, but also as a female scholar and author, and it was in these

---

[33] Richard Baker, *A chronicle of the kings of England* (1670), 635.

[34] Quoted in John Davies, *The Works in Verse and Prose*, ed. A.B. Grosart ([n. p.], 1869–1876), ii, cxxiii; Baker, *Chronicle*, 635.

[35] *An Essay to Revive the Ancient Education of Gentlewomen* in *The Female Spectator: English Women Writers before 1800*, ed. M.R. Mahn and H. Koon (Bloomington, 1977), 134.

latter capacities rather than as a prophet or Christian witness that she was subsequently celebrated as a woman of letters by George Ballard in his *Memoirs of several ladies of Great Britain* (1751).[36] Ballard's anthology also included a rare example of a posthumous edition of one of Eleanor Davies' tracts,[37] alongside a brief mention of the printed extracts of *The Book of Margery Kempe*, and works by writers as varied as Julian of Norwich, Margaret Roper, Queen Elizabeth, Katherine Philips and Mary Astell. Ballard comments on the difficulty of understanding her writing (his own interest is largely confined to what she reveals about her familial relationships), and confirms that Davies' fame was not long standing: in her time she had been 'the subject of much discourse, even from the Prince to the Peasant, tho' now almost wholly forgotten'.[38]

To conclude, Margery Kempe, Elizabeth Barton, Anne Askew, and even Eleanor Davies were charismatic figures in their day, but their posthumous fates varied considerably. Barton and Askew, who along with Kempe no doubt expected their reputations as holy women to survive, were remembered in recusant and Protestant circles respectively. In the case of Barton, it is clear that for political reasons her works were deliberately suppressed and her name defamed. To predict the King's death was a dangerous act. Eleanor Davies did not explicitly do so until the execution of Charles I was imminent; no doubt this explains her survival, but the difficulty in interpreting her texts meant that their popularity must have been limited, especially after her death. Quite apart from the vagaries of chance in one instance (*The Book of Margery Kempe*) and the success of a developing system of censorship in another (Barton's works), a further factor which has contributed to the obscurity of much women's writing is the marginalization of certain kinds of literary text. Increasingly in recent years, the marginal status of prophetic writings has been reconsidered, and the realization that the full range of texts and methods of textual production must be considered in the study of women's writing has resulted in all of these women becoming the subject of historical and literary interest. It is heartening to remember that even Margery Kempe's apparent obscurity only lasted from the sixteenth century until the rediscovery of her book in the early twentieth. Despite their diverse backgrounds, Kempe, Barton, Askew and Davies can usefully be considered as being part of a long-standing, culturally recognizable and often politically powerful tradition of female prophecy: believing that they were called to utter a divine message and witness to the world, they all saw themselves as secretaries of God.

36 George Ballard, *Memoirs of several ladies of Great Britain* (Oxford, 1752), 62–78. For an analysis of Ballard's contribution to women's literary history, see M.J.M. Ezell, *Writing Women's Literary History* (Baltimore, 1993), 79–103.

37 Ballard, *Memoirs*, 271–80.

38 Ballard, *Memoirs*, 271.

Bibliography

Primary Sources

Manuscripts

London, BL, MS Cleopatra Eiv.
    Documents relating to Elizabeth Barton.

London, BL, MS Harley 4990.
    Documents relating to Elizabeth Barton.

London, PRO, SP 1/50; SP 1/73; SP 1/77; SP 1/79; SP 1/80; SP 1/82; SP 1/138;
    SP 1/139; SP 1/140; SP 1/143.
    Documents relating to Elizabeth Barton.

London, PRO, SP 16/248 and SP 16/345.
    Unpublished poems by or attributed to Eleanor Davies, 'Hand writeing.
    October 1633. Exaudi Deus. psalme. 55', and 'When hee was come to the
    other side of the contrye'.

London, PRO, SP 16/380.
    Documents relating to Eleanor Davies.

Oxford, Bodleian Library, MS Rawlinson C 208.
    Account of William Thorpe's trial.

Oxford, Bodleian Library, MS Cherry 36.
    Elizabeth Tudor's prose translation of 'Le Miroir de l'Âme Pécheresse' of
    Marguerite d'Angouléme.

Early Printed Books and Tracts Published before 1800

Place of publication is London or unknown unless otherwise stated. Works are given
STC, and/or Wing's *STC* numbers. In the cases of works by Eleanor Davies and
Lucy Hastings, numbers in Hindle's *Bibliography* are also given. Where possible
confusion has rendered it necessary, I have annotated entries.

Askew, Anne, *The first examinacyon of Anne Askewe, latelye martyred in Smyth-*
    felde (Wesel, 1546), *STC* 848.
    ———, *The first examination of Anne Askew, lately martyred in Smith-fielde*
    (1585), *STC*, 849.
    ———, *The lattre examinacyon of Anne Askewe, with the elucydacyon of Johan*
    Bale (Wesel, 1547), *STC*, 850.
    ———, *The first examinacion of Anne Askewe. (The latter examynacyon)* (1547),
    STC 851.

————, *The firste examinacion of Anne Askew. (The latter examination)* (1548), *STC* 852.

————, *The fyrst examinacion of Anne Askewe. (The latter examinacion)* (1550), *STC* 852.5.

————, *The first examination of Anne Askew. (The lattre examinacion)* (1560), *STC* 853.

————, 'I am a woman poore and blind' (1624), *STC* 853.5.

Ayscu, Edward, *A historie contayning the warres, treaties, marriages, between England and Scotland* (1607), *STC* 1014.

Baker, Richard, *A chronicle of the kings of England* (1670), Wing, *STC* B506.

Bale, John, *The actes of Englysh votaryes, comprehendynge their vnchast practyses and examples by all ages* (Antwerp, 1546), *STC* 1270.

————, *The image of bothe churches after the moste wonderfull and heuenly reuelacion of Sainct John the euangelist* (Antwerp, 1548), *STC* 1297.

————, *A brefe chronycle concerning the examination and death of the blessed martir of Christ, Sir John Oldecastell the Lord Cobham* (1548), *STC* 1276.

Ballard, George, *Memoirs of several ladies of Great Britain* (Oxford, 1752).

Bayly, Thomas, *The life and death of that renowned John Fisher Bishop of Rochester* (1655), Wing, *STC* B1513.

Bourchier, Thomas, *Historia ecclesiastica da martyrio fratrvm ordinis divi Francisci* (Paris, 1582).

Cary, Mary, *The little horn's doom and downfall* (1651), Wing, *STC* C737.

————, *The resurrection of the witnesses* (1648), Wing, *STC* C737A.

Collins, An, *Divine Songs and meditacions* (1653), Wing, *STC* C5355.

Crowley, Robert, *The confutation of .xiii. articles wherunto Nicholas Shaxton, late bishop subscribed* (1548), *STC* 6083.

Davies, Eleanor, *All the kings of the earth shall prayse thee* (Amsterdam, 1633), *STC*, 903.5, Hindle, *Bibliography*, 2.

————, *Amend, amend; Gods kingdome is at hand* (1643), Wing, *STC* D1967, Hindle, *Bibliography*, 6.

————, *And without proving what we say* (1648), Wing, *STC* D1968, Hindle, *Bibliography*, 33.

————, *Apocalyps, chap. 11. Its accomplishment* (1648), Wing, *STC* D1969, Hindle, *Bibliography*, 52.

————, *Apocalypsis Jesu Christi* (1644), Wing, *STC* D1970, Hindle, *Bibliography*, 10.

————, *The appearance* (1650), Wing, *STC* D1972A, not in Hindle, *Bibliography*.

————, *The arraignment* (1650), Wing, *STC* D1972B, not in Hindle, *Bibliography*.

————, *As not unknowne, . . . this petition* (1645), Wing, *STC* D1973, Hindle, *Bibliography*, 14.

————, *Before the Lords second coming* (1650), Wing, *STC* D1974, Hindle, *Bibliography*, 43.

————, *The benidiction* (1651), Wing, *STC* D1975, Hindle, *Bibliography*, 46a.

————, *The benidiction* (1651), Wing, *STC* D1976, Hindle, *Bibliography*, 46b.

————, *The benediction* (1651), Wing, *STC* D1977, Hindle, *Bibliography*, 46c.

————, *Bethlehem signifying the house of bread* (1652), Wing, *STC* D1978, Hindle, *Bibliography*, 51.

———, *The bill of excommunication* (1650), Wing, *STC* D1979, Hindle, *Bibliography*, 40.

———, *The blasphemous charge against Her* (1649), Wing, *STC* D1980, Hindle, *Bibliography*, 37.

———, *The blasphemous charge against her* (1649), Wing, *STC* D1981, Hindle, *Bibliography*, 38.

———, *The brides preparation* (1645), Wing, *STC* D1982, Hindle, *Bibliography*, 15.

———, *The crying charge* (1649), Wing, *STC* D1982A, not in Hindle, *Bibliography*.

———, *The day of ivdgements modell* (1646), Wing, *STC* D1983, Hindle, *Bibliography*, 23.

———, *The dragons blasphemous charge* (1651), Wing, *STC* D1984, cf. Hindle, *Bibliography*, 48. Another edition of *The blasphemous charge*.

———, *Elijah the Tishbite's supplication* (1650), Wing, *STC* D1985, Hindle, *Bibliography*, 44.

———, *The everlasting gospel* (1649), Wing, *STC* D1986, Hindle, *Bibliography*, 36.

———, *The excommunication out of paradice* (1647), Wing, *STC* D1987, Hindle, *Bibliography*, 27.

———, *Ezekiel, Cap. 2.* (1647). Wing, *STC* D1988, Hindle, *Bibliography*, 53.

———, *Ezekiel the prophet explained* (1647), Wing, *STC* D1988A, not in Hindle, *Bibliography*.

———, *For the blessed feast of Easter* (1646), Wing, *STC* D1989, Hindle, *Bibliography*, 22.

———, *For the most honourable states sitting at White-Hall* (1649), Wing, *STC* D1989A, not in Hindle, *Bibliography*.

———, *For the right noble, Sir Balthazar Gerbier* (1649), Wing, *STC* D1989B, not in Hindle, *Bibliography*.

———, *For Whitson Tyds last feast* (1645), Wing, *STC* D1990, Hindle, *Bibliography*, 17.

———, Fragment: 'hour, Europe the Worlds third part . . .' (1646), not in Wing, *STC*, Hindle, *Bibliography*, 26.

———, *From the Lady Eleanor, her blessing* (1644), Wing, *STC* D1991, Hindle, *Bibliography*, 9.

———, *The Gatehouse salutation from* (1647), Wing, *STC* D1991A, not in Hindle, *Bibliography*.

———, *Given to the Elector Prince Charles of the Rhyne from the Lady Eleanor* (1648), Wing, *STC* D1992, Hindle, *Bibliography*, 29.

———, *Given to the Elector Prince Charls of the Rhyne from the Lady Eleanor* (1651), Wing, *STC* D1993, Hindle, *Bibliography*, 48.

———, *Great Brittains visitation* (1645) Wing, *STC* D1994, Hindle, *Bibliography*, 18.

———, *Hells destruction* (1651), Wing, *STC* D1995, Hindle, *Bibliography*, 45.

———, *Her appeal from the court to the camp* (1649), not in Wing, *STC* or Hindle, *Bibliography*. Copy seen: Washington DC, Folger Shakespeare Library, ac 186721.19.

————, *Je le tien. The general restitvtion* (1646), Wing, *STC* D1996A, not in Hindle, *Bibliography*.

————, *The Lady Eleanor Douglas, dowager, her iubilees plea* (1650), Wing, *STC* D1996B, not in Hindle, *Bibliography*.

————, *The Lady Eleanor her appeal* (1646), Wing, *STC* D1972, Hindle, *Bibliography*, 25.

————, *The Lady Eleanor, her appeale to the High Covrt of Parliament* (1641), Wing, *STC* D1971, Hindle, *Bibliography*, 4.

————, *The Lady Eleanor her remonstrance* (1648), Wing, *STC* D2006, Hindle, *Bibliography*, 30.

————, *The mystery of general redemption* (1647), Wing, *STC* D1996C, not in Hindle, *Bibliography*.

————, *The new Jerusalem at hand* (1649), Wing, *STC* D1997, Hindle, *Bibliography*, 34.

————, *Of errors ioyned with Gods word* (1645), Wing, *STC* D1999, Hindle, *Bibliography*, 16.

————, *Of the general great days approach* (1648), Wing, *STC* D1999A, not in Hindle, *Bibliography*.

————, *Of times and seasons* (1651), Wing, *STC* D2000, Hindle, *Bibliography*, 49.

————, *A prayer or letter for the peoples conversion and deliverance from their distraction* (1649), not in Wing, *STC* or Hindle, *Bibliography*. Printed on continuous signatures with *A prayer or petition for peace* (1649). Copy seen: Washington DC, Folger Shakespeare Library, ac 186721.6.

————, *A prayer or letter for the peoples conversion and deliverance from their distraction* (1649), not in Wing, *STC* or Hindle, *Bibliography*. Printed on continuous signatures with *Sions Lamentation* (1649). Copy seen: Oxford, Bodleian Library, 12 Θ 1336 (11).

————, *A prayer or petition for peace* (1644), Wing, *STC* D2001, Hindle, *Bibliography*, 11.

————, *A prayer, or petition of peace* (1645), Wing, *STC* D2002, Hindle, *Bibliography*, 19.

————, *A prayer or petition for peace* (1647), Wing, *STC* D2003, Hindle, *Bibliography*, 28.

————, *A prayer, or petition for peace* (1649), not in Wing, *STC* or Hindle, *Bibliography*. Copy seen: Washington DC, Folger Shakespeare Library, ac 186721.6.

————, *A prayer or petition for peace* (1649), not in Wing, *STC* or Hindle, *Bibliography*. Copy seen: Oxford, Worcester College Library, B.B.1.6. (112).

————, *Presented a letter or petition from their tedious distraction for a speedy deliverance* (1649), not in Wing, *STC* or Hindle, *Bibliography*. Another edition of *A prayer or letter for the peoples conversion and deliverance from their distraction* printed on continuous signatures with *A prayer, or petition for peace* (1649). Copy seen: Oxford, Worcester College Library, B.B.1.6 (112).

————, *A prophesie of the last day* (1645), Wing, *STC* D2004, Hindle, *Bibliography*, 20. A fragment of this tract is recorded as *I am the first, and the last*, Wing, *STC* D1996, Hindle, *Bibliography*, 13.

————, *Prophetia de die* (1644), Wing, *STC* D2005, not in Hindle, *Bibliography*.

167

————, *Reader, the heavy hour at hand* (1648), Wing, *STC* D2005.5, not in Hindle, *Bibliography*.

————, *The restitution of prophecy* (1651), Wing, *STC* D2007, Hindle, *Bibliography*, 47.

————, *The restitvtion of reprobates* (1644), Wing, *STC* D2008, Hindle, *Bibliography*, 8.

————, *The revelation interpreted* (1646), Wing, *STC* D2009, Hindle, *Bibliography*, 24.

————, *Samsons fall* (1642). Wing, *STC* D2010, Hindle, *Bibliography*, 42.

————, *Samsons legacie* (1643), Wing, *STC* D2011, cf. Hindle, *Bibliography*, 5.

————, *The second comming of Our Lord* (1645), Wing, *STC* D2012, Hindle, *Bibliography*, 21.

————, *The serpents excommunication* (1651), Wing, *STC* D2012A, not in Hindle, *Bibliography*.

————, *A sign given them* (1649), Wing, *STC* D2012AA, not in Hindle, *Bibliography*.

————, *Sions lamentation* (1649), Wing, *STC* D2012B, cf. Hindle, *Bibliography*, 41. Some copies are catalogued by Wing as *Zach.12. And they shall look*, Wing, *STC* D2020, Hindle, *Bibliography*, 41.

————, *The star to the wise* (1643), Wing, *STC* D2013, Hindle, *Bibliography*, 7.

————, *Strange and wonderful prophesies* (1649), Wing, *STC* D2014, Hindle, *Bibliography*, 35.

————, *Tobits book, a lesson* (1652), Wing, *STC* D2016, Hindle, *Bibliography*, 50.

————, *To the Kings most excellent majesty: the humble petition* (1648), not in Wing, *STC*, cf. Hindle, *Bibliography*, 29. This tract is attached to the end of *Given to the Elector* (1648). Copies seen: Oxford, Worcester College Library, A.A.1.11 (18), A.A.1.12 (2) and B.B.X.6 (1).

————, *To the most honorable the High Covrt of Parliament assembled &c. My Lords; ther's a time* (1643), Wing, *STC* D2015, Hindle, *Bibliography*, 5.

————, *To the most honorable the High Covrt of Parliament assembled &c. My Lords, As theres a time* (1649), not in Wing, *STC* or Hindle, *Bibliography*. Printed on continuous signatures with *Samsons fall*. Copy seen: Washington DC, Folger Shakespeare Library, ac 186721.2

————, *A warning to the dragon and all his angels* (1625), *STC* 904, Hindle, *Bibliography*, 1.

————, *Wherefore to prove the thing* (1648), Wing, *STC* D2017, Hindle, *Bibliography*, 32.

————, *Woe to the house* (Amsterdam, 1633), *STC* 904.5, Hindle, *Bibliography*, 3.

————, *The word of God* (1644), Wing, *STC* D2018, Hindle, *Bibliography*, 12.

————, *The writ of restitution* (1648), Wing, *STC* D2019, Hindle, *Bibliography*, 31.

Elizabeth I, *A godly medytacyon of the christen sowle* (Wesel, 1548), *STC*, 17320.

Fell, Margaret, *Women's speaking justified* (1666), Wing *STC* F642.

Foxe, John, *Actes and monuments of these latter and perillous dayes, touching matters of the church* (1563), *STC* 11222.

————, *Actes and monuments of matters most speciall in the church* (4th ed. 1583), *STC* 11225.

Goodwin, John, *Redemption redeemed* (1651), Wing, *STC* G1149.

Hakewill, George, *An apologie or declaration of the power and providence of our God* (Oxford, 1635), *STC* 12613.

Hastings, Lucy, *The new proclamation in answer* (1649),Wing, *STC* D1998, Hindle, *Bibliography*, 39. Wing attributes this work to Eleanor Davies.

Heylyn, Peter, *Cyprianus Anglicus* (1668), Wing, *STC* H1699.

Hogarde, Miles, *The displaying of the Protestantes, with a description of diuers their abuses* (1556), *STC* 13557.

James I, *King James his divine prophecie* (1645), Wing, *STC* J134.

Jessey, Henry, *The exceeding riches off grace advanced* (1647), Wing, *STC* J687.

Lambarde, William, *A perambulation of Kent: conteining the description . . . of that shyre* (1576), STC 15175.

————, *A perambulation of Kent . . . now increased and altered* (1596), *STC* 15176.

More, Thomas, *The workes of Sir Thomas More*, ed. W. Rastell (1557), *STC* 18076.

Morison, Richard, *Apomaxis calvmniarum* (1537), *STC* 18109.

N. N., *Maria triumphans. Being a discourse, wherein the B. Virgin Mary is defended* (St Omer, 1635), *STC* 18331.

Sanders, Nicholas, *De origine progressu schismatis Anglicani* (Cologne, 1585).

Thorpe, William, *The examinacion of master William Thorpe preste accused of heresye. The examinacion of syr John Oldcastell* (Antwerp, 1530), *STC* 24045.

Touchet, Mervin, *The arraignement and conviction of Mervin Lord Avdley* (1643), Wing, *STC* A3743.

————, *The trial of the Lord Audley* (1679), Wing, *STC* T2227.

————, *The tryal and condemnation of Mervin, Lord Audley* (1699), Wing, *STC* T2144.

Trapnel, Anna, *The cry of a stone* (1654), Wing, *STC* T2031.

————, *Anna Trapnel's report and plea* (1654), Wing, *STC* T2033.

Voragine, Jacobus de, *The legende named in latyn legenda aurea*, trans. W. Caxton (Westminster, 1483), *STC* 24873.

Winstanley, Gerrard, *The new law of righteousnes* (1649), Wing, *STC* W3049.

————, *The saints paradice: or, the fathers teaching* (1648), Wing, *STC* W3051.

Medieval and Early Modern Works Edited or Reprinted after 1800

Listed alphabetically under author or, where appropriate, under title, rather than under editor.

Aquinas, St Thomas, *Summa theologiæ*, ed. and trans. T. Gilby (London, 1964–1976), 60 vols.

Askew, Anne, *The Examinations of Anne Askew*, ed. E. Beilin (Oxford, 1996).

Audelay, John, *The Poems of John Audelay*, ed. E.K. Whiting, EETS o.s. 184 (London, 1931).

Bale, John, *The Complete Plays of John Bale*, ed. P. Happé, Tudor Interludes 4 and 5 (Cambridge, 1985–1986), 2 vols.

————, *The Vocacyon of Johan Bale*, ed. P. Happé and J.N. King, Medieval and Renaissance Texts and Studies 70 (Binghamton, N.Y., 1990).

169

Ballads from the Manuscripts, ed. F.J. Furnivall (London, 1868), 2 vols.

Bridget of Sweden, *The Liber Celestis of St Bridget of Sweden*, ed. R. Ellis, EETS o.s. 291 (Oxford, 1987).

———, *The Revelations of Saint Birgitta*, ed. W. P. Cumming, EETS o.s. 178 (London, 1929).

Bridgett, T.E., *Life of Blessed John Fisher, Bishop of Rochester, Cardinal to the Holy Roman Church, and Martyr under Henry VIII* (London, 1888)

Catherine of Siena, *The Orcherd of Syon*, ed. P. Hodgson and G. Liegey, EETS o.s. 258 (London, 1966).

Cavendish, George, *The Life and Death of Cardinal Weolsey*, ed. R. S. Sylvester, EETS o.s. 243 (London, 1959).

The Cell of Self-Knowledge: Seven Early English Mystical Treatises printed by Henry Pepwell in 1521, ed. E.G. Gardner (London, 1910).

The Chastising of God's Children and the Treatise of Perfection of the Sons of God, ed. J. Bazire and E. Colledge (Oxford, 1957).

Christine de Pisan, *The Book of the City of Ladies*, trans. E. R. Richards (New York, 1983).

———, *Ditié de Jehanne d'Arc*, ed. A.J. Kennedy and K. Varty, Medium Ævum Monographs n.s. 9 (Oxford, 1977).

———, *The Treasure of the City of Ladies*, trans. S. Lawson (Harmondsworth, 1985).

Chronicle of the Grey Friars of London, ed. J. G. Nichols, CS o.s. 53 (London, 1852).

Cobbett's Complete Collection of State Trials and Proceedings for High Treason and Other Crimes and Misdemeanors (London, 1809–1828), 34 vols.

A Collection of Ranter Writings from the Seventeenth Century, ed. N. Smith (London, 1983).

Cranmer, Thomas, *A Confutation of Unwritten Verities* in *The Remains of Thomas Cranmer*, ed. H. Jenkyns (Oxford, 1833), iv, 143–244.

———, *The Works of Thomas Cranmer*, ed. J. E. Cox (Cambridge, 1846), 2 vols.

Cromwell, Thomas, *Life and Letters of Thomas Cromwell*, ed. R.B. Merriman (Oxford, 1968), 2 vols.

Davenant, William, *The Shorter Poems, and Songs from the Plays and Masques*, ed. A.M. Gibbs (Oxford, 1972).

Davies, Eleanor, *Prophetic Writings of Eleanor Davies*, ed. E.S. Cope (Oxford, 1995).

Davies, John, *The Poems of Sir John Davies*, ed. R. Krueger (Oxford, 1975).

———, *The works in Verse and Prose of Sir John Davies*, ed. A.B. Grosart ([np], 1869–1876), 3 vols.

Elizabeth I, *The Mirror of the Sinful Soul: a Prose Translation*, intro. P.W. Ames (London, 1897).

———, *Elizabeth's Glass with 'The Glass of the Sinful Soul' (1544) by Elizabeth I and 'Epistle Dedicatory' & 'Conclusion' (1548) by John Bale*, intro. M. Shell (Lincoln, Nebraska, 1993).

Elizabeth of Hungary, 'The reuelacions of saynt Elysabeth of Hungary,' ed. C. Horstmann *Archiv für Neuere Sprachen* lxxvi (1866), 392–400.

An English Chronicle of the Reigns of Richard II., Henry IV., Henry V., and Henry VI. Written before the Year 1471, ed. J.S. Davies, CS o.s. 64 (London, 1861).

170

English Wycliffite Sermons, ed. A. Hudson and P. Gradon (Oxford, 1983–1990), 3 vols.

Eusebius Pamphili, *Ecclesiastical History, Books 1–5*, trans. R. J. Deferrari, The Fathers of the Church 19 (Washington DC, 1953).

Foxe, John, *The Acts and Monuments of John Foxe*, ed. J. Pratt (4th ed. London, 1877), 8 vols.

Gardiner, Stephen, *The Letters of Stephen Gardiner*, ed. J.A. Muller (Cambridge, 1933).

Geoffrey of Monmouth, *History of the Kings of England*, trans. S. Evans, rev. C.W. Dunn (London, 1963).

Gerson, Jean, 'De Probatione Spirituum' in *Oeuvres Complètes*, ed. Mnr. P. Glorieux (Paris, 1960–1973), ix, 177–85.

Hall, Edward, *Hall's Chronicle; containing the History of England*, ed. H. Ellis London, 1809).

Hall, Richard, *Vie du bienheureux martyr Jean Fisher, Cardinal, Evêque de Rochester (†1535)*, ed. Fr. van Ortroy (Brussels, 1893).

Harpsfield, Nicholas, *The life and death of Sir Thomas Moore, knight*, ed. E.V. Hitchock, intro. R.W. Chambers, EETS o.s. 186 (London, 1932).

Herbert, George, *The Works of George Herbert*, ed. F.E. Hutchinson (Oxford, 1953).

Heresy Trials in the Diocese of Norwich, 1428–1431, ed. N.P. Tanner, CS 4th series 20 (London, 1977).

Hilton, Walter, [possibly] *The Prickynge of Love*, ed. H. Kane, Salzburg Studies in English Literature: Elizabethan and Renaissance Studies 92: 10 (Salzburg, 1983).

————, *The Scale of Perfection*, ed. E. Underhill (London, 1923).

Hoccleve, Thomas, *Hoccleve's Works: the Minor Poems*, ed. F.J. Furnivall and I. Gollancz, rev. J. Mitchell and A.I. Doyle, EETS e.s. 61 and 73 (London, 1970).

Howard, Henry, *Henry Howard, Earl of Surrey: Poems*, ed. E. Jones (Oxford, 1964).

St Jerome, *The Principle Works of Saint Jerome*, trans. W.H. Freemantle, G. Lewis and W.G. Martley, A Select Library of Nicene and Post-Nicene Fathers of the Christian Church 2nd series 4 (Oxford, 1893).

Julian of Norwich, *A Book of Showings to the Anchoress Julian of Norwich*, ed. E. Colledge and J. Walsh (Toronto, 1978), 2 vols.

————, *A Revelation of Love*, ed. M. Glasscoe (Exeter, 1976).

Kempe, Margery, *The Book of Margery Kempe*, ed. S.B. Meech and H.E. Allen, EETS o.s. 212 (Oxford, 1940).

————, *The Book of Margery Kempe*, trans. B.A. Windeatt (Harmondsworth, 1985).

The Lay Folks Mass Book or the Manner of Hearing Mass, ed. T.F. Simmons, EETS o.s. 71 (London, 1879).

The Life of Christina of Markyate: a Twelfth Century Recluse, ed. and trans. C.H. Talbot (Oxford, 1959).

The Lisle Letters, ed. M. St C. Byrne (Chicago, 1981), 6 vols.

Love, Nicholas, *Mirrour of the Blessed Lyf of Jesu Christ*, ed. J. Hogg and L.F. Powell, Analecta Cartusiana 91 (Salzberg, 1989), 2 vols.

The Monk of Farne: The Meditations of a Fourteenth-Century Monk, trans. a Benedictine of Stanbrook, ed. H. Farmer (London, 1961).

More, Thomas, *A Dialogue Concerning Heresies*, ed. T.C. Lawler, G. Marc'hadour and R.C. Marius, The Yale Edition of the Complete Works of St Thomas More 3 (New Haven, 1981), 2 parts.

——, *The Correspondence of Sir Thomas More*, ed. E.F. Rogers (Princeton, 1947).

Milton, John, *Complete Poems and Major Prose*, ed. M.Y. Hughes (New York, 1957).

Narratives of the Days of the Reformation chiefly from the Manuscripts of John Foxe the Martyrologist with Two Contemporary Biographies of the Archbishop Cranmer, ed. J.G. Nichols, CS o.s. 77 (London, 1859).

Nashe, Thomas, *The Works of Thomas Nashe*, ed. R.B. McKerrow, rev. F.P. Wilson (Oxford, 1966), 5 vols.

Netter, Thomas, *Doctrinale antiquitatum fidei catholicae ecclesiae*, ed. F.B. Blanciotte (Venice, 1757–1759; republished Farnborough, 1967), 3 vols.

Nova legenda anglicæ: as Collected by John of Tynemouth, John Capgrave and Others, ed. C. Horstmann (Oxford, 1901), 2 vols.

Nucius, Nicander, *The Second Book of the Travels of Nicander Nucius of Corcyra*, ed. J.A. Cranmer, CS o.s. 17 (London, 1841).

Overton, Richard, *The Araignment of Mr. Persecution*, reprinted in *Tracts on Liberty in the Puritan Revolution 1638–1647*, ed. W. Haller (New York, 1934), iii, 205–56.

'Prosalegenden. Die legenden des ms Douce 114', ed. C. Horstmann, *Anglia* viii (1885), 102–96.

Raymond of Capua, *The Life of Saint Catherine of Siena*, trans. G. Lamb (London, 1960).

A Revelation of Purgatory by an Unknown Fifteenth Century Woman Visionary: Introduction, Critical Text and Translation, ed. M.P. Harley, Studies in Women and Religion 18 (Lewiston, N.Y., 1985).

Rolle, Richard, *The Fire of Love and the Mending of Life or the Rule of Living*, trans. R. Misyn, ed. R. Harvey, EETS o.s. 106 (London, 1896).

——, *The English Writings of Richard Rolle, Hermit of Hampole*, ed. H.E. Allen (Oxford, 1931).

Roper, William, *The Lyfe of Sir Thomas Moore, knighte*, ed. E.V. Hitchock, EETS o.s. 197 (London, 1935).

'The Sermon against the Holy Maid of Kent and her Adherents, delivered at Paul's Cross, November the 23rd, 1533, and at Canterbury, December the 7th', ed. L.E. Whatmore, *English Historical Review* lviii (1943), 463–75.

Statutes of the Realm, ed. A. Luders et al. (1810–1828), 11 vols.

Tacitus, *On Britain and Germany: A New Translation of the 'Agricola' and the 'Germanica'*, trans. H. Mattingley (Harmondsworth, 1948).

St Teresa of Avila, *The Lyf of the Mother Teresa of Jesus*, English Recusant Literature 1558–1640 212 (Antwerp, 1611; reproduced Ilkley, 1974).

——, *The Life of St Teresa of Àvila by Herself*, trans. J.M. Cohen (Harmondsworth, 1957).

Three Chapters of Letters Relating to the Suppression of Monasteries, ed. T. Wright, CS o.s. 26 (London, 1843).

The Trial of Jeanne d'Arc, trans. W.P. Barrett (London, 1931).

Two Wycliffite Texts: the Sermon of William Taylor 1406; the Testament of William Thorpe 1407, ed. A. Hudson, EETS o.s. 301 (Oxford, 1993).

Tyndale, William, *An Answer to Sir Thomas More's Dialogue*, ed. H. Walter (Cambridge, 1850).

———, *The New Testament 1534*, ed. N.H. Wallis (Cambridge, 1938).

———, *The Obedience of a Christian Man* in *Doctrinal Treatises and Introductions to Different Portions of the Holy Scripture*, ed. H. Walter (Cambridge, 1848), 127–344.

Voragine, Jacobus de, *The Golden Legend*, trans. G. Ryan and H. Ripperger (Toronto, 1941).

Winstanley, Gerrard, *The Law of Freedom and Other Writings*, ed. C. Hill (Cambridge, 1983).

Wriothesley, Charles, *A Chronicle of England during the Reigns of the Tudors from AD 1485 to 1559*, ed. W.D. Hamilton, CS 2nd series 11 and 20 (London, 1875–1877), 2 vols.

Yorkshire Writers: Richard Rolle of Hampole an English Father of the Church and His Followers, ed. C. Horstmann (London, 1895–1896), 2 vols.

Selected Secondary Works

Aers, D., *Community, Gender, and Individual Identity: English Writing 1360–1430* (London, 1988), 73–116.

———, ed., *Culture and History 1350–1600: Essays on English Communities, Identities and Writing* (London, 1992).

Ahlgren, G.T., 'Visions and Rhetorical Strategy in the Letters of Hildegard of Bingen' in *Dear Sister: Medieval Women and the Epistolary Genre*, ed. K. Cherewatuk and U. Wiethaus (Philadelphia, 1993), 46–63.

Alter, R., *The Art of Biblical Narrative* (New York, 1981).

Armstrong, C.A.J., 'The Piety of Cicely, Duchess of York: A Study in Late Medieval Culture' in *For Hilaire Belloc: Essays in Honour of his Seventy-Second Birthday*, ed. D. Woodruff (London, 1942), 73–94.

Armstrong, I., ed., *New Feminist Discourses: Critical Essays on Theories and Texts* (London, 1992).

Aston, M., *England's Iconoclasts: Laws against Images* (Oxford, 1988).

———, 'Lollard Women Priests?' *Journal of Ecclesiastical History* xxxi (1980), 441–61.

———, *Lollards and Reformers: Images and Literacy in Late Medieval Religion* (London, 1984).

———, 'Lollardy and Literacy', *History* lxii (1977), 347–71.

Atkinson, C.W., *Mystic and Pilgrim: The Book and the World of Margery Kempe* (Ithaca, N.Y., 1983).

Aughterson, K., *Renaissance Woman, Constructions of Femininity in England: a Sourcebook* (London, 1995).

Bainton, R.H., *Women of the Reformation in France and England* (Minneapolis, 1973), 211–29.

Baker, D., ed., *Medieval Women: Dedicated and Presented to Professor Rosalind M.T. Hill on the Occasion of Her Seventieth Birthday*, Studies in Church History subsidia 1 (Oxford, 1978).

Barratt, A., ed., *Women's Writing in Middle English* (London, 1992).

Bartlett, A.C., ed., *Vox Mystica: Essays on Medieval Mysticism* (Cambridge, 1995).

Bauckham, R., *Tudor Apocalypse. Sixteenth Century Apocalypticism, Millennarianism and the English Reformation: from John Bale to John Foxe and Thomas Brightman*, Courtenay Library of Reformation Classics 8 (Oxford, 1978).

Beckwith, S., 'A Very Material Mysticism: The Medieval Mysticism of Margery Kempe' in *Medieval Literature: Criticism, Ideology and History*, ed. D. Aers (Brighton, 1986), 34–57.

———, 'Problems of Authority in Late Medieval Mysticism: Language, Agency and Authority in *The Book of Margery Kempe*', *Exemplaria* iv (1992), 171–99.

Beer, F., *Women and Mystical Experience in the Middle Ages* (Woodbridge, 1992).

Beilin, E.V., 'Anne Askew's Dialogue with Authority' in *Contending Kingdoms: Historical, Psychological and Feminist Approaches to the Literature of Sixteenth-Century England and France*, ed. M.R. Logan and P.L. Rudnytsky (Detroit, 1991), 313–22.

———, 'Anne Askew's Self-Portrait in the *Examinations*' in *Silent but for the Word: Tudor Women as Patrons, Translators, and Writers of Religious Works*, ed. M.P. Hannay (Kent, Ohio, 1985), 77–91.

———, *Redeeming Eve: Women Writers of the English Renaissance* (Princeton, 1987).

Bell, M., G. Parfitt and S. Shepherd, eds., *A Bibliographical Dictionary of English Women Writers 1580–1720* (Hemel Hempstead, 1990).

Bell, R., *Holy Anorexia* (Chicago, 1985).

Bennett, J.M., 'Medieval Women, Modern Women: Across the Great Divide' in *Culture and History 1350–1600: Essays on English Communities, Identities and Writing*, ed. D. Aers (London, 1992), 147–75.

Benton, J.F., 'Consciousness of Self and Perceptions of Individuality' in *Renaissance and Renewal in the Twelfth Century*, ed. R.L. Benson and G. Constable (Oxford, 1982), 263–96.

Berg, C. and P. Berry, 'Spiritual Whoredom: an Essay on Female Prophets in the Seventeenth Century' in *1642: Literature and Power in the Seventeenth Century*, ed. F. Barker, J. Bernstein, J. Coombes, P. Hulme, J. Stone and J. Stratton (Colchester, 1981), 37–54.

Bilinkoff, J., 'A Spanish Prophetess and Her Patrons: the Case of María de Santo Domingo', *Sixteenth Century Journal* xxiii (1992), 21–34.

Bingham, C., 'Seventeenth-Century Attitudes Toward Deviant Sex', *Journal of Interdisciplinary History* i (1971), 447–72.

Blamires, A., 'The Limits of Bible Study for Medieval Women' in *Women, the Book and the Godly*, ed. L. Smith and J. Taylor (Cambridge, 1995), 1–12.

Blamires, A., K. Pratt and C.W. Marx, eds., *Woman Defamed and Woman Defended: An Anthology of Medieval Texts* (Oxford, 1992).

Boffey, J., 'Women Authors and Women's Literacy in Fourteenth- and Fifteenth-Century England' in *Women and Literature in Britain, 1150–1500*, ed. C.M. Meale, Cambridge Studies in Medieval Literature 17 (Cambridge, 1993), 159–82.

Bolton, B.M., '*Vitae Matrum*: A Further Aspect of *Frauenfrage*' in *Medieval Women: Dedicated and Presented to Professor Rosalind M.T. Hill on the Occasion of Her Seventieth Birthday*, ed. D. Baker, Studies in Church History subsidia 1 (Oxford, 1978), 253–73.

Bosse, R.B., 'Margery Kempe's Tarnished Reputation: a Reassessment', *Fourteenth Century English Mystics Newsletter* v (1979), 9–19.

Boyd, B., ed., *The Middle English Miracles of the Virgin* (San Marino, Calif., 1964).

Brant, C., and D. Purkiss, eds., *Women, Texts, and Histories: 1575–1760* (London, 1992).

Breasted, B., '*Comus* and the Castlehaven Scandal', *Milton Studies* iii (1971), 201–24.

Bridenthal, R., C. Koonz and S. Stuard, eds., *Becoming Visible: Women in European History* (Boston, 1987).

Brigden, S., *London and the Reformation* (Oxford, 1989).

Brown, D.C., *Pastor and Laity in the Theology of Jean Gerson* (Cambridge, 1987).

Brown, P., *The Cult of the Saints* (London, 1981).

Burckhardt, J., *The Civilization of the Renaissance*, trans. S.G.C. Middlemore (London, 1944).

Burke, P., 'How to be a Counter-Reformation Saint', in *Religion and Society in Early Modern Europe 1500–1800*, ed. K. von Greyerz (London, 1984), 45–55.

Butler, J., *Gender Trouble: Feminism and the Subversion of Identity* (New York, 1990).

Bynum, C.W., 'Did the Twelfth Century Discover the Individual?' *Journal of Ecclesiastical History* xxxi (1980), 1–17.

———, *Holy Feast and Holy Fast: the Religious Significance of Food to Medieval Women* (Berkeley, 1987).

———, *Jesus as Mother: Studies in the Spirituality of the High Middle Ages*, Publications of the Center for Medieval and Renaissance Studies UCLA 16 (Berkeley, 1982).

Capp, B., *The Fifth Monarchy Men: a Study in Seventeenth-Century Millenarianism* (London, 1972).

Chaytor, H.J., *From Script to Print: an Introduction to Medieval Vernacular Literature* (London, 1966).

Chedgzoy, K., M. Hansen and S. Trill, eds., *Voicing Women: Gender and Sexuality in Early Modern Writing* (Keele, 1996).

Cheney, A.D., 'The Holy Maid of Kent', *Transactions of the Royal Historical Society* n.s. xviii (1904), 107–29.

Certeau, M. de, *Heterologies: Discourse on the Other*, trans. B. Massumi, Theory and History of Literature 17 (London, 1986).

———, *The Mystic Fable Volume One: the Sixteenth and Seventeenth Centuries*, trans. M.B. Smith (Chicago, 1992).

Cherewatuk, K., and U. Wiethaus, *Dear Sister: Medieval Women and the Epistolary Genre* (Philadelphia, 1993).

Christian, W.A., *Apparitions in Late Medieval and Renaissance Spain* (Princeton, 1981).

Christie-Murray, D., *A History of Heresy* (Oxford, 1989).

Cixous, H., 'The Laugh of the Medusa', trans. K. Cohen and P. Cohen, *Signs* i (1976), 876–99.

Clanchy, M.T., *From Memory to Written Record: England 1066–1307* (2nd ed. London, 1993).

Clark, A., *Working Life of Women in the Seventeenth Century* (rpt. London, 1982).

Clarke, D., 'The Iconography of the Blush: Marian Literature of the 1630s' in *Voicing Women: Gender and Sexuality in Early Modern Writing*, ed. K. Chedgzoy, M. Hansen and S. Trill (Keele, 1996), 111–28.

Clay, R.M., *The Hermits and Anchorites of England* (London, 1914).

Cleve, G., 'Margery Kempe: A Scandinavian Influence on Medieval England' in *The Medieval Mystical Tradition in England*, ed. M. Glasscoe, Exeter Symposium 5 (Cambridge, 1992), 163–78.

Cohn, N., *The Pursuit of the Millennium: Revolutionary Millenarians and Mystical Anarchists of the Middle Ages* (London, 1970).

Colledge, E., '*Epistola solitarii ad reges*: Alphonse of Pecha as Organizer of Brigittine and Urbanist Propaganda', *Medieval Studies* xviii (1956), 19–49.

Constable, G., 'Ælred of Rievaulx and the Nun of Watton: an Episode in the Early History of the Gilbertine Order' in *Medieval Women: Dedicated and Presented to Professor Rosalind M.T. Hill on the Occasion of Her Seventieth Birthday*, ed. D. Baker, Studies in Church History subsidia 1 (Oxford, 1978), 205–26.

Cope, E.S., ' "Dame Eleanor Davies Never Soe Mad a Ladie" ', *Huntington Library Quarterly* i (1987), 133–44.

———, *Handmaid of the Holy Spirit: Dame Eleanor Davies, Never Soe Mad a Ladie* (Ann Arbor, 1992).

Costa, M. Ortega, 'Spanish Women in the Reformation' in *Women in Reformation and Counter-Reformation Europe: Public and Private Worlds*, ed. S. Marshall (Bloomington, 1989), 89–119.

Crawford, P., *Women and Religion in England, 1500–1720* (London, 1993).

Cressy, D., *Literacy and the Social Order: Reading and Writing in Tudor and Stuart England* (Cambridge, 1980).

Cross, C., ' "Great Reasoner's in Scripture": the Activities of Women Lollards 1380–1530' in *Medieval Women: Dedicated and Presented to Professor Rosalind M.T. Hill on the Occasion of Her Seventieth Birthday*, ed. D. Baker, Studies in Church History subsidia 1 (Oxford, 1978), 359–80.

Cuming, G.J., and D. Baker, eds., *Popular Belief and Practice*, Studies in Church History 8 (Cambridge, 1972), 195–202.

Dailey, B.R., 'The Visitation of Sarah Wight: Holy Carnival and the Revolution of the Saints in Civil War London', *Church History* lv (1986), 438–55.

Davies, W.T., 'A Bibliography of John Bale,' *Proceedings and Papers of the Oxford Bibliographical Society* v (1936–1939), 201–79.

Davis, J., 'Joan of Kent, Lollardy and the English Reformation', *Journal of Ecclesiastical History* xxxiii (1982), 225–33.

Davis, N.Z., *Society and Culture in Early Modern France* (London, 1975).

Delaney, S., ' "Mothers to Think Back Through": Who are They? The Ambiguous Example of Christine de Pizan' in *Medieval Texts and Contemporary Readers*, ed. L.A. Finke and M.S. Shichtman (Ithaca, N.Y., 1987), 177–97.

Devereux, E.J., 'Elizabeth Barton and Tudor Censorship', *Bulletin of the John Rylands Library* xlix (1966–1967), 91–106.

Dickens, A.C., *The English Reformation* (London, 1964).

Dickman, S., 'Margery Kempe and the Continental Tradition of the Pious Woman' in *The Medieval Mystical Tradition in England: Papers read at Dartington Hall, July 1984*, ed. M. Glasscoe (Cambridge, 1984), 150–68.

——, 'Margery Kempe and the English Devotional Tradition' in *The Medieval Mystical Tradition in England: Papers read at the Exeter Symposium, July 1980*, ed. M. Glasscoe (Exeter, 1980), 156–72.

Dillon, J., 'Holy Women and their Confessors or Confessors and their Holy Women? Margery Kempe and Continental Tradition' in *Prophets Abroad: the Reception of Continental Holy Women in Late-Medieval England*, ed. R. Voaden (Cambridge, 1996), 115–40.

Dinzelbacher, P., 'The Beginnings of Mysticism Experienced in Twelfth-Century England' in *The Medieval Mystical Tradition in England*, ed. M. Glasscoe, Exeter Symposium 4 (Cambridge, 1987), 111–13.

Dobin, H., *Merlin's Disciples: Prophecy, Poetry and Power in Renaissance England* (Stanford, Calif., 1990).

Dodds, M.D., 'Political Prophecies in the Reign of Henry VIII', *Modern Languages Review* xi (1916), 276–84.

Dronke, P., *Women Writers of the Middle Ages: A Critical Study of Texts from Perpetua († 203) to Marguerite Porete († 1310)* (Cambridge, 1984).

Dubois, D.J., 'Thomas Netter of Walden, OC (*c.*1372–1430)' (B.Litt. thesis, University of Oxford, 1978).

Duffy, E., *The Stripping of the Altars: Traditional Religion in England, c.1400–c.1580* (New Haven, 1992).

Eco, U., *Travels in Hyperreality: Essays*, trans. W. Weaver (London, 1987).

Elkins, S., *Holy Woman of Twelfth Century England* (Chapel Hill, N.C., 1988).

Elliot, D., *Spiritual Marriage: Sexual Abstinence in Medieval Wedlock* (Princeton, N.J., 1993).

Ellis, R., '*Floris ad Fabricandam . . . Coronam*: an Investigation into the Use of the Revelations of St Bridget of Sweden in Fifteenth-Century England', *Medium Ævum* li (1982), 163–86.

——, 'Margery Kempe's Scribe and the Miraculous Books' in *Langland, the Mystics and the Medieval English Religious Tradition: Essays in Honour of S.S. Hussey*, ed. H. Phillips (Cambridge, 1990), 161–75.

Elton, G., *Policy and Police: the Enforcement of the Reformation in the Age of Thomas Cromwell* (Cambridge, 1972).

——, *Reform and Renewal: Thomas Cromwell and the Common Weal* (Cambridge, 1973).

Emmerson, R.K., 'The Prophetic, the Apocalyptic, and the Study of Medieval Literature' in *Poetic Prophecy in Western Literature*, ed. J. Wojcik and R.J. Frontain (London, 1984), 40–54.

Erskine, J.A., 'Margery Kempe and her Models: the Role of the Authorial Voice', *Mystics Quarterly* xv (1989), 75–85.

Ezell, M.J.M., *Writing Women's Literary History* (Baltimore, 1993).

Fairfield, L.P., 'John Bale and the Development of Protestant Hagiography in England', *Journal of Ecclesiastical History* xxiv (1973), 145–60.

——, *John Bale: Mythmaker for the English Reformation* (West Lafayette, 1976).

Feather, J., *A History of British Publishing* (London, 1988).

Feroli, T., 'The Sexual Politics of Mourning in the Prophecies of Eleanor Davies', *Criticism* xxxvi (1994), 359–82.

———, 'Sodomy and Female Authority: the Castlehaven Scandal and Eleanor Davies's *The Restitution of Prophecy* (1651)', *Women's Studies* xxiv (1994), 31–49.

Firth, K.R., *The Apocalyptic Tradition in Reformation Britain 1530–1645* (Oxford, 1979).

Fisher, S., and J. E. Halley, *Seeking the Woman in Late Medieval and Renaissance Writings: Essays in Feminist Contextual Criticism* (Knoxville, 1989).

Flanagan, S., *Hildegard of Bingen, 1098–1179: a Visionary Life* (London, 1989).

Foster, F.A., 'Legends of the Afterlife' in *A Manual of the Writings in Middle English, 1050–1500*, ed. J. Burke Severs (Hamden, Conn., 1970), ii, 452–7; 645–9.

Foucault, M., *Discipline and Punish: the Birth of the Prison*, trans. A. Sheridan (London, 1975).

Fox, A., 'Prophecies and Politics in the Reign of Henry VIII' in *Reassessing the Henrician Age: Humanism, Politics and Reform 1500–1550*, A. Fox and J. Guy (Oxford, 1986), 77–94.

Fraser, A., *The Weaker Vessel: Woman's Lot in Seventeenth-Century England* (London, 1989).

Gairdner, C.B., *Lollardy and the Reformation in England: An Historical Survey* (London, 1908–1913), 4 vols.

Gardiner, E., *Medieval Visions of Heaven and Hell: a Sourcebook* (New York, 1993).

———, *Visions of Heaven and Hell before Dante* (New York, 1989).

Gentles, I., 'London Levellers in the English Revolution: the Chidleys and Their Circle', *Journal of Ecclesiastical History* xxix (1978), 281–309.

Gibson, G.M., *The Theatre of Devotion: East Anglian Drama and Society in the Late Middle Ages* (Chicago, 1989).

Gilbert, S.M., and S. Gubar, eds., *The Norton Anthology of Literature by Women: the Tradition in English* (New York, 1985).

Glasscoe, M., ed., *The Medieval Mystical Tradition in England: Papers read at the Exeter Symposium, July 1980* (Exeter, 1980).

———, ed., *The Medieval Mystical Tradition in England: Papers read at Dartington Hall, July 1982* (Exeter, 1982).

———, ed., *The Medieval Mystical Tradition in England: Papers read at Dartington Hall, July 1984* (Cambridge, 1984).

———, ed., *The Medieval Mystical Tradition in England*, Exeter Symposium 4 (Cambridge, 1987).

———, ed., *The Medieval Mystical Tradition in England*, Exeter Symposium 5 (Cambridge, 1992).

Goodman, A., 'The Piety of John Brunham's Daughter of Lynn' in *Medieval Women: Dedicated and Presented to Professor Rosalind M.T. Hill on the Occasion of Her Seventieth Birthday*, ed. D. Baker, Studies in Church History subsidia 1 (Oxford, 1978), 347–58.

Gradval, K., *Ravishing Maidens: Writing Rape in Medieval French Literature and Law* (Philadelphia, 1991).

Graef, H., *Mary: A History of Doctrine and Devotion* (London, 1963–1965), 2 vols.

Graham, E., H. Hinds, E. Hobby and H. Wilcox, eds., *Her Own Life: Autobiographical Writings of Seventeenth-Century Englishwomen* (London, 1989).

Gray, D., 'Popular Religion and Late Medieval English Literature' in *Religion in the Poetry and Drama of the Late Middle Ages in England*, ed. P. Boitani and A. Torti (Cambridge, 1990), 1–28.

Greaves, R.L., ed., *Triumph Over Silence: Women in Protestant History*, Contributions to the Study of Religion 15 (Westport, 1985).

——, and R. Zaller, eds., *Biographical Dictionary of British Radicals in the Seventeenth Century* (Brighton, 1982), 3 vols.

Green, M., *Celtic Goddesses: Warriors, Virgins and Mothers* (London, 1995).

Greer, G., S. Hastings, J. Medoff and M. Sansone, eds., *Kissing the Rod: An Anthology of Seventeenth-Century Women's Verse* (London, 1988).

Greer, G., *Slip-Shod Sibyls: Recognition, Rejection and the Woman Poet* (London, 1995).

Greg, W.W., *Some Aspects and Problems of London Publishing between 1550 and 1650* (Oxford, 1956).

Grundy, I., 'Women's History? Writings by English Nuns' in *Women, Writing, History 1640–1740*, ed. I. Grundy and S. Wiseman (London, 1992), 126–38.

Guy, J., *Tudor England* (Oxford, 1988).

Hackett, H., *Virgin Mother, Maiden Queen: Elizabeth I and the Cult of the Virgin Mary* (London, 1995).

Hadfield, A., *Literature, Politics and National Identity: Reformation to Renaissance* (Cambridge, 1994).

Haines, R.M., ' "Wilde Wittes and Wilfulnes": John Swetstock's Attack on those "Poyswunmongeres", the Lollards' in *Popular Belief and Practice*, ed. G.J. Cuming and D. Baker, Studies in Church History 8 (Cambridge, 1972), 143–53.

Haller, W., *Foxe's Book of Martyrs and the Elect Nation* (London, 1963).

Hamilton, D.B., and R. Strier, eds., *Religion, Literature, and Politics in Post-Reformation Britain, 1540–1688* (Cambridge, 1996).

Hannay, M.P., ed., *Silent But For The Word: Tudor Women as Patrons, Translators, and Writers of Religious Works* (Kent, Ohio, 1985).

Happé, P., 'Recent Sudies in John Bale', *English Literary Renaissance* xvii (1987), 103–13.

Hardacre, P.H., 'Gerrard Winstanley in 1650', *Huntington Library Quarterly* xxii (1959), 345–9.

Harding, W., 'Body into Text: *The Book of Margery Kempe*' in *Feminist Approaches to the Body in Medieval Literature*, ed. L. Lomperis and S. Stanbury (Philadelphia, 1993), 168–87.

Harley, M.P., 'The Origin of a Revelation of Purgatory', *Reading Medieval Studies* xii (1986), 87–91.

——, 'A Fifteenth-Century Revelation of a Cistercian Nun', *Vox Benedicta* vi (1989), 120–7.

——, 'The Vision of Margaret Edward and Others at Canterbury, 29 July 1451', *Manuscripta* xxxii (1988), 146–51.

Harries, R., 'On the Brink of Universalism' in *Julian: Woman of Our Day*, ed. R. Llewelyn (London, 1985), 41–60.

Haugaard, W.P., 'Katherine Parr: the Religious Convictions of a Renaissance Queen', *Renaissance Quarterly* xxii (1969), 346–59.

Higgins, P., 'The Reactions of Women, with Special Reference to Women Petitioners', in *Politics, Religion and the English Civil War*, ed. B. Manning (London, 1973), 177–222.

Hill, C., *The Century of Revolution 1603–1714* (London, 1978).

———, 'The Religion of Gerrard Winstanley', *Past and Present* supplement 5 (1987).

———, *The World Turned Upside Down: Radical Ideas during the English Revolution* (London, 1972).

Hindle, C.J., *A Bibliography of the Printed Pamphlets and Broadsides of Lady Eleanor Douglas the Seventeenth-Century Prophetess* (Edinburgh, 1936).

Hirsh, J.C., 'Author and Scribe in *The Book of Margery Kempe*', *Medium Ævum* xliv (1975), 145–50.

———, *The Revelations of Margery Kempe: Paramystical Practices in Late Medieval England*, Medieval and Renaissance Authors 10 (Leiden, 1989).

Hobby, E., *Virtue of Necessity: English Women's Writing 1649–88* (London, 1988).

Hogg, J., ed., *Studies in St Birgitta and the Brigittine Order*, Analecta Cartusiana 35:19 (Salzburg, 1993), 2 vols.

Holbrook, S.E., 'Margery Kempe and Wynkyn de Worde' in *The Medieval Mystical Tradition in England*, ed. M. Glasscoe, Exeter Symposium 4 (Cambridge, 1987), 27–46.

Holdsworth, C.J., 'Christina of Markyate' in *Medieval Women: Dedicated and Presented to Professor Rosalind M.T. Hill on the Occasion of Her Seventieth Birthday*, ed. D. Baker, Studies in Church History subsidia 1 (Oxford, 1978), 185–204.

———, 'Visions and Visionaries in the Middle Ages', *History* xlviii (1963), 141–53.

Hudson, A, 'The Examination of Lollards', *Bulletin of the Institute of Historical Research* xlvi (1973), 145–59.

———, *Lollards and Their Books* (London, 1985).

———, ' "No newe thyng": the Printing of Medieval Texts in the Early Reformation Period', in *Middle English Studies Presented to Norman Davis in Honour of his Seventieth Birthday*, ed. D. Gray and E.G. Stanley (Oxford, 1983), 153–74.

———, *The Premature Reformation: Wycliffite Texts and Lollard History* (Oxford, 1988).

———, 'William Thorpe and the Question of Authority' in *Christian Authority: Essays in Honour of Henry Chadwick*, ed. G.R. Evans (Oxford, 1988), 127–37.

———, and P. Biller, eds., *Heresy and Literacy, 1000–1531* (Cambridge, 1994).

Hughes, J., *Pastors and Visionaries: Religion and Secular Life in Late Medieval Yorkshire* (Woodbridge, 1988).

Hughey, R., 'A Note on Queen Elizabeth's "Godly Meditation" ', *The Library* 4th series xv (1934–1935), 237–40.

Hutchinson, A, 'Beyond the Margin: the Recusant Bridgettines' in *Studies in St. Birgitta and the Brigittine Order*, ed. J. Hogg, Analecta Cartusiana 35: 19 (New York, 1993), ii, 267–84.

———, 'Three (Recusant) Sisters' in *Vox Mystica: Essays on Medieval Mysticism*, ed. A.C. Bartlett (Cambridge, 1995), 147–58.

Irigaray, L., *The Irigaray Reader*, ed. M. Whitford (Oxford, 1991).

———, *Speculum of the Other Woman*, trans. G. C. Gill (Ithaca, 1985).

Irwin. J., ed., *Womanhood in Radical Protestantism: 1525–1675* (New York, 1979).

Jansen, S.L., *Political Protest and Prophecy under Henry VIII* (Woodbridge, 1991).

Jardine, L., *Reading Shakespeare Historically* (London, 1996).

Jørgensen, J., *Saint Bridget of Sweden*, trans. I. Lund (London, 1954), 2 vols.

Johnson, F. R., 'The English Cult of St Bridget of Sweden', *Analecta Bollandiana* ciii (1985), 75–92.

Johnson, L. S., 'The Trope of the Scribe and the Question of Literary Authority in the Works of Julian of Norwich and Margery Kempe', *Speculum* lxvi (1991), 820–38.

Jones, A.R., ' "Writing the Body": Toward an Understanding of *l'Ecriture féminine*' in *The New Feminist Criticism: Essays on Women, Literature and Theory*, ed. E. Showalter (London, 1986), 361–77.

Jordan, C., *Renaissance Feminism: Literary Texts and Political Models* (Ithaca, 1990).

Kastan, D.S, 'An Early English Metrical Psalm: Elizabeth's or John Bale's?' *Notes and Queries* n.s. xxi (1974), 404–5.

Keiser, G.R., 'The Mystics and the Early English Printers: the Economics of Devotionalism' in *The Medieval Mystical Tradition in England*, ed. M. Glasscoe, Exeter Symposium 4 (Cambridge, 1987), 9–26.

———, 'St Jerome and the Brigittines: Visions of the Afterlife in Fifteeth-Century England' in *England in the Fifteenth Century: Proceedings of the 1986 Harlaxton Symposium*, ed. D. Williams (Woodbridge, 1987), 143–52.

Kelly, D.R., *The Beginning of Ideology: Consciousness and Society in the French Reformation* (Cambridge, 1981).

Kelly, J., *Women, History and Theory* (Chicago, 1984).

Kendall, R.K., *The Drama of Dissent: the Radical Poetics of Nonconformity, 1380–1590* (Chapel Hill, N.C., 1986).

Kerby-Fulton, K., *Reformist Apocalypticism and 'Piers Plowman'*, Cambridge Studies in Medieval Literature 7 (Cambridge, 1990).

Kieckhefer, R., *Unquiet Souls: Fourteenth-Century Saints and Their Religious Milieu* (Chicago, 1984).

King, J.N., *English Reformation Literature: the Tudor Origins of the Protestant Tradition* (Princeton, 1982).

———, 'The Godly Woman in Elizabethan Iconography', *Renaissance Quarterly* xxxviii (1985), 41–84.

———, 'Patronage and Piety: the Influence of Catherine Parr' in *Silent but for the Word: Tudor Women as Patrons, Translators, and Writers of Religious Works*, ed. M.P. Hannay (Kent, Ohio, 1985), 43–60.

———, *Tudor Royal Iconography: Literature and Art in an Age of Religious Crisis* (Princeton, 1989).

Klapisch-Zuber, C., ed., *Silences of the Middle Ages*, A History of Women in the West 2 (Cambridge, Mass., 1992).

Knott, J.R., *Discourses of Martyrdom in English Literature, 1563–1694* (Cambridge, 1993).

Knowles, D., *The English Mystical Tradition* (London, 1961).

———, *The Religious Orders in England* (Cambridge, 1948–1959), 3 vols.

Kristeva, J., *The Kristeva Reader*, ed. T. Moi (Oxford, 1986).

————, *Powers of Horror: an Essay on Abjection*, trans. L.S. Roudiez (New York, 1982).

Kruger, S.F., *Dreaming in the Middle Ages*, Cambridge Studies in Medieval Literature 14 (Cambridge, 1992).

Kurtz, P.D., 'Mary of Oignies, Christine the Marvelous, and Medieval Heresy', *Mystics Quarterly* xiv (1988), 186–96.

Lagorio, V.M., 'The Medieval Continental Women Mystics: An Introduction' in *An Introduction to the Medieval Mystics of Europe*, ed. P. Szarmach (Albany, 1984), 161–93.

Larner, C., *Witchcraft and Religion: the Politics of Popular Belief*, ed. A. Macfarlane (Oxford, 1984).

Larrington, C., *Women and Writing in Medieval Europe: a Sourcebook* (London, 1995).

Leff, G., *Heresy in the Later Middle Ages: The Relation of Heterodoxy to Dissent c.1250–c.1450* (Manchester, 1967), 2 vols.

Le Goff, J., *The Birth of Purgatory* (Chicago, 1984).

Lerner, R.E., *The Heresy of the Free Spirit in the Later Middle Ages* (Berkeley, 1972).

————, 'Medieval Prophecy and Religious Dissent', *Past and Present* lxxii (1976), 3–24.

Levack, B.P., *The Witch-hunt in Early Modern Europe* (2nd ed. London, 1995).

Levin, C., 'Power, Politics, and Sexuality: Images of Elizabeth I' in *The Politics of Gender in Early Modern Europe*, ed. J.R. Brink, A.P. Coudert and M.C. Horowitz, Sixteenth-Century Essays and Studies 12 (Kirksville, Missouri, 1989), 95–110.

————, 'Women in *The Book of Martyrs* as Models of Behaviour in Tudor England', *International Journal of Women's Studies* iv (1981), 196–207.

Lieb, M., *The Visionary Mode: Biblical Prophecy, Hermeneutics and Cultural Change* (Ithaca, N.Y., 1991).

Loades, D., *Politics, Censorship and the English Reformation* (London, 1991).

————, 'The Theory and Practices of Censorship in Sixteenth-Century England', *Transactions of the Royal Historical Society*, 5th series, xxiv (1974), 141–57.

Lochrie, K., '*The Book of Margery Kempe*: the Marginal Woman's Quest for Literary Authority', *Journal of Medieval and Renaissance Studies* xvi (1986), 33–55.

————, *Margery Kempe and Translations of the Flesh* (Philadelphia, 1991).

Logan, M.R., and P.L. Rudnytsky, eds., *Contending Kingdoms: Historical, Psychological, and Feminist Approaches to the Literature of Sixteenth-Century England and France* (Detroit, 1991).

McConica, J.K., *English Humanists and Reformation Politics under Henry VIII and Edward VI* (Oxford, 1965).

————, 'The Recusant Tradition of Sir Thomas More' in *Essential Articles for the Study of Thomas More*, ed. R.S. Sylvester and G.P. Marc'hadour (Hamden, Conn., 1977), 136–49.

Macdonald, M., *Mystical Bedlam: Madness, Anxiety, and Healing in Seventeenth-Century England* (Cambridge, 1981).

McDonnell, E.W., *The Beguines and Beghards in Medieval Culture with Special Emphasis on the Belgian Scene* (New Brunswick, N.J., 1954).

Macek, E., 'The Emergence of a Feminine Spirituality in *The Book of Martyrs*', *Sixteenth-Century Journal* xix (1988), 63–80.

McEntire, S., *Margery Kempe: a Book of Essays* (New York, 1992).

Macfarlane, A., *Marriage and Love in England: Modes of Reproduction 1300–1840* (Oxford, 1986).

———, *The Origins of English Individualism: The Family, Property and Social Transition* (Oxford, 1978).

McGinn, B., trans., *Apocalyptic Spirituality: Treatises and Letters of Lacantius, Adso of Montier-en-Der, Joachim of Fiore, the Spiritual Franciscans, Savonarola* (New York, 1979).

———, *Apocalypticism in the Western Tradition* (Aldershot, 1994).

———, *Visions of the End: Apocalyptic Traditions in the Middle Ages* (New York, 1979).

McGrath, A.E., *Reformation Thought: an Introduction* (Oxford, 1988).

McGregor, J.F. and B. Reay, eds., *Radical Religion in the English Revolution* (Oxford, 1984).

Mack, P., *Visionary Women: Ecstatic Prophecy in Seventeenth-Century England* (Berkeley, 1992).

———, 'Women as Prophets During the English Civil War', *Feminist Studies* viii (1982), 19–45.

McKee, J.R., *Dame Elizabeth Barton, O.S.B, The Holy Maid of Kent* (London, 1925).

Maclean, I., *The Renaissance Notion of Woman: A Study in the Fortunes of Scholasticism and Medical Science in European Intellectual Life* (Cambridge, 1980).

McNamer, S., 'The Exploratory Image: God as Mother in Julian of Norwich's *Revelations of Divine Love*', *Mystics Quarterly* xv (1989), 21–8.

McQuade, P., ' "Except that they had offended the Lawe": Gender and Jurisprudence in *The Examinations of Anne Askew*', *Literature and History* 3rd series iii.2 (1994), 1–14.

McSheffrey, S., *Gender and Heresy: Women and Men in Lollard Communities 1420–1530* (Philadelphia, 1996).

———, 'Literacy and the Gender Gap in the Late Middle Ages: Women and Reading in Lollard Communities' in *Women, the Book and the Godly*, ed. L. Smith and J. Taylor (Cambridge, 1995), 157–70.

Mahn, M.R, and H. Koon, eds., *The Female Spectator: English Women Writers before 1800* (Bloomington, 1977).

Maisonneuve, R. 'Margery Kempe and the Eastern Tradition of the "Perfect Fool" ' in *The Medieval Mystical Tradition in England: Papers read at Dartington Hall, July, 1982*, ed. M. Glasscoe (Exeter, 1982), 1–17.

Marshall, S., ed., *Women in Reformation and Counter-Reformation Europe: Public and Private Worlds* (Bloomington, 1989).

Mason, H.A., *Humanism and Poetry in the Early Tudor Period* (London, 1959).

Mason, M.G., 'The Other Voice: Autobiographies of Women Writers' in *Autobiography: Essays Theoretical and Critical*, ed. J. Olney (Princeton, 1980), 207–35.

Matchinske, M., 'Holy Hatred: Formations of the Gendered Subject in English Apocalyptic Writing, 1625–1651', *English Literary History* lx (1993), 349–77.

Meale, C.M., ' ". . . alle the bokes that I haue of latyn, englisch, and frensch": Laywomen and their Books in Late Medieval England' in *Women and Literature in Britain, 1150–1500*, ed. C.M. Meale, Cambridge Studies in Medieval Literature 17 (Cambridge, 1993), 128–58.

Millett, B., and J. Wogan-Browne, eds., *Medieval English Prose for Women: Selections from the Katherine Group and Ancrene Wisse* (Oxford, 1990).

Minnich, N.H., 'Prophecy and the Fifth Lateran Council (1512–1517)' in *Prophetic Rome in the High Renaissance Period*, ed. M. Reeves (Oxford, 1992), 63–87.

Monter, W., 'Women and the Italian Inquisition' in *Women in the Middle Ages and the Renaissance: Literary and Historical Perspectives*, ed. M.B. Rose (Syracuse, 1986), 73–87.

Moi, T., *Sexual/Textual Politics: Feminist Literary Theory* (London, 1985).

Montrose, L.A. ' "Shaping Fantasies": Figurations of Gender and Power in Elizabethan Culture' in *Representing the English Renaissance*, ed. S. Greenblatt (Berkeley, 1988), 31–64.

Morgan, A., *Dante and the Medieval Otherworld*, Cambridge Studies in Medieval Literature 8 (Cambridge, 1990).

Morris, C., *The Discovery of the Individual, 1050–1200* (London, 1972).

Mueller, J., 'Autobiography of a New "Creatur": Female Spirituality, Selfhood, and Authorship in *The Book of Margery Kempe*', *New York Literary Forum* xii–xiii (1984), 63–75.

———, 'A Tudor Queen Finds Voice: Katherine Parr's *Lamentation of a Sinner*' in *The Historical Renaissance: New Essays on Tudor and Stuart Literature and Culture*, ed. H. Dubrow and R. Strier (Chicago, 1988), 15–47.

Naish, C., *Death Comes to the Maiden: Sex and Execution 1431–1933* (London, 1991).

Neame, A., *The Holy Maid of Kent: the Life of Elizabeth Barton, 1506–1534* (London, 1971).

Nelson, B., 'Lady Eleanor Davies: the Prophet as Publisher', *Women's Studies International Forum* viii (1985), 403–9.

Nevanlinna, S., 'The First Translation of a Young Princess: Holograph Manuscript Versus Printed Text' in *Proceedings from the Third Nordic Conference for English Studies, Hässebly, Sept 25–27, 1986*, ed. I. Lindblad and M. Ljung, Stockholm Studies in English 73 (Stockholm, 1987), i, 243–56.

Newman, B., *Sister of Wisdom: St Hildegard's Theology of the Feminine* (Berkeley, 1987).

Norbrook, D., *Poetry and Politics in the English Renaissance* (London, 1984).

Norman, M., 'Dame Gertrude More and the English Recusant Tradition', *Recusant History* xiii (1976), 196–211.

Nuttall, A.D., *Overheard by God: Fiction and Prayer in Herbert, Milton, Dante and St John* (London, 1980).

Olson, V.N., *John Foxe and the Elizabethan Church* (Berkeley, 1973).

Partner, N., 'Reading *The Book of Margery Kempe*', *Exemplaria* iii (1991), 29–66.

Patch, H.A., *The Other World According to Descriptions in Medieval Literature* (Cambridge, Mass., 1950).

Patrides, C.A., and J. Wittreich, eds., *The Apocalypse in English Renaissance Thought and Literature: Patterns, Antecedents and Repercussions* (Manchester, 1984).

Patterson, A., 'Sir John Oldcastle as Symbol of Reformation Historiography' in *Religion, Literature, and Politics in Post-Reformation England, 1540–1688*, ed. D.B. Hamilton and R. Strier (Cambridge, 1996), 6–26.

Patterson, L., *Negotiating the Past: the Historical Understanding of Medieval Literature* (Madison, WI, 1987).

———, 'On the Margin: Postmodernism, Ironic History, and Medieval Studies', *Speculum* lxv (1990), 87–108.

Petroff, E.A., *Body and Soul: Essays on Medieval Women and Mysticism* (Oxford, 1994).

———, ed., *Medieval Women's Visionary Literature* (New York, 1986).

Porter, R., 'The Prophetic Body: Lady Eleanor Davies and the Meanings of Madness', *Women's Writing* i (1994), 51–63.

Power, E., *Medieval English Nunneries c.1272 to 1535* (Cambridge, 1922).

———, *Medieval Women*, ed. M.M. Postan (Cambridge, 1975).

Prescott, A.L., 'The Pearl of Valois and Elizabeth I: Marguerite de Navarre's *Miroir* and Tudor England' in *Silent But For The Word: Tudor Women as Patrons, Translators and Writers of Religious Works*, ed. M.P. Hannay (Kent, Ohio, 1985), 61–76.

Prior, M., ed., *Women in English Society 1500–1800* (London, 1985).

Purkiss, D., 'Producing the Voice, Consuming the Body: Women Prophets of the Seventeenth Century' in *Women, Writing, History 1640–1740*, ed. I. Grundy and S. Wiseman (London, 1992), 139–58.

Rahner, *Visions and Prophecies*, Quæstiones Disputatæ 10 (London, 1963).

Reeves, M, 'History and Prophecy in Medieval Thought', *Medievalia et Humanistica* n.s. 5 (1974), 51–75.

———, *The Influence of Prophecy in the Later Middle Ages: a Study of Joachimism* (Oxford, 1969).

Rex, R., 'The Execution of the Holy Maid of Kent', *Historical Research* lxiv (1991), 216–20.

Rich, A., *On Lies, Secrets and Silence: Selected Prose, 1966–1978* (London, 1980).

Riddy, F., 'Women Talking about the Things of God: a Late Medieval Subculture' in *Women and Literature in Britain, 1150–1500*, ed. C.M. Meale, Cambridge Studies in Medieval Literature 17 (Cambridge, 1993), 104–27.

Robbins, R.H., 'Political Prophecies' in *A Manual of the Writings in Middle English 1050–1500*, v, ed. A.E. Hartung (New Haven, Conn., 1975), 1516–36.

Rollins, H.E., 'Notes on Some English Accounts of Miraculous Fasts', *Journal of American Folklore* xxxiv (1921), 357–76.

Rosaldo, M.Z., and L. Lamphere, eds., *Women, Culture and Society* (Stanford, Calif., 1974).

Rowlands, M.B., 'Recusant Women 1560–1640' in *Women in English Society 1500–1800*, ed. M. Prior (London, 1985), 149–80.

Rubin, M., *Corpus Christi: the Eucharist in Late Medieval Culture* (Cambridge, 1991).

Ruether, R.R., *Mary: The Feminine Face of the Church* (London, 1979).

Russo, M, 'Female Grotesques: Carnival and Theory' in *Feminist Studies/Critical Studies*, ed. T. de Laurentis (Basingstoke, 1988), 213–29.

S.W.G., 'Dougle Fooleries', *Bodleian Quarterly Record* vii (1932), 95–8.

Sargent, M.G., 'The Transmission by English Carthusians of some Late Medieval Spiritual Writings', *Journal of Ecclesiastical History* xxvii (1976), 225–40.

Schmidtke, J.A., ' "Saving" by Faint Praise: St. Birgitta of Sweden, Adam Easton and Medieval Antifeminism', *American Benedictine Review* xxxiii (1982), 149–61.

Schulenburg, J.T., 'Female Sanctity: Public and Private Roles, ca. 500–1100' in *Women and Power in the Middle Ages*, ed. M. Erler and M. Kowaleski (Athens, Georgia, 1988), 102–25.

Scott, J. 'Women's History' in *New Perspectives on Historical Writing*, ed. P. Burke (Cambridge, 1991), 42–66.

Scott, K., ' "Io Catarina": Ecclesiastical Politics and Oral Culture in the Letters of Catherine of Siena' in *Dear Sister: Medieval Women and the Epistolary Genre*, ed. K. Cherewatuk and U. Wiethaus (Philadelphia, 1993), 87–121.

Shell, M., *Elizabeth's Glass with 'The Glass of the Sinful Soul' (1544) by Elizabeth I and 'Epistle Dedicatory' & 'Conclusion' (1548) by John Bale*, intro. M. Shell (Lincoln, Nebraska, 1993).

Smith, C.F., 'Jane Lead: The Feminist Mind and Art of a Seventeenth-Century Protestant Mystic' in *Women of Spirit: Female Leadership in the Jewish and Christian Traditions,* ed. R.R. Ruether and E. McLaughlin (New York, 1979), 183–203.

——, 'Jane Lead: Mysticism and the Woman Cloathed with the Sun' in *Shakespeare's Sisters: Feminist Essays on Women Poets*, ed. S.M. Gilbert and S. Gubar (Bloomington, 1979), 3–18.

Smith, L., and J. Taylor, eds., *Women, the Book and the Godly* (Cambridge, 1995).

Smith, N., *Perfection Proclaimed: Language and Literature in English Radical Religion 1640–1660* (Oxford, 1989).

Southern, R.W., *Western Society and the Church in the Middle Ages*, Pelican History of the Church 2 (Harmondsworth, 1970).

Spenser, T., 'The History of An Unfortunate Lady', *Harvard Studies and Notes in Philology and Literature* xx (1938), 43–59.

Staley, L., *Margery Kempe's Dissenting Fictions* (Pennsylvania, 1994).

Stewart, A., 'The Early Modern Closet Discovered', *Representations* i (1995), 76–100.

Stock, B., *The Implications of Literacy: Written Languages and Models of Interpretation in the Eleventh and Twelfth Centuries* (Princeton, 1983).

Strohm, P., *Hochon's Arrow: the Social Imagination of Fourteenth-Century Texts* (Princeton, 1992).

Stone, L., *The Family, Sex and Marriage in England 1500–1800* (London, 1977).

Sumption, J., *Pilgrimage: An Image of Mediæval Religion* (London, 1975).

Szittya, P., 'Domesday Bokes: The Apocalypse in Medieval English Literary Culture' in *The Apocalypse in the Middle Ages*, ed. R.K. Emmerson and B. McGinn (Ithaca, N.Y., 1992), 374–97.

Tanner, N.P., *The Church in Late Medieval Norwich, 1370–1532* (Toronto, 1984).

Taylor, R., *The Political Prophecy in England* (New York, 1967).

Temkin, O., *The Falling Sickness: a History of Epilepsy from the Greeks to the Beginnings of Modern Neurology* (Baltimore, 1945).

Thomas, D., *A Long Time Burning: The History of Literary Censorship in England* (London, 1969).

Thomas, K.V., 'The Meaning of Literacy in Early Modern England' in *The Written Word: Literacy in Transition*, ed. G. Baumann (Oxford, 1986), 97–131.

——, *Religion and the Decline of Magic: Studies in Popular Beliefs in Sixteenth and Seventeenth Century England* (London, 1971).

——, 'Women and the Civil War Sects', *Past and Present* xiii (1958), 42–65.

Thompson, S., *Women Religious: the Founding of English Nunneries after the Norman Conquest* (Oxford, 1991).

Thomson, J.A.F., *The Later Lollards, 1414–1520* (Oxford, 1965).

Todd, J., *Dictionary of British Women Writers* (London, 1989).

Uhlman, D.R., 'The Comfort of Voice, the Solace of Script: Orality and Literacy in *The Book of Margery Kempe*', *Studies in Philology* xci (1994), 50–69.

Underhill, E., *The Essentials of Mysticism and Other Essays* (London, 1920).

Veevers, E., *Images of Love and Religion: Queen Henrietta Maria and Court Entertainment* (Cambridge, 1989).

Voaden, R., ed., *Prophets Abroad: the Reception of Continental Holy Women in Late Medieval England* (Cambridge, 1996).

Walker, D.P., *The Decline of Hell. Seventeenth-Century Discussions of Eternal Torment* (Chicago, 1964).

Warner, M., *Alone of All Her Sex: the Myth and the Cult of the Virgin Mary* (London, 1990).

——, *Joan of Arc: The Image of Female Heroism* (London, 1981).

Warnicke, R.M., *The Rise and Fall of Anne Boleyn* (Cambridge, 1989).

——, *Women of the English Renaissance and Reformation*, Contributions to Women's Studies 38 (Westport, Conn., 1983).

Warren, A.K., *Anchorites and their Patrons in Medieval England* (Berkeley, 1985).

Watson N., 'The Composition of Julian of Norwich's *The Revelation of Love*', *Speculum* lxviii (1993), 637–83.

——, ' "Yf wommen by double naturelly": Remaking "Woman" in Julian of Norwich's *Revelation of Love*', *Exemplaria* viii (1996), 1–34.

Watt, D., ed., *Medieval Women in their Communities* (Cardiff, 1997).

——, 'The Prophet at Home: Elizabeth Barton and the Influence of Bridget of Sweden and Catherine of Siena' in *Prophets Abroad: the Reception of Continental Holy Women in Late-Medieval England*, ed. R. Voaden (Cambridge, 1996), 161–76.

——, 'Reconstructing the Word: the Prophecies of Elizabeth Barton', *Renaissance Quarterly* l (1997), 132–59.

——, 'The Posthumous Reputation of the Holy Maid of Kent', *Recusant History* xxiii (1996), 148–58.

Watt, T., *Cheap Print and Popular Piety, 1550–1640* (Cambridge, 1991).

Weber, M., *Economy and Society: an Outline of Interpretative Sociology*, ed. G. Roth and C. Wittich (New York, 1968), 3 vols.

Weinstein, D., and R.M. Bell, *Saints and Society: the Two Worlds of Western Christendom, 1000–1700* (Chicago, 1982).

Weissman, H.P., 'Margery Kempe in Jerusalem: *Hysterica Compassio* in the Late Middle Ages' in *Acts of Interpretation: The Text and Its Context 700–1600*, ed. M.J. Carruthers and E.D. Kirk (Norman, Oklahoma, 1982), 201–17.

White, H.C., *Tudor Books of Saints and Martyrs* (Madison, 1963).

Wiesner, M.E., *Women and Gender in Early Modern Europe* (Cambridge, 1983).

Willis, D., *Malevolent Nurture: Witch-hunting and Maternal Power in Early Modern England* (Ithaca, N.Y., 1995).

Wilson, D., *A Tudor Tapestry: Men, Woman and Society in Reformation England* (London, 1972).

Wilson, J., 'Communities of Dissent: the Secular and Ecclesiastical Communities of Margery Kempe's *Book*' in *Medieval Women in their Communities*, ed. D. Watt (Cardiff, 1997), 155–85.

Wilson, K.M., ed., *Medieval Women Writers* (Athens, Georgia, 1984).

——, ed., *Women Writers of the Renaissance and Reformation* (Athens, Georgia, 1987).

——, and F.J. Warnke, eds., *Women Writers of the Seventeenth Century* (Athens, Georgia, 1989).

Windeatt, B.A., 'Julian of Norwich and Her Audience', *Review of English Studies* xxviii (1977), 1–17.

Wiseman, S., 'Unsilent Instruments and the Devil's Cushions: Authority in Seventeenth-Century Women's Prophetic Discourse' in *New Feminist Discourses: Critical Essays on Theories and Texts*, ed. I. Armstrong (London, 1992), 176–96.

Wittenburg, J., *Disorderly Women and Female Power in the Street Literature of Early Modern England and Germany* (Charlottesville, 1992).

Wojcik, J., and R.J. Frontain, eds., *Poetic Prophecy in Western Literature* (London, 1984).

Woolf, R., 'Saints' Lives' in *Continuations and Beginnings: Studies in Old English Literature*, ed. E.G. Stanley (London, 1966), 37–66.

Wright, M.J., 'What They Said to Margery Kempe: Narrative Reliability in her *Book*', *Neophilologus* lxxix (1995), 497–508.

Zim, R., *English Metrical Psalms: Poetry and Prayer 1535–1601* (Cambridge, 1987).

Index